MARK PHILLIPS

The Man and His Horses

MARK PHILLIPS

The Man and His Horses

Angela Rippon

DAVID & CHARLES
Newton Abbot   London

The publishers would like to acknowledge the considerable help
given by Jim Bennett in the photography for this book. He has
provided all the colour photographs except those on pages 49
and 50, as well as the black-and-white photographs individually
acknowledged. We gratefully acknowledge permission to
reproduce the map and sketches of the Badminton fences on
pages 242–259.

This book has been written under the auspices of the British
Equestrian Federation to whom a donation from the royalties
has been made.

British Library Cataloguing in Publication Data
Rippon, Angela
    Mark Phillips: the man and his horses.
    1. Phillips, Mark   2. Horsemanship
    I. Title   II. Phillips, Mark
    798.2'3'0924   SF309

ISBN 0–7153–8224–1

Typeset by Keyspools Ltd
Golborne, Lancs,
and printed in Great Britain
by Butler & Tanner Ltd, Frome and London
for David & Charles (Publishers) Limited
Brunel House   Newton Abbot   Devon

Contents

Chapter One

'Sit up, look up, hands down, heels down.' Anne Phillips chanted that eight-word litany over and over again to her young son Mark as she walked him round and round the show-rings perched on top of a diminutive pony in the leading-rein classes.

There was no way of knowing that those four basic instructions were laying the foundation on which Mark Phillips would build the career that has made him one of the leading three-day-event riders in the world. At the tender age of two they were merely a set of instructions to be obeyed, with the brightly coloured ribbons of another 'pretty' or rosette as a reward for his patience at the end of the day.

There had never been any doubt that Mark Phillips would ride. He'd been born into a family where for two generations the horse had been an essential part of life. 'And I was absolutely determined that he should ride,' says his mother emphatically. 'When he was a very little boy I used to ask him "Would you like to go for a walk with Nanny, or a ride with me?" It was guaranteed that he would say he'd come for a ride.'

Anne Phillips has been described as a homely and capable woman – which she undoubtably is. She's also humorous, candid, has a strength of character that makes her determined to achieve goals and, I suspect, formidable as an opponent, and she is positively 'mad about horses' which isn't surprising when you consider that her own childhood was full of them.

The only daughter of Brigadier John Tiarks, a member of the wealthy Tiarks banking family, she'd travelled with her father's regiment, the King's Dragoon Guards, to Egypt, Camberley, India and finally Aldershot where 'Sharks', as he was known, commanded the regiment from 1937–9. The KDGs was a cavalry regiment. 'There was no way that my father would have been anything *but* a cavalry soldier.' And in those years between the wars when they still had horses, not the tanks that have since replaced them, it was an accepted part of regimental life that the cavalry officers would showjump or play polo in the summer, and hunt in the winter.

'And hunting was the love of my father's life,' recalls Anne Phillips, 'so the horses were always there. There are photographs of me going hunting as a very small child on a leading rein with my father. When we went to Camberley, father was Master of the Camberley Drag

Hounds, and when I went to Downe House School near Newbury in 1939 my father had every intention of picking me up to take me hunting every Saturday during the season.' But war was declared and 'Sharks' and the regiment went off to the Middle East, so the headmistress's indulgence towards Miss Tiark's hunting exploits was never put to the test!

Towards the end of the war Anne Tiarks joined the WRNS and at a party in London met a young major – Peter Phillips of the King's Dragoon Guards. His family had hunted in Warwickshire, where his father was a mining engineer, and whilst at the Royal Agricultural College he'd ridden with the Berkeley, so it would be fair to assume that a common love of horses and hunting drew them together.

'But if I was totally honest I don't believe it was,' says Peter Phillips, 'though I do know that as we started seeing quite a bit of each other I was put on a horse and taken out for a ride just above Wotton-under-Edge to see how I would cope – and Anne took off like a rocket.'

Mrs Phillips remembers being 'mildly disappointed that you didn't ride as well as I'd hoped – but at least you liked horses' and that was enough to put the seal on their romance. They were married on 17 December 1946 at St Mark's, North Audley Street, and the young bride established a temporary home with her parents while Peter Phillips, having left the army, went off to Cirencester College of Agriculture for two years to learn to be a farmer.

'Originally the idea had been for me to follow in my father's footsteps and become a mining engineer,' says Peter Phillips, 'and just before I joined the army at the outbreak of war, I worked down a pit for nine months. I went down the shaft in darkness and came up in darkness, so never saw daylight except at week-ends.' Perhaps it was the memory of that eternal night that made Peter Phillips look instead towards the outdoor existence of a farmer, though he admits: 'I don't *really* know why I chose the job. My home was always in the middle of the countryside, so I've always had a basic interest in it – and liked animals. It just appealed to me in the same way that it appealed to Mark.' So Peter Phillips became a farmer almost by accident rather than design, much as his son was to do nearly thirty years later.

At the end of his two years at Cirencester, the Phillips bought a 400-acre mixed farm at Long Green near Tewkesbury. On 22 September 1948 Mark Phillips was born at the Cotswold Maternity Home, Tetbury, and three days later the family moved into their new home.

'It really belonged to the Agricultural Mortgage Company rather than us,' says Mrs Phillips. Together they managed a milking herd, a flock of sheep, a gaggle of chickens, turkeys and ducks, and an arable crop of corn, wheat, barley and oats. It was still a love of horses, and hunting, that filled their leisure hours and Mark was destined to share that love. His first pony, a minute Shetland called appropriately Tiny Wee, arrived when he was eighteen months old. He was hoisted on its

Mark at eighteen months old on his first pony, Tiny Wee, with his mother at their home near Tewkesbury

back and led around the yard for his first 'ride' before he could even walk, and had won his first rosette in a leading-rein class before he was two. He'd also made his first visit to the Badminton Horse Trials as a nappy-clad babe in arms, naturally oblivious of the importance that place was to have in his life.

Sarah Phillips, Mark's sister, was born in 1951, and their mother was just as determined that the new addition to the family would also be a rider. Tiny Wee was clearly destined to be handed on to young Sarah, so by the time he was three a new pony was needed for Mark and number two arrived through a stroke of good fortune. Longdon Beauty was just over 11 hands high and belonged to close friends and neighbours of the Phillips who had planned to move to Rhodesia, but before they went they gave the pony to Mark. Anne Phillips believes: 'Beauty probably had a very great influence on his life. She was a pony that, when he kicked, she went, and when he pulled the reins, she stopped. But she was a very lively lady, very quick and sensitive. There might be a pheasant jumping out of a hedge in front of him – or anything – so he had to anticipate, think ahead. He couldn't just sit there – he really had to think about riding.'

By the time he was four he was off the leading rein and trotting with some confidence beside his parents on their comparatively massive hunters.

Mark at about four years old, now off the leading rein, riding his second pony, Beauty

'But in no way did he and the pony always remain together,' recalls his mother. Mark's own memory of those early days is understandably patchy: 'I don't remember particularly wanting or not wanting to ride – but I must have enjoyed it, and when you're small, winning rosettes and sometimes a silver cup is very nice. But I know I used to fall off fairly regularly. I used to count the number of times – it got up to seventy-eight – after that I lost count. But it didn't put me off.'

Perhaps also there was the advantage of not having to do any of the hard work associated with horses, like catching the pony in the field, grooming it and cleaning the tack – his mother did all that for him: 'I was determined that riding should be fun, not a drudge' she says.

By the time Mark was six, Sarah was queueing up to ride Beauty, and so once again his parents started looking for a new pony and found it in the 'For Sale' columns of *Horse and Hound*. Pickles – or Picky as he became known – was a strong 13-hand hunter pony from Norfolk, 'a real boy's pony' is how he's remembered by the family, and it was with him that Mark joined the Ledbury Pony Club and began competing in junior working hunter classes, showjumping and hunter trials. He also hunted regularly with his parents and on at least one occasion joined his grandfather for a day with the Berkeley where, Anne Phillips remembers: 'The fences were much bigger than anything he'd jumped before. But from a very early age it never occurred to him not to jump an obstacle. He would just aim his pony at the fence and jump.'

It wasn't long before riding had to take second place to school. At five he'd been sent to Wells Court, a junior school near his home, and at eight he became a boarder at Stouts Hill Preparatory School in Gloucestershire where, before it closed, parents used to pay nearly £700 a term and were shown into the headmaster's study by a butler.

Some boys at the school went riding at a nearby equitation centre but Mark never joined them: 'I used to enjoy going to shows and competing in the holidays on my own ponies, but to ride one behind the other on the third cousin to a Thelwell pony on a hot summer's afternoon, being bitten by flies, didn't say a lot to me really. And besides, it wasn't really aimed at me. It was for those people who didn't have a chance to ride during the holidays – which I did.' But apart from that, Mark discovered a natural ability for a variety of sport. 'I much preferred to play football and rugby, or take part in athletics. Really the only time I seriously considered the horses was when a lot of my friends went off ski-ing in the Christmas holidays. It was slightly galling not being able to go, but my parents said I couldn't ski *and* have a pony so I stayed with the pony, and went hunting – which I thoroughly enjoyed.'

For Mark and his sister Sarah life had few complications. Although never immensely wealthy, Mark's family belonged to that band of the comfortably-off upper middle classes known as 'The County Set' – what one newspaper was much later moved to describe as the modern English Squirearchy.

Mrs Phillips describes their life in those early years as being 'a bit Irish really', but there were always funds to cover the hunters in the stable, a holiday cottage in Cornwall, a small dinghy – 'it was called the *Sea Pony*, we never could get away from horses' – and Mark's school fees at two not-inexpensive public schools. So the Phillips were never poor in the way that an agricultural labourer was poor, but life was nevertheless not all plain sailing. They loved the Tewkesbury countryside, the life and the friends around them, but the farm itself was cold and damp and fell prey to a series of disasters. Two hundred and fifty acres of it lay in what was locally called 'The Marsh', and when the Severn broke its banks one June in an unprecedented flood, their whole hay crop was destroyed. Their flock of a hundred ewes suffered a spate of sheep-worrying just before lambing, some of the dairy herd were affected with arsenic poisoning, and one of the local hotels they supplied with duck and poultry went bankrupt, owing them a large sum of money.

'Things were getting very tight financially,' recalls Peter Phillips, 'and because I was totally committed to the Mortgage Company I had no money left to change the policy of the farm to make it more profitable. Then came the final straw. I was out riding my horse, quietly because it had been lame, and on the way home I saw they were

(*left*) Mark and his sister Sarah aged six and four respectively and in contrast (*right*) Mark in the uniform of a 12th Lancer as a page at a wedding at the same age

pegging out the route for the M5 – right across the best part of the farm. I was absolutely furious and thought – this is it. Now we've really had it.' But that week's edition of the *Farmer and Stock Breeder* carried an advertisement that was to change the family's lives, and fortunes. 'It was asking for someone between thirty-five and forty, which I was, with six to ten years' farming experience, which I had, and who was prepared to live in Wiltshire, which I was. So I applied for the job amongst four hundred others, and got it.'

The job was with Wall's sausage company, and made him responsible for the company's pig-buying throughout the Westcountry, a position that eventually led to him being offered a directorship with Walls. Which is how the Phillips came to live at Great Somerford in the rambling sixteenth-century house of mellow Cotswold stone that's been their home ever since. Mrs Phillips hated leaving Tewkesbury and admits to going to Great Somerford very reluctantly: 'For a long, long time I harked back to that farm,' she says, 'and it took

me years to feel settled here. But from Mark's point of view it had a
major effect on his life because almost immediately he came under the
influence of Frank Weldon and Alec Scott.'

The young members of the Beaufort Pony Club could hardly have
believed their luck. Two of their senior instructors were both Olympic
horsemen; Col Alec Scott was a member of the team which won the
bronze medal at the 1936 Berlin Olympics, and Col Frank Weldon was
one of the heroes of the winning British three-day-event team at the
Stockholm Olympics in 1956. In retrospect it is likely that the two
instructors considered themselves equally fortunate, for the class of
1958 included Jennie Bullen, now as Jennie Loriston-Clarke one of the
country's leading dressage exponents, her sister Jane who was a
member of the 1968 Olympic three-day-event team and won
Badminton in 1968 and – as Jane Holderness-Roddam – in 1978, Mike
Tucker, an international three-day-event rider – and Mark Phillips,
who joined the Beaufort soon after his parents moved from
Tewkesbury to Great Somerford.

At this stage in his life – and by now Mark was nine – he'd had no
formal riding tuition. His mother's litany of 'sit up, look up, hands
down, heels down' was still being drummed into him, but apart from
that Anne Phillips allowed his riding talent to develop naturally by
riding a succession of ponies that were, as she says, 'total contrasts. He
learned at a very young age that you couldn't ride the same way on
everything. And I really do believe that it's the pony that makes the
child – not the other way around – so we always attempted to buy him
the best ponies within our means.' She also believed that Mark should
grow up having the right attitude towards the sport. 'I never allowed
him to carry a stick under any circumstances whatsoever until he was
twelve,' she says. 'It used to infuriate me to see children's ponies
getting the blame for children's bad riding. He used to say "The
blooming pony won't do this, that or the other" and I would say "I
don't know what you mean – it's not the pony's fault – it's your
fault".' The lessons obviously sank in. His exceptional ability is
reflected in two wins at the Working Pony classes at Badminton aged
about nine and ten on Picky.

Even now, when Mark is schooling his horses, he never carries a
whip, and if you ask him to analyse what went wrong after a poor
dressage score or badly-jumped fence, he'll always look to himself for
the fault – rarely, if ever, the horse. He was also taught the value of
being a good loser. 'I can see it now,' says his mother. 'We went to a
hunter trial near Blunsdon, and he finished the round with a face like
thunder. I can remember saying "I will not have it – I do not wish to see
by your face how many fences you've knocked down" and I think he
learned fairly quickly that he wasn't going to be very popular if he
came out looking like a thundercloud.'

So Mark Phillips arrived at the Beaufort, a good loser, a keen

Mark riding Pickles, and Jane Bullen – fellow-members of the Beaufort Pony Club instructed by the Olympic horsemen Col Alec Scott and Col Frank Weldon (*Photonews*)

competitor and a fine natural horseman – but without a clue how to ride the basic, elementary dressage movements, and totally incapable of doing a sitting trot. 'I can remember going into a dressage arena for the first time and bumping and bouncing around all over the place – because I just couldn't do a sitting trot. So Alec Scott put me on a lunge rein, and that was very unfunny. Oh dear. As a young boy being put on the lunge – damned uncomfortable. But someone must have convinced me that it was doing some good, because I obviously kept at it. And when I say I didn't have a clue about dressage – I really didn't. I didn't know you had to ride into the corners, and the first time I tried to ride in a circle it looked more like a lopsided pear.'

That first summer camp was an eye-opener for young Phillips and, even now when he speaks of those early lessons, there's still a tinge of the awe that he and the rest of the class felt for the skills and achievements of Alec Scott and Frank Weldon. 'When he was teaching Col Frank didn't stand on his feet – he used to ride in front of us. On one occasion he brought his Badminton horse, Young Pretender, and gave us a demonstration of how to get a horse to lengthen and come back. This thing was just floating across the ground – and there we were on our little ponies, trying to copy him.'

The example of Alec Scott and Frank Weldon, together with lessons from Molly Sivewright at Talland Equitation Centre, had the right effect and eventually the sitting trot became less of a painful experience and Mark began to achieve quite creditable dressage scores.

Not long after the move to Great Somerford, another pony arrived in the Phillips' yard. Rocky had been showjumped by Lady Sarah Fitzalan-Howard, the Duke of Norfolk's daughter, and was acquired by Mark's Aunt Flavia, who'd been a close friend of the Norfolks for many years. As a young girl Aunt Flavia had been keen on hunting; she also played polo and, with her showjumper Lightwater, enjoyed a run of success which took her to the finals of the Foxhunter Championship at Wembley in the '50s. Aunt Flavia never married. Instead she spent many years looking after the children of the Duke and Duchess of Norfolk and their ponies, accompanying them on their travels to shows and competitions up and down the country. Later, when her father died, she moved to Great Somerford with her mother, barely two hundred yards from brother Peter and his young family, and quite naturally took a kindly interest in Mark's riding. So for almost three years, Rocky and Picky took Mark hunting in the winter and to pony club camp in the summer.

'And then the moment seemed to come when it was time to go up a step,' recalls his mother. 'Mark was twelve and we still felt that he

Mark, now aged about eleven, competing in a local show on Rocky, a pony acquired by Aunt Flavia from Lady Sarah Fitzalan-Howard (*Reed Photography*)

wasn't ready to "make" his own pony – so we went back to Norfolk and bought Archer. He was quite old – twelve at least – but had been in the Norfolk Pony Club team for a couple of years.' The combination of Archer's age and experience undoubtably helped Mark to win his first place in the pony club team of 1961, along with Jennie Bullen, Mike Tucker and George Weldon. The rest of the team were at least two years older than Mark. 'It was a tremendous thrill to ride with people who were older, and far more experienced than me – and that in itself was an encouragement.'

But the real thrill for all those young riders at that time was that the Pony Club Championships were held on the Sunday of the Burghley Three-Day-Event every September. They performed their dressage test on the area in front of the Marquis of Exeter's imposing home, did the showjumping in an arena near the main ring, and then rode across country over a course which included some of the fences – like the trout hatchery – that had been jumped by their seniors the day before, and then rode into the main arena to collect their prizes.

Mark believes: 'It really was a crying shame when they took the championship away from Burghley and staged it at the National Equestrian Centre at Stoneleigh, because it was such an incredible thrill for us young riders to be actually riding at Burghley when the major competition was taking place.'

In 1967 Mark would write his own bit of history at Burghley in that major competition but seven years earlier, in his first attempt to reach the Pony Club Championship finals, he failed miserably. In the qualifying rounds, after an encouraging dressage score with Archer, he set off across country full of enthusiasm, only to be eliminated after three refusals at the water jump. The following year Mark broke an arm highjumping at school, but then, in 1963, the Beaufort Club won their area trial and headed north to Stamford for the Championship. By now Mark had changed schools – he'd graduated to Marlborough College where he immediately made his mark in the colts rugby team and at athletics. Archer was sold (and is still alive today) and Mark's new pony, a 15-hand thoroughbred called Pirate, had arrived from Cornwall. The four young members of the team, Mark, Jane Bullen, Mike Petre and Liz Dotesio, were stabled and housed at Exton Hall, the home of the Gainsborough family. Mark remembers: 'They were very kind to us, and on the night we arrived gave us a very smart dinner. There was a huge dining room with lots of silver, and because we were still very young we didn't really know very much about that sort of formal carry-on. They started by offering us a napkin, off a tray. Poor Jane was the first in line, and she didn't know what to do. I didn't have a clue either, but by the time it got round to me, it became clear that inside these napkins there was a corn on the cob – and we were supposed to unwrap them to pour butter on them as a starter. We overcame that confusion alright but then they brought round the main

Mark aged 12 on Archer at Ascot Jumping Show in 1961 where he took part in the Ponies of Britain event (*Graphic Photos*)

Mark and Pirate competing in the area trial on the way to the Pony Club Championships at Burghley in 1963 (*Reed Photography*)

course, which looked like chicken in a cream sauce. Jane loved chicken, and took a huge portion – I don't think I'll ever forget the look on her face when she discovered that it wasn't chicken but fish – which she hated.'

But any discomfort over dinner was more than made up for by the adventure of being away from home to take part in a major competition, and the thrill of being at Burghley itself. It would be nice to say that the adventure ended in victory for the Beaufort team – but it didn't – in fact they finished fourth. They returned to Gloucestershire without the trophy, but with three friendships firmly established. Mike Petre has remained one of Mark's friends, and Jane Holderness-Roddam was one of the first people he thought of when nominating godmothers for his son Peter in 1977.

Pirate – or Wuz as he was nicknamed – had not been an easy horse to ride. According to Mrs Phillips: 'When you were doing dressage, if you had any contact with the front end at all, up went his head – so you had to kid the judge all the time.' Pirate was eventually sold to Chris Collins' sister, and Mark graduated to a 16-hand chestnut gelding called Kookaburra. Mark had been in the senior ride at the pony club since 1960, instructed by Col Frank Weldon.

'A well brought up boy – always ready with his please's and thank you's,' is how Frank Weldon remembers Mark, and 'a careful rider – not overly courageous – but he had a bit of spark about getting on with the job that suggested he had enormous potential as a three-day-event rider'.

That potential was given full rein over the next few years with Mark competing in the Pony Club Championship at Burghley again in 1965, when the Beaufort finished second with Mark in individual fourth position. Mark was able to draw on the wealth of knowledge and experience Frank Weldon had gained as an international rider. His own riding improved enormously as a result, especially crosscountry, and it was given an extra boost when he was sixteen – not from another trainer, but from simply wearing contact lenses. Until then, he admits, he'd ridden around hunter trial and crosscountry courses 'half blind'.

From his earliest days at Stouts Hill when Mark could hardly see the blackboard he'd been diagnosed as short-sighted and had to wear glasses. His mother believes that 'breaking his arm at a children's party and catching measles at the same time' didn't exactly help the situation.

'But vanity, vanity, always vanity – I never wore my glasses when I rode.' Nor indeed when he played rugby, and admits that even though

The Beaufort team placed fourth in the 1964 Pony Club Championships at Burghley (*l to r*) Mark on Kookie, Elizabeth Dotesio, Jane Bullen and George Weldon (*John Nestle*)

he was reckoned to be a pretty handy threequarter, he rarely saw the ball come out of the scrum. 'I'd wait for everyone else to move, then I knew I had to set off. And it was hopeless trying to wear glasses out hunting, they'd get covered in great splats of mud.' So when he was hunting, or playing rugby, it was just a question of 'follow the pack'.

But on a crosscountry course there is no-one to follow – only your nose. 'Unless the fences were close together I couldn't see from one obstacle to the next, and I couldn't read the numbers on the markers either, so I always walked the course very carefully, taking in all the landmarks that would get me from fence to fence – otherwise I'd have got lost. And once I'd set off – oh the bliss to see the fences coming up and knowing I was on the right track.' It may sound a bit hit and miss but it obviously paid off because he never once took the wrong course, and believes that all those years of meticulous planning help him now in picking the quickest and most accurate route between fences.

Wearing contact lenses meant that he was actually able to 'see' his way round the course for the first time in his life, but to begin with he was only able to wear them for a few hours a day and so every riding competition would end with the ritual of Mark holding his head over an upturned bowler while he removed the precious slivers of glass.

'If I'd dropped them on the grass, I'd have been there now looking for them,' he explains. 'At least in the bowler I had a chance of finding them!' After that initial 'running-in' period, he was able to wear them throughout the day so that now putting the lenses in as soon as he wakes and taking them out last thing at night has become an automatic part of his daily routine.

Following his success at the Pony Club Championships in the autumn of 1965, Mark returned to Marlborough College to face his final year at school. He was made a prefect and elected Captain of Athletics. He competed in the high jump and triple jump. In the long jump he cleared 22ft 3in – a track record; although some years later the record was broken he still has the satisfaction of knowing that the long jump record he established at Stouts Hill of 14ft 9in has never been bettered.

Not considered fast enough to be an individual sprinter, Mark earned a place in the 4 × 100yd relay team and was 'thrilled on the first occasion we ran the 440 yards in under 44 seconds'. He played rugby for the Colts XV, but failed to win a position in the First XV after an accident on the athletics track left him with an injured back, though he did train with the First XV. Clearly, as far as Mark was concerned, academic work took a back seat to his activities as a sportsman at school, but in that final year he knuckled down and added two 'A' levels in history and geography to the eight 'O' levels he'd already achieved.

It was a foregone conclusion that Mark would follow the family tradition of a career in the army, and so in the summer of 1966 he attended the Regular Commissions Board at Warminster in the hope of winning a place at Sandhurst – and failed.

'The school was horrified, we were shattered,' says his mother. The Board gave no reason for their decision, but Mark had never been a 'pushy' individual and admits to being 'shy' in the company of strangers, so presumably the combination of quiet reserve that had made him such a popular individual at school and in the pony club, and the fact that he was 'always a bit speechless', as his mother puts it, did not convince the members of the Selection Board that they were looking at potential officer material.

Mark's own disappointment was crowned by a bout of glandular fever that kept him in bed for ten days and brought his career with the pony club team, to an ignominious end.

'I was the last one left of the old brigade and saw myself as the Big White Chief. But being ill meant that I didn't ride for ages, and I almost got straight out of bed to go to the area trials.' He finished fifth and failed to qualify. 'So I left the club slightly with my tail between my legs.'

But Mark is nothing if not a supreme optimist. 'It's been the same all my life,' he says without recrimination. 'As soon as I hit a high spot –

Mark at seventeen riding Kookie in the Wylye Novice One-Day Event; with Kookie he made the transition from Pony Club to adult eventing (*Reed Photography*)

crash, down I go to the bottom, and have to start all over again.'

The climb back on that occasion began with a suggestion from the Army Careers Board that Mark might get into Sandhurst on what was known as an 'S' type engagement. It would mean joining the army as an ordinary soldier for four months before trying again at the Regular Commissions Board. While his application was being processed, Mark studied for a third 'A' level in British Constitution, and embarked on his first series of adult horse trials.

Kookaburra was a tough, obstinate, quality cob that would rather stop in front of fences than jump over them, and needed to be ridden with skill and determination to get a clear round. And so it was with a mixture of excitement and trepidation that the family headed north in September for the Everdon One-Day Event.

'My goodness, was I ignorant in those days!' says Mark candidly. 'In fact, compared to the way I ride now, I was a proper cowboy. We did quite a nice 'pony club' dressage test, and went clear in the showjumping. In those days I used to pull my stirrups up and ride short for the showjumping, then let them down a couple of holes before I went across country.' The ploy had worked well going over the smaller fences of the pony club courses, but developed a major flaw over the larger obstacles of the BHS course. 'Before I even got to the first fence I'd lost both my pedals, and then we had a snowstorm – in September. As I went over the last fence, it had an inch of snow on the top. But we still managed to finish fourth.'

A sixth at Sherborne, fifth at Stokenchurch and second at Wylye all followed in quick succession and then, in early October, he won the novice section of the one-day event run by the army at Tweseldown racecourse near Aldershot. A further win at Mixbury a few weeks later upgraded Kookaburra from a novice to an intermediate horse, and he celebrated the promotion by coming second at Kemsing.

A silver ashtray at the Phillips' home in Great Somerford recalls Kooky's brief and spectacular career, but by the end of the season it was clear that Kooky had reached his limit. 'A heavyweight horse' is how Mark describes him, 'and while he was just fine at intermediate or open intermediate, he just didn't have the quality, the speed, or the stamina to go on from there.'

So Kooky was retired to hunting, and Mark began a new partnership with the wild, courageous Rock On.

Chapter Two

During the time that the Phillips had lived in Tewkesbury, the Biddlecombe family had been near-neighbours. Whenever there'd been a question of buying a new horse, Anne Phillips had turned to Walter Biddlecombe for advice – and that was the course she followed towards the end of 1966 when they began looking for a replacement for Kooky.

Rock On was a 16.1-hand bay gelding, out of the Irish stallion Black Rock. The horse had already been returned to the Biddlecombe yard after a week with another prospective buyer who proclaimed him 'unrideable'. But the Phillips liked him, handed over the £400 asking price, and took him home to Great Somerford where they discovered that he 'jumped like a flying bedstead, and was as wild as a horse possibly could be'. He also proved himself to have incredible speed across country, limitless courage, and such a sweet and affectionate nature in the stable, away from the atmosphere of competition, that he earned the nickname 'Sloppy Jo' – Jo for short.

At the beginning of 1967, while Mark was still waiting to go into the army, the Phillips decided that the only way to harness Rock On's spirit and potential, and at the same time improve their son's riding, was to send them both to a professional trainer. Frank Weldon suggested the Olympic three-day-event rider Bertie Hill, who had just set up a training yard at Great Rapscott in North Devon.

The two men immediately established a liking and respect for each other which, over the years, has developed into a firm and lasting friendship. Mary Hill remembers him as 'a very nice young man – almost too nice – who needed the edges knocked off a bit'. Certainly up until then life had been pretty cushy. Boarding school had been fairly carefree, there had been good horses to ride in the holidays, his Aunt Flavia was always generous with offers of stabling, grazing, transport and horses when the resources of the family were stretched, and his mother still took the drudgery out of riding by catching the horse, grooming it, feeding it and cleaning the tack.

But the North Devon farming community and the routine of a working yard soon brought him down to earth. On his first night at Great Rapscott, he 'had one drink too many,' says Bertie, 'and discovered that life wasn't quite as simple as he'd imagined. After that I would say we sort of roughed him up a bit by making him ride a lot of young horses so that he learned how to pick them up off the ground.' But Bertie knew this was no greenhorn he was teaching. 'Mark had all the ability in the world,' he says, 'he was a natural, a gifted rider and all-round horseman – it was just a matter of adding a bit of polish.'

That polish came over the next three long, hard, months, when Mark learned what it really meant to own and look after a horse: that stable duties started at dawn and finished at dusk, that riding a horse wasn't a matter of pushing buttons but meant hours of backbreaking work in the saddle with the sharp edge of Bertie Hill's tongue for company.

As for Rock On, Mark described him in a letter home to his parents as a 'frightening' horse to ride – but an understanding and partnership developed between horse and rider that led Bertie Hill to declare that in his opinion the horse had enough ability to compete at Burghley that autumn, Badminton the following spring, and possibly even the next Olympics in Mexico during the summer of 1968.

Considering that Mark had barely been out of the pony club for 6 months, talk of the Olympic Games seemed premature, to say the least, to his astonished parents, who were given this 'plan for the future' during a picnic on Exmoor. But Bertie was convinced that the horse had international potential.

'He was so courageous it wouldn't occur to him to stop – he'd rather fall than stop – so it took a courageous jockey to ride him.' But Bertie's faith in the horse was based on a trainer's observation rather than competition performance. It needed a full one-day event to put his ability to the test.

So the partnership were entered for the Crookham Horse Trials in March, and while Rock On won the novice section, Mark lost four front teeth. After a characteristically fast and furious round, just three fences from the end of the course Rock On suddenly leapt over a tyre rut on the flat. He had the reputation for jumping cavaletti as though they were five-bar gates, so a small rut got the big ditch treatment. He caught Mark completely unawares and as Rock On's head came up it smashed into his face and knocked four front teeth loose. He finished the course covered in glory and blood, and although he was able to stuff the teeth back into their sockets, the nerves never really took and over the years they gradually went greyer and greyer, until he had to have them capped.

But at the time the possible loss of four front teeth was a minor consideration compared to the job of qualifying Rock On for Burghley. Just four days after their triumph at Crookham, they entered at Liphook but, because there was a waiting list for competitors in the novice section, he tackled the intermediate course instead – and came second. In those days horses were not graded on a points system but in accordance with the amount of prize money won, and the accumulated sum from Liphook and Crookham was enough to have Rock On up-graded to open competitions – all within the space of four days.

On 17 April 1967 Mark enlisted in the army and was sent to the Royal Greenjackets in Winchester as a twenty-seven shillings a day rifleman, so when Rock On was entered to run at Sherborne in May, it was with Bertie Hill as his jockey and not Mark Phillips.

The dressage and showjumping sections of the competition are something of a blurr to Bertie – though he does remember that Rock On was very one-sided. 'I can feel it now – he was so hard on the right rein, the only way to ride a dressage test was to be a bit clever and not let the judges see just how bad he was.' It was the crosscountry ride that left a lasting impression on Bertie – mainly because he seems to have completed the round in a state of near terror.

Although Mark couldn't ride in the competition, he did manage to get one day's leave from camp and arrived on the course in time to see Rock On thundering downhill towards a tree in full flight, and Bertie hanging on to the buckle end with his face as white as a sheet.

For most of the course Rock On had been flying like an express train, which presented no problems to a rider who'd been point-to-point racing since he was a teenager, and had ridden in the gold-winning Olympic three-day-event team at Stockholm in '56. But when he reached the Sherborne ski jump, it took all Bertie's courage and skill as a horseman to stay with the exuberant Rock On. The drop on the far side of the jump was about six foot, 'but he just flew at this thing and jumped out so far that it made it a hell of a bigger jump. I thought we were never going to touch down, and when we did he was going flat out down the hill towards a tree. I'd let the reins slip through my fingers to give him all the head he needed on landing, but then I had to gather up the reins to turn him for the next. My God – did I have a ride!'

Towards the end of May the army held their own horse trials at Tidworth in Hampshire, and as a serving soldier it wasn't too difficult for Mark to get leave to tackle what would be his first major three-day event. As it turned out there were no rosettes for the pair. They had a crashing fall at the second fence when Rock On tried to jump a brook and two steps, which should have been taken in three strides, in one mighty leap. Later on the course he skidded around a corner going flat out and had another crashing fall. But neither the rider, nor his trainer, were disheartened. Rock On had proved that his courage was greater than any fence, and the ride round Burghley was no longer a pipe dream, but a practical reality.

As Mark was still in training at Winchester as a rifleman he could only ride his impetuous, brilliant young horse on those rare days when he got leave from camp. He would drive through the night to Bertie's farm in Devon, where Rock On was now a permanent stable guest, to school him for a few precious hours before driving back to base at the end of a twelve- or twenty-four-hour pass.

As the competition at Burghley drew nearer, the horse did nothing but confirm the early promise of brilliance, and only one small cloud appeared on an otherwise clear horizon. Mark had successfully attended the Regular Commissions Board at Westbury in Wiltshire, and was selected for officer training at Sandhurst. The new term opened at the beginning of September, just one week before the competition, and as cadets were confined to the Academy for their first three weeks, this meant Mark would be unable to ride. Fortunately Col Bill Lithgow, the *chef d'equipe* of the British three-day-event team, was then commanding a college at Sandhurst, and a telephone call from Bertie Hill ensured that Mark was posted to his college. Col Bill, who was already well aware of the outstanding potential shown by the Phillips/Rock On partnership, agreed that Mark should have the opportunity to ride at Burghley, and promptly authorised the appropriate leave without reference to the commandant, confident that no-one would miss him for just three days.

Nowadays when Mark prepares for a major competition he rides to a carefully-prepared training programme that starts weeks before and culminates in seven days of intensive work with his trainer in Devon. But for his first ride at Burghley that autumn of 1967, his 'training' was non-existent. He hadn't sat on Rock On for almost six weeks. In all that time the horse had been with Bertie Hill, who drove from Devon to the competition stables at Stamford on the Wednesday of Burghley week. Mark's parents collected him from Sandhurst on Thursday afternoon, and when he arrived to be re-united with the horse the night before his dressage test – he was sick. The combination of a stomach upset, and a horse that found dressage difficult at the best of times, produced a test that Mark would sooner forget and gave him a position second from last. He spent the Friday afternoon walking the crosscountry course and started out on the speed and endurance section on Saturday morning, knowing that he was placed thirty-seventh out of thirty-nine competitors. Rock On flew round the steeplechase course, and arrived in the starters' box after the roads and tracks, immediately before the crosscountry phase, obviously ready to run for his life. Mr Phillips set to washing him down, greasing his legs, and walking him round quietly during the ten-minute halt 'but I didn't dare take his saddle off – as you're supposed to,' he says. 'Jo was so wild, that we'd never have got it back on again.' But the unconventional 'rest' did nothing to slow Jo up. 'He went round like an absolute bomb,' says Peter Phillips, making Bill Thompson's beautiful championship course look effortless, and thundering over the finishing-line an astonishing one minute under the optimum time allowed. Rock On's speed and brilliance across country pulled them up the scoreboard to tenth place, and after jumping one of only eight clear rounds in the showjumping ring on the final day, they finished the competition in fourth place. Mark was jubilant, his family ecstatic, and the commandant of Sandhurst somewhat perplexed.

(*above*) Mark clearing a fence at Burghley in 1967 on Rock On, known as Jo (*Nicholas Meyjes*); (*below*) showjumping in the rain with Rock On later in the same competition (*Findlay Davidson*)

According to Mark's father, the story goes that, over breakfast on Monday morning, the commandant's daughter said, 'I see one of your cadets has done quite well at Burghley.'

'Not possible,' says the commandant, 'none of my cadets is at Burghley.'

'Well,' she says, 'a cadet, Mark Phillips, was placed fourth.' Whereupon Bill Lithgow was sent for and asked to explain.

Col Bill *did* explain, and from then on the army took a far more indulgent view towards Mark's riding exploits. Fortunately, the next big milestone in their career, the Badminton Horse Trials, took place during April when the college was on Easter leave, so no favours had to be asked or given. Mark's father had been a timekeeper at Badminton for ten years, and each April the family had made a pilgrimage to this premier three-day event.

'I used to look at the fences as a youngster and think "I'll never jump that! It's impossible!",' Mark says, 'but as I got older, it became a major objective.'

That spring the British Olympic selectors were looking for riders and horses that could represent Britain at the Mexico Olympics. As always in an Olympic year, the trial at Badminton was something of a curtain-raiser, with the fences deliberately constructed to test the possible Olympic contenders. Mark describes it even now as 'the biggest Badminton course I've ever ridden'; his mother remembers

Mark and Rock On in their first Badminton Three-Day Event in 1968 when they finished fourth, here clearing Fence 15 (*Findlay Davidson*)

'pacing up and down in the stables when Lorna Sutherland came back after the crosscountry. She'd gone about number two or three and she said "This is the first time I don't want to get up on my second ride". Then someone else came back with blood pouring from a horse, and I thought, "Oh Lord, Mark will never get round!".' In fact the pair made mincemeat of the course, and moved up from an overnight position of twentieth to third place, after Rock On's usual exhibition of gallop and dash. But the record books will show that that year they finished fourth, because in the showjumping on the final day Mark admits that he 'foolishly took the advice of someone who didn't know my horse, about how I should jump the last fence. It was a tricky treble which could be jumped with either one long stride or two short ones between the last two elements. If ever a horse would have done it in one, it was Rock On. But I did as I was told and tried two, and went crashing into the last element. We collected ten penalties, and dropped to fourth.'

It was a personal disappointment, and a lesson learned the hard way, but the Olympic team selectors were far from disappointed. When they published their short-list of eight prospective riders a few days later, Mark and Rock On found themselves in company with Richard Meade, Staff-Sgt Ben Jones, Derek Allhusen, Fiona Pearson, Lorna Sutherland, Martin Whitley, and the rider who had won at Badminton and was another former Beaufort Pony Club member, Jane Bullen.

Jo was returned to Great Somerford and Mark went back to Sandhurst to continue his studies, and it was there that he received a phone call from a member of the Canadian team, offering to buy Rock On for the amazing sum of five thousand pounds. He rang his parents 'with awe in his voice and asked what shall we do?' Mr Phillips smiles at the memory and his wife says, with some pride, 'to his eternal credit Peter said, "We're in this for fun aren't we? You can't go out and buy an Olympic horse, so no, he's not for sale.".'

Later in the year Rock On went lame, so it wasn't just the Canadians who were deprived of his brilliance – so was Mark. In retrospect, the Phillips believe it was almost inevitable that the horse would have leg trouble.

'He would just fling himself into the air with such glorious abandon,' says Mrs Phillips. 'We've seen him jump over a drop fence with six feet to spare, which meant that he was always coming down from such a height that inevitably his legs took the toll.'

Later that summer, on the advice of the Olympic selectors, Rock On was hobdayed (an operation to improve his wind) because of the altitude of Mexico City. 'We were so green in those days,' says Mark, 'we just did as we were told without really questioning them. I wouldn't do it now, and although it's clever to be wise after the event, I don't think we should have done it then.'

It left his Aunt Flavia with weeks, rather than months, to get Rock On fit and well for the final Olympic trial at Burghley. She took him to Arundel, the Duke and Duchess of Norfolk's home, and nursed him into condition on the gentle, rolling parkland. 'We must have been crazy to even think about doing it, but we did,' recalls Mark. But it didn't pay off. Rock On broke down on his final gallop before the trial on Cheltenham racecourse, and 19-year-old Cadet Mark Phillips saw his chance of riding for Britain in the Mexico Olympics slip away.

If the Olympic selectors began the year thinking they had an embarrassment of riches, by the time they named their team in September the list had diminished considerably. Sgt Ben Jones' mount Foxdor had died, both Richard Meade's horses, Turnstone and Barbary, were injured, and Rock On had broken down. It left the selectors with the unenviable choice of either sending a team largely composed of young horses and riders, or pairing off their best riders with the best of the horses left to them. In the end, that's just what they did, and the final team consisted of the already proven partnerships of Derek Allhusen on Lochinvar and Jane Bullen on the gallant little Our Nobby, with Richard Meade riding The Poacher who'd been lent by one of the unsuccessful riders on the short list, Martin Whiteley, while Brigadier Gordon-Watson offered his great young horse, Cornishman V, to Ben Jones – though when the team was announced after Burghley, Richard and Ben swapped horses, and it was Richard Meade who rode Cornishman to victory with Ben Jones on The Poacher.

A hardly-recognisable Rock On enjoying the Christmas sunshine when Mark was about eighteen

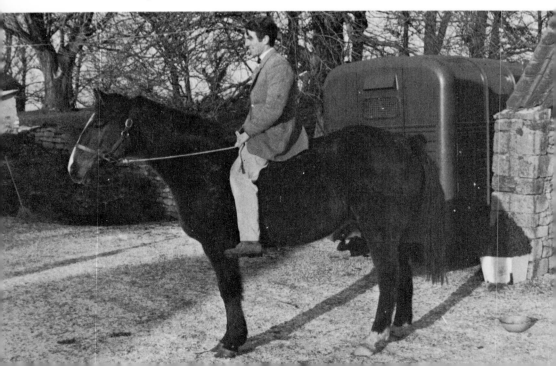

As for Mark, he'd resigned himself to the fact that he'd be left behind, especially after Sheila Wilcox won at Burghley and was offered a place in the team as reserve rider. But while the team was in training at Ascot, Sheila turned the selectors down as she could not get a guarantee that she would ride in Mexico. So Mark was called in, offered the role of reserve, and jumped at the chance. The thrill of being part of the team – albeit as reserve – was inevitably tinged with the disappointment that he would fly to Mexico without Rock On. But, says Mark, 'I was just grateful at having had the opportunity to go – it was a great experience for me.'

The team arrived in Mexico almost a month before the games were due to start to give competitors and their horses a chance to get acclimatized to the altitude. Mark had already resigned himself to the fact that he wouldn't get a chance to ride unless one of the team fell ill, and as they all looked the picture of health, it wasn't even a possibility, though things did get a little uncomfortable after a rather spirited party at which Mark and Harvey Smith threw Richard Meade into a swimming pool.

'He landed awkwardly,' recalls Mark, 'and bruised his ribs. So much so that he had to have some concentrated physiotherapy and wasn't able to join the team at Avandero, the site of the equestrian competition, for nearly two days after the rest of the team. As you can imagine, there was rather a lot of leg-pulling about whether I'd done it on purpose or not.' Of course he hadn't – and so instead of riding he fulfilled the only role left to him, that of general factotum and dogsbody, and in his own way did his best to relieve some of the tension of competition by taking on many of the mundane, but necessary, jobs and errands.

Avandero is a hundred miles west of Mexico City, and six thousand feet above sea level. The three-day-event course had been built in a valley on the edge of a golf course through which ran a small stream.

When the team inspected the fences on the day before the dressage, they found a course that was big but straight forward and Mark admits: 'I would like to have ridden round it. It was a tremendous challenge – though whether I would have been equal to it is another matter.'

But what ultimately made the course such a challenge to the skill and courage of the riders was not the size, not the construction of the fences – but the weather.

Midway through the morning on crosscountry day Avandero was hit by a rainstorm which turned the ground into a treacherous morass and the tiny stream into a raging torrent. The first two riders of each national team rode in good conditions, but by the time the last two began their rounds, the stream had burst its banks and it was impossible to see either the take-off or landing points for the fences that straddled the water.

Mark had spent the first half of the day helping on the steeplechase course, but as the weather deteriorated he positioned himself at the second of the water jumps, towards the end of the course. When the teams had seen the fence in dry conditions it had presented a jump up onto a bank over a wide ditch, with the stream in the middle. Says Mark: 'The banks were at different levels but when the river flooded the take-off side was under water – so you couldn't see where to take off. So we stuck twigs and bits of bush along the edge of the bank so they'd stick up through the water and give the riders a guide. Then, as they galloped in, they got to where the twigs where, they gave the horse a bit of a kick and just hoped for the best.'

One horse after another slid and splashed its way through the obstacles, and tragically one animal died at one of the stream crossings. It suffered a heart attack on landing and was washed downstream, ironically before the floods started. Derek Allhusen blazed the trail for Britain early in the day and rode himself into the silver medal position in the individual tables. Jane Bullen had two falls on Our Nobby when his legs got stuck in the mud, while Richard Meade on Cornishman and Ben Jones on The Poacher went clear in some of the most atrocious conditions ever experienced in an Olympic three-day event.

Britain emerged after the showjumping phase as the gold medal winners and Mark admits to feeling: 'Green with envy. I kept thinking, if only I could have had a ride; if only things had gone differently. But in riding, unlike most sports, your own ability often plays a comparatively small part in deciding whether you can compete or not. It's simply whether you've got the right horse at the right time.'

But his envy quickly turned to pride when the team received their gold medals, and the National Anthem rang out across the stadium. It was his first taste of Olympic triumph, albeit secondhand, and made him more determined than ever to secure a place four years later in the Munich team. He admits 'ever since I've been a four-year man', meaning that while most riders think in terms of competitions year by year, he's always aiming for the next Olympics, and preparing his horses on a four-year cycle.

Mexico also offered his first real encounter with the national press. As a small boy he'd been 'chuffed' at seeing his name in the *Daily Telegraph* when they recorded the results of the Pony Club Championships, and the local press and television had taken an interest in him after his successes at Burghley and Badminton and when he joined the Olympic squad. But in Mexico he discovered that what appears in print isn't always an accurate record of events.

'There were student riots in Mexico City – and to read some of the papers you'd think they were upsetting the whole games, but as far as the athletes were concerned we never even noticed it was going on.' And when it came to reporting conditions on crosscountry day, stories were so exaggerated that Mark says, 'I had to look again to make sure that the writers were actually talking about the same place.'

Later in his career Mark was to have many brushes with the press and discover that honesty and integrity have not always been their priorities when reporting his own affairs, but during those mellow days in Mexico he was simply left wondering 'if I'd ever really been there'.

Although he hadn't ridden, Mark was still an official member of the team, and enjoyed much of the euphoria that surrounded the winners on their return to Britain and as a result had his first meeting with Princess Anne, on what must be one of the classiest blind dates on record.

Mark had been invited to a celebration party for the Mexico team in the Whitbread Cellars, just off Ludgate Circus in London. By now he was back at Sandhurst at the start of his second year, and a few days before the party he was summoned to the adjutant's office.

'The adjutant at Sandhurst was rather a frightening chap, really,' he says, 'and definitely when a little lowly cadet was summoned by the adjutant it meant trouble – so I went there in fear and trepidation. He told me that Princess Anne was going to be a guest at the Whitbread thing, then going on for dinner afterwards, and that I was considered to be a suitable candidate to go along and make up the numbers. I took a deep breath, gulped, and that was that.'

The rest of the dinner party included John Miller, the Crown Equerry, and Mary Morrison, one of the Queen's ladies-in-waiting. A table had been booked at Bucks Club; when Princess Anne prepared to leave the Whitbread reception, Mark was told to follow her car. The official party got into the Royal car, 'an Austin Princess, I think – anyway, it was a big black job' and cadet Phillips tucked in behind, driving his Mini van.

'I didn't have a clue where we were going,' he says, 'as no-one had thought to tell me the name of the restaurant. So I didn't dare lose sight of the car, and when we went through a set of red traffic lights I just kept going and hoped to goodness that no-one would stop me.'

It turned out to be a memorable meal. The conversation, naturally, revolved around horses as Princess Anne was herself just about to embark on an eventing career. But then, halfway through the meal, Mark turned his head quickly and out popped one of his contact lenses. It hardly seemed appropriate to start groping under the table in search of the lens when his dinner companion was a member of the Royal Family, so Mark's view of the rest of the evening was slightly out of focus. When the party broke up, Mark walked with them to say his goodnights, 'but when I turned round to go back in and look for the lens – they'd locked me out'. He eventually found his way round the back of the restaurant and persuaded the waiters to let him in through the kitchens and then proceeded to hunt, on all fours, across the carpet pile for the sliver of glass!

Throughout the winter of 1968 Rock On continued his convalescence in the lush, green fields around Great Somerford. Although Mark had plans for him to compete again in 1969, it was what he describes as 'the beginning of the end for him'. There was no question of him doing anything for at least another six months, and so Mark turned his attention instead to the young bay gelding his family had bought for him the year before.

Great Ovation spent his early years in the Porlock stables of Les Scott. Bertie Hill had broken the horse as a three-year-old, and on one of Mark's many visits to Great Rapscott suggested he might like to look at the animal as a future prospect.

'He was a big, good-looking horse,' recalls Bertie. 'He had bags of ability, and I thought he'd be just right for Mark.'

The first time Mark saw Great Ovation, Les Scott wasn't interested in selling as the horse had already been entered for the Doncaster Sales. But he didn't reach his reserve, so Mark, with his mother and Aunt Flavia, drove to Porlock to see him.

'And I didn't even ride him. We just saw him trot up and down the road. He was a beautiful horse and a beautiful mover. He had great presence and pointed his toes beautifully – I thought this is bound to be another Merely-a-Monarch.'

The family were very impressed, and settled on a price of £800. 'That was a lot of money for a four-year-old,' says Mrs Phillips, 'so Flavia paid for two legs, my mother bought one, and Peter and I bought the fourth.'

Later Mark's grandmother and parents gave him their share of the horse, which is why Great Ovation always appeared in the joint ownership of aunt and nephew.

His good looks qualified him for the working hunter class at the Horse of the Year Show, and in the winter after the Mexico Olympics he had his first taste of hunting. By the spring of 1969, Great Ovation was ready to begin the round of hunter trials and novice one-day events, and had earned himself the stable name of Cheers.

Chapter Three

'Not a particularly illustrious start' is how Mark Phillips describes the beginning of Great Ovation's career. A series of hunter trials prepared him for his first BHS novice one-day event at Windsor in April 1969. 'But he certainly didn't win everything he entered,' says Mark, 'and although I had high hopes of winning at Windsor on Smith Lawn, we were beaten into second place – by Princess Anne on a horse called Royal Ocean.'

Although it's easy to imagine that at this time Mark's life revolved entirely around horses he was, in fact, only riding and competing during leave from Sandhurst. In term time, while Mark continued his studies, it was his Aunt Flavia who provided stabling and grazing for Rock On and Cheers, and kept them fit with daily exercise. She also provided the transport to and from competitions in the shape of a trailer and Bedford van. 'I was really just the "girl groom",' she says, 'and delighted to be able to help.'

But in the first half of 1969 there was a lull in Aunt Flavia's equestrian travels. Rock On was not fit enough to compete at Badminton, so there'd been none of the preliminary trips to events before the competition in April, and Cheers was still very much the baby of the family; his two outings to Windsor and then Farleigh, where he was fourth, were confined to the Easter holidays. But it's doubtful if Mark would have looked for more opportunities to ride that summer, as he was approaching the end of his two years at Sandhurst and was determined to do well in his final examinations.

After being told in no uncertain terms that their son was not considered suitable officer material by the Regular Commissions Board in 1966, it was with considerable pride, that Anne and Peter Phillips watched their son pass out as a senior under-officer and heard him named, out of more than three-hundred cadets, as runner-up for the sword of honour, the second most outstanding cadet in his year. On 25 July 1969 Mark was commissioned as a second lieutenant in 1st The Queen's Dragoon Guards, following his father, grandfather, uncle and godfather into what was considered to be the 'family regiment'.

Mark admits that for a while it was a toss-up between the QDGs and the Scots Greys 'simply because I knew a lot of people in the Greys like Hamish Lochore, Roger Horn and Norman Arthur, all from the eventing world'. But in the end he settled for the QDGs, not the least of his reasons being that he thought they would look more kindly on his equestrian activities!

Mark was detailed to join his regiment in Detmold, Germany, that September, and he planned to spend his two-months' leave preparing for, then competing in, the Punchestown Three-Day Event in August and the European Championships three weeks later at Haras du Pin in France.

Rock On had now completely recovered after almost a year out of competition, but the European team selectors felt he needed the pipe-opener at Punchestown before they would finally confirm Mark's involvement in the championship. Flavia drove the Land-Rover and trailer to Fishguard to make the overnight crossing to Ireland, only to be told that the sea was too rough and she'd have to wait till morning. A scattering of straw on the floor of the trailer provided a reasonably comfortable makeshift bed; with Jo for company she settled down for the night. Dawn brought calm seas and a passage to Ireland.

In spite of his long rest away from major competitions, Rock On had lost none of his old fire. As usual his dressage test was hard work – but there was more of a battle to come on the crosscountry course. With the exception of a technical refusal at the sheep pen, Rock On cleared everything on the course and launched himself with gusto at the final four fences, which ran parallel with the Punchestown racetrack. The stables were behind the grandstand and, according to Mark, 'as we rode down in front of the grandstand he was off, back to the stables. That was where he wanted to go and I had to ride with both hands on one rein just to keep him on course.'

Rock On's performance convinced the selectors that he was worthy of his place in the British contingent, and in September Mark achieved what had become a major ambition – to ride with the Union Jack under his saddle.

The slipping saddlecloth during the dressage phase of the European Horse Trials at Haras du Pin in 1969 (*Findlay Davidson*)

Mark and Rock On having a narrow escape at Fence 8, the Normandy Bank, during the European Championships at Haras du Pin (*Findlay Davidson*)

'And when he did, the blooming thing fell off,' Anne Phillips now talks about the incident with a chuckle in her voice – but at the time it could have been explosive. As Mark began his dressage test, the saddlecloth started to work its way out from under the saddle.

'It was agony,' he says, while Mrs Phillips remembers that 'the test seemed interminable as the cloth slipped further and further back till it finally fluttered to the ground. When Mark got to the far end of the arena a steward dashed in and picked it up.' As Mark says, 'If we'd come off the corner at the end of the test and it had still been lying in our path – that would have been that.' But to his eternal credit, Jo didn't react at all, and ever since saddlecloths have been securely stitched to Mark's saddle.

When they'd inspected the crosscountry course the day before the dressage competition, the British contingent had been staggered by the size and complexity of the fences, and to this day Mark rates that European Championship course as 'the biggest I've ever ridden over'. It included the first Normandy bank, later adapted by Frank Weldon, and included as one of the spectacular fences at the Badminton trials.

'But unlike Frank's version,' says Mark, 'which had a square bank with a ditch in front and a rail behind, this had a sort of dip, then a round hump, then a set of rails three or four feet beyond that. The

The last fence on the Haras du Pin crosscountry course, when Mark and Rock On had the fastest time of the day (*Findlay Davidson*)

object was to clear the ditch, jump onto the hump and then bounce out over the rails.'

But Rock On – who's been described by Mark as 'agony to coax through the dressage, but a real "hold on to your hats boys" chap on the second day', defied the logic of the course-builders, not to mention the laws of gravity – and cleared it in one – just.

'It was the most extraordinary thing,' he says as if, even now, he can hardly believe it, 'but he didn't quite make it, leaving one front leg behind. When he landed he went right down on his nose. I was going to get off, but from somewhere in the crowd I heard Dick Stillwell shouting "Hang on – don't get off!" so I didn't and damn me, he stood up again, and off we went.'

It seemed that nothing on the course could defeat him – even the ditch-and-rail where so many riders came to grief was dismissed by Rock On with a leap that took him from bank to bank 'and very cleverly too'. As they thundered on towards the end of the course, Mark's confidence was high and then, unbelievably, at one of the easiest fences on the course, 'we got our wires crossed, he hit the front rail at an angle, flipped right over, and down we went'.

Neither horse nor rider was defeated. Mark remounted and continued the round. He had a stop at the quarry later on the course but in spite of that, and the fall, still clocked up the fastest time of the day. Apart from the fact that Mark cursed himself for losing concentration, he was none the worse for his fall. The only person left completely shattered by the experience was his mother.

'I've never liked the life and limb bit of the crosscountry,' she admits, 'so at Haras du Pin I picked out the easiest fence on the course – and he just landed at my feet. It wasn't a bad fall, and they were on their way again very quickly, but I said to myself 'that's the last time I watch''.' And she never has since. In fact it's become something of a family superstition that on crosscountry day Mrs Phillips stays well clear of the course and either sits in the car, or watches the action on television. To go anywhere near a jump would spell disaster!

The massive Championship course claimed almost half the competitors, leaving only twenty-two to compete in the showjumping phase on day three. A good round on Rock On confirmed Mark's overall position as seventh and he finished with the third best overall marks of the British squad.

It was a memorable week for Mark. On 22 September, right in the middle of the competition, he'd celebrated his twenty-first birthday.

The successful British team at Haras du Pin (*l to r*) Derek Allhusen, Richard Walker, Pollyann Hely-Hutchinson and Sgt Ben Jones; Mary Gordon-Watson and Mark Phillips, the two individual riders, are behind (*Findlay Davidson*)

Members of the British team, which included Derek Allhusen, Mary Gordon-Watson, Ben Jones and Richard Walker, clubbed together and bought him a silver-topped riding whip which he's carried at every competition since, and has become one of his unofficial lucky mascots.

Mary Gordon-Watson clocked up the first of an impressive run of wins on her horse, Cornishman V, that would eventually include the World Championship and a second Olympic team gold medal. But Mark was delighted with his first international result, and confidently looked forward to earning a place in the World Championship team the following year. Unfortunately there was little time for celebration. After the competition Rock On was loaded into the horsebox and driven back to England, while Mark set off to drive through the night to join his regiment in Detmold. He was cutting it fine. The competition in France ended on the Sunday afternoon and the following Monday morning he had to report for duty.

Armed with an RAC route, he set off from Normandy in his 1100 Ford Escort Estate, and by three o'clock in the morning was only halfway across Belgium. 'I don't think I'd appreciated how far it was,' he admits, 'and in the small hours I started to run out of petrol.' An all-night garage solved the fuel problem; Mark's only difficulty was paying for it! 'I didn't have any Belgian money – just pound notes – and would you believe it? At three o'clock in the morning, this Belgian garage owner got out a copy of the *Financial Times*, worked out the exchange rate, and took enough money in sterling to cover the cost.'

By dawn he'd crossed the border into Germany, and pulled off the autobahn to wash and shave. Just after nine o'clock, he drove through the gates of the regimental headquarters of The Queen's Dragoon Guards in Detmold – Second Lieutenant Mark Phillips was about to embark on his career as a professional soldier.

The Queen's Dragoon Guards is still, rather quaintly I think, described as a cavalry regiment, but by the time Mark Phillips joined in 1969, the horses were long gone. They'd had their final parade in India in 1936 when his grandfather was serving with the regiment and had been replaced by that less elegant but more functional war machine – the tank.

As the New Boy, Mark spent his first three months in Detmold as an understudy to Lt Eric Grounds. A course at Bovington had given him all the technical knowledge he needed to operate the tank, but from Lt Grounds he got an invaluable practical demonstration of how to work together with men and machines.

'When I arrived to join the regiment, they were out on exercise, and I was just thrown into Eric's tank. I'd been on the preliminary young officers' course, but at that stage I really didn't know one end of a tank from the other. They gave me a set of headphones, and I became his rather useless radio operator. But he kept me in order, told me what to do and what not to do – and eventually I was able to take over the troop from him.' This referred to the fact that, in January, he was made a troop leader. Mark then embarked on what he now regards as 'the best times I ever had in the army'.

His troop consisted of four Centurion tanks, a sergeant, two corporals and twelve men. 'We were a team,' he says, 'and there was always a tremendous spirit working within each unit.' His troop nicknamed him 'Chief' 'and that', says Mark emphatically, 'is the *only* nickname I've ever had'. He was referring to the tag 'Foggy' which some gossip columnists claim is the name he was given at Sandhurst by his cadets, suggesting that he was wet and thick. But Mark discounts that: 'If you've got a nickname you eventually get to hear about it – but the first that any of us knew about it was when it appeared in the Hickey column.' Understandably he, and the rest of his family, regard the label as unfair and cruel and admit to being 'rather annoyed' whenever it appears in print. But if 'Fog' is the invention of a Fleet Street hack, 'Chief' was the accolade of a crack troop and Mark Phillips says, with some pride: 'They were fantastic times, and I think we ran a very good troop. I know if it hadn't been, I would never have been allowed to go and do as much riding as I did. But because the job was right, the Colonel was happy to let me go.'

It is a feature of Mark's army career that he always seems to have kept his priorities firmly established – Army first, riding second. It would be naive to suggest that he didn't get special leave to compete in the Olympics or major national and international competitions; like any other talented sportsman in the armed services, he was given every help and encouragement to compete in premier events but, at the same time, he seems to have made a genuine effort to keep ahead of his work so that his absence from camp didn't put an extra load on his colleagues. And it certainly wasn't a one-way deal, for every time that Lt Phillips appeared in a dressage or showjumping arena he wore the striking dark-blue and silver uniform of an officer of the QDGs and indirectly provided the army with a mobile recruiting poster.

Not that there were many occasions for him to ride during the first half of 1970. His own horses were still stabled with Flavia in Wiltshire and the horses of the Detmold Saddle Club were tame fare after the heroic achievements of Rock On, and although for a while Mark owned a polo pony and played in regimental chukkas, it wasn't a game he particularly enjoyed, or mastered. Hunting and eventing were his prime interests as a rider, and to enjoy either meant snatching a weekend at home in England whenever he could afford the petrol and face the rigours of the drive. He organised his timetable for the journeys home with all the planning and precision of a military exercise.

'I could leave Detmold at half-past four, drive to Ostend and arrive by eleven in time to catch the overnight ferry to Dover. We could be through customs by about four-thirty, in London by seven, and home by nine on Saturday morning.' That left him the whole of Saturday and Sunday to compete, or ride to hounds, before heading back on Sunday evening on the eleven o'clock ferry from Dover, arriving back at his regiment on Monday morning after a drive through the night across half of Western Europe.

'It wasn't something I did every weekend,' Mark says, 'just every four or six weeks.' But Rock On was being prepared for Badminton, and Mark wanted a crack at the World Championships later that year; as the horses couldn't be brought to him, he *had* to go to them.

In between these frantic visits, there was the problem of keeping fit. Like any rider, Mark acknowledges that 'the only way to be fit to ride is to ride'. But as that was impossible, the regimental PTI devised a series of exercises to strengthen all the 'riding' muscles after watching him ride a Saddle Club horse, and kept Mark to a punishing routine of circuit training. At the end of the day, when his fellow officers were relaxing in the mess before dinner, he would be working up a sweat to the relentless bark of the instructor. Sit-ups and squats, press-ups and skipping. Exercises using weights and pulleys, balance and sheer physical strength. Everything geared to work on wrists and arms, then back and stomach, thighs and ankles, then back to wrists again. Round and round, against the stopwatch and his own fatigue barrier. And as Mark drily put it, 'The PTI would have a word in my ear if I wasn't working hard enough.'

As it turned out the sessions in the gym at the beginning of the year were all in vain. During his preparations for Badminton, Rock On broke down yet again, and it would be over a year before Mark could ride him in a first-class competition. It was a major blow. Not only because it robbed him of the chance of taking Rock On around the Badminton course in the spring of 1970 but, more importantly, because he'd hoped that the partnership might be considered by the British team selectors for a place at the World Championships that autumn.

Instead Mark concentrated on improving the form of his young novice Great Ovation, and Bertie Hill offered him a ride on the promising grey, Chicago, who'd caught the selectors' eye when Bertie had taken him to Badminton that year. Because Bertie was a professional there was no way he could ride Chicago himself at the Championships, and says, 'A good horse needs a good pilot and Mark was the only one I would have enjoyed seeing ride him.'

The final trial for the World Championships was to be held at Eridge in August. The week before, Aunt Flavia drove Great Ovation north so that he and Mark could have their first crack at the Scottish circuit.

Nowadays, when the network of motorways makes driving north a relatively simple affair, it's perhaps difficult to imagine the complexity of the drive from Wiltshire to Ayr with a Land-Rover and trailer (the

Bedford van had long since been exhausted!). But Aunt Flavia's stamina clearly equalled her nephew's and she completed the journey in two days, with an overnight stop in Yorkshire.

In spite of the fact that Cheers distinguished himself by coming fourth at Lockerbie, Mark describes it as 'not a very successful trip'. Cheers crashed over an artificial wall which is still an obstacle on the course and, although he didn't fall, he gave himself a huge knee. That night the trio stayed on the racecourse at Ayr and the following morning they parked the trailer on the seafront and walked Cheers into the surf, hoping that the chill Atlantic breakers would bring down the swelling, convinced that at any minute they'd be arrested either for parking illegally or for riding on the beach. But before the local constabulary got round to taking any action, Flavia, Mark and Cheers drove twelve miles further up the west coast to Irvine, for the Annick One-Day Event.

It's a feature of the course that a number of the fences are provided by the natural local obstacles of thick hawthorn hedges and wide ditches – and that was to prove Cheers' downfall. After jumping a tiger trap, riders had to immediately turn sharp right and pop over a ditch. But Cheers didn't make it. 'He put his great feet in the ditch, and I was chucked against the bank. The impact twisted my backbone – and that was it – I was absolutely crippled.'

The event at Annick was on the Wednesday; three days later, on Saturday morning, Mark was due to ride Chicago at Eridge in the final trial for the World Championships. But after the fall he could hardly walk, let alone ride, so Flavia was left to take the horse home, while Mark went to London in search of an instant cure. Needless to say, he didn't find one, and on Friday night, when he arrived at Eridge, it looked as though he'd be unable to ride. As a last resort, Col 'Babe' Mosley, who was then chairman of the selectors, took Mark to a local osteopath, 'and although he didn't cure me,' says Mark, 'at least I was able to ride.'

He did the dressage test and showjumping, but was excused from the ride across country. Instead the selectors agreed to wait a few days while Mark's back improved, before making a final judgement. He went to a chiropractor and an osteopath who eased the pain enough for him to be able to ride a few days later. Subsequently Mark admits: 'There wasn't any form of treatment I didn't try. I went to a physiotherapist, osteopath, chiropractor, an acupuncturist, I had injections into my spine, I even went to a faith healer.'

Their combined efforts haven't cured him – even now there are times when his back 'goes' leaving him doubled up with pain for days at a time – but after that initial treatment he rode over a specially constructed course at Ascot. Not surprisingly Mark found the exercise, 'very nerve-wracking. The entire selection committee turned up to watch just me jump a dozen fences, partly to see if my back really

The winning British team at the World Championships, Punchestown, 1970 (*l to r*) Richard Meade, Mark Phillips, Stewart Stevens and Mary Gordon-Watson (*Findlay Davidson*)

was all right, and partly to see how I got on with the horse.' That last statement is perhaps the more important of the two because, at that stage, Mark had only sat on the horse twice – once at Bertie's farm when he'd popped him over a few fences and again at Eridge – but he'd never ridden him across country.

It may not have been an ideal selection test, but the committee was convinced that the partnership would work, and the names of Mark Phillips and Chicago joined those of Richard Meade with The Poacher, Mary Gordon-Watson on Cornishman and Stuart Stevens on Benson, as the official British team for the World Championships at Punchestown in September 1970, with Lorna Sutherland, as an individual, riding Popadom.

If Mark had missed out on riding Chicago before they left for Ireland, he more than made up for it in the two weeks before the competition, and very quickly realised that the big nine-year-old grey was something special.

Bertie Hill had shown faith in the horse from the very beginning. As a six-year-old he'd been placed in novice and intermediate competitions, and when upgraded to open competitions had won at Wylye, Chatsworth and Kinlet. In 1970 Bertie had ridden him round Badminton, passed him on to his son, Tony, who took second place in the Junior European Championships in August, and then offered him to Mark for Punchestown, confident that two years later the partnership would go on to the Olympics. As it turned out, that partnership was only short-lived but, even now, Mark refers to Chicago as 'one of the greatest horses I've ever ridden'.

After their dressage test they were in fifteenth position – not a leader, but still in touch – and with everything to ride for across country. Nowadays the course at Punchestown is regarded as one of the best half-dozen or so in Europe, but in 1970, the course-builders had made a major blunder. Mark's description of the fences as 'big and made of matchsticks' says it all, with a postscript from Mary Gordon-Watson that 'none of the riders liked what they saw and the spectators liked it even less'.

A night of rain before the crosscountry phase turned the ground into a mud rink, and when Mark set off as the second man in the British team he realised that the competition had become 'a matter of survival – it was just like a battlefield out there'. Instead of the usual ten-minute halt in the starters' box between the roads and tracks, and crosscountry phase, he had to hang around for almost forty minutes while the carpenters rebuilt those fences that had been demolished by

Mark and Chicago during the crosscountry phase of the World Championships at Punchestown (*Clive Hiles*)

earlier riders. And there was little comfort in the knowledge that not one of the thirteen horses that had gone before him had completed the course.

But in Mark's words 'Chicago went like an absolute dream' and cleared the first four fences without even a hint of trouble. Then at fence five, a sheep pen, his problems started. The obstacle offered three possible routes – over a parallel bar on the right, a big bounce through the middle, or a very wide parallel on the left.

'I came over the brow of the hill and aimed for the right-hand side, but a steward started waving a yellow flag at me and I saw that the fence had been smashed to bits on the right, and they'd closed that alternative off. So – instant change of plan. I didn't know too much about bouncing, so I aimed him at the big parallel on the left – with my heart in my mouth – and he jumped it beautifully.'

The big grey made fence after fence look easy. The ditch-and-rail that had claimed most of the horses before him 'he just slipped through, as clever as a cat'. It wasn't until he got to fence twenty-eight, a rail halfway down a slippery bank, that he made his first semblance of a mistake. He just caught the rail with a hind foot – but it didn't

The final phase at the World Championships at Punchestown; Mark and Chicago sailing over Fence 8 during their showjumping clear round (*Clive Hiles*)

check the great horse as he blazed his way towards the homeward run.

Fence twenty-nine had taken the heaviest toll of the day. It offered a two-foot-high parallel rail with a six-foot spread and a drop of seven to eight feet on the other side. Horse after horse had come to grief at this obstacle and, in an attempt to make it easier for the horses to jump, halfway through the competition the course-builders altered the fence by filling the gap with brush.

What happened when he jumped is still a vivid scar on Mark's memory: 'I came swanning into it – mad fool – and as we took off, Chicago saw all the greenery and tried to bank it. His feet went down in all the brush – and crash, that's us on the deck.' In those days, providing a horse had gone through the marker flags on a fence, even after a fall, they didn't have to jump again, and as Mark had cleared the first pole, he could have walked Chicago under the far rail and continued the course. 'Instead some bloody fool led him out of the side, which meant I had to jump the fence again because we hadn't gone through both sets of flags.'

It took at least five minutes for the carpenters to rebuild the demolished fence; 'talk about being frightened – the thought of having to jump that damn thing again didn't fill me with an enormous amount of glee. But when I put him to it, he jumped right over – absolutely marvellous.' And in that instant, Mark found himself heading straight for a huge crowd of onlookers. In the time it had taken to rebuild the fence, the spectators had crowded round the landing side – inside the penalty zone. It's extraordinary to think that at a World Championship people were not stewarded behind the fences, but they weren't and as Mark says: 'I had the choice of either ploughing straight through the people or turning right to avoid them, and being a sucker, I tried to turn right. We were going quite fast after taking a run at the jump and as I turned, he lost his legs on the slippery ground, so down we went again. That was two falls I'd had at the same fence.' Understandably Mark feels the incident was 'totally unfair' as Chicago went on to jump the last three fences without even a hint of a mistake and produce a clear showjumping round on the third and final day.

The British were the only team to get three riders home, and took the world title. Mary Gordon-Watson won the individual gold, Richard Meade came second, and Mark finished eleventh overall – in spite of his enormous penalty score of 120 from the infamous twenty-ninth, with his opinion of the horse firmly established.

'He was brilliant, absolutely brilliant.'

Chapter Four

Mark drove back to his regiment in September 1970 hoping that the partnership he'd established with Chicago would be strong enough to carry them both into the European Championships the following year, and the Olympics the year after that. Rock On was still taking life easy in Wiltshire but, with luck, would be back in competition by the summer, and although he hadn't demonstrated any flashes of brilliance, Great Ovation had upgraded from novice to intermediate competitions. Whichever way you looked at it, for a professional soldier who thought of his equestrian activities as a hobby Mark Phillips had almost an embarrassment of riches.

In October Cheers made his first appearance at an overseas competition – and it was very nearly his last! Mark's parents and Aunt Flavia drove with the horse to Deurne in Holland where Mark rode as an individual, and the pair ended up in a muddy heap on the ground after the horse had planted his feet in the middle of a ditch and collected sixty penalties. 'He didn't give me a very good ride,' admits Mark and as a result, before the family left for England, he and his father spent an hour agonising over what to do with the horse. 'I can see us now,' says Mark, 'sitting in the railway station buffet, drinking coffee, saying shall we keep him, or shall we sell him. There was a lot of heart-searching, in the end I decided to give him one more chance.' That chance took the form of a season's hunting – and completely changed Mark's opinion of the horse.

The Berkeley country covers huge tracts of Gloucestershire, what Mark describes as a 'rum sort of country with ditches and dykes, and hedges that might only be the height of a stool, but have a yawning chasm on the other side'.

Cheers had hunted before – mostly with the Duke of Beaufort's pack across more predictable countryside. He'd already been labelled as 'not a particularly generous horse' by the Phillips, and the trappy going of the Berkeley could have been disastrous. But according to Mark 'I don't know what got in to him, but he really got going, and gave me one of the best days I've ever had'.

Following hard on the heels of huntsman Tim Langley he negotiated a bullfinch and iron gate into a pub car park, deftly popped over a stone wall onto a slope with a stream and ditch at the bottom,

Mark and Columbus with the Whitbread Trophy – Badminton 1974 (*Peter Harding*)

Mark and Great Ovation at Deurne in October 1970 where they finished eleventh, after which it was nearly decided to sell Cheers (*Findlay Davidson*)

survived endless encounters with solid hedges and finally cleared a fence straight into a pond. 'He really did jump into some fiendish places,' says Mark, 'and I thought, well, after that he can't be all bad.'

So when Mark was posted to Catterick in January 1971 he took Cheers with him and for the first time in his life was able to ride every day, and organise his own training programme in preparation for the spring events.

Hunting with the Zetland and Beadale kept Cheers on his toes, but the essential work on schooling and jumping was fitted in before breakfast, during the lunch hour or whenever Mark had a free evening from his military duties as an army instructor. Catterick itself had only the most limited facilities – 'a postage stamp of grass with four poles and two tins' is how Mark describes the training area. But next door on the RAF base there was a huge triangle of flat ground between the two main runways and taxi-ing strip. It offered a perfect schooling area, so thanks to 'an enlightened CO' and a bit of inter-service co-operation, that's where Great Ovation did all his fast work; Mark admits, 'I can't believe that the RAF would let me do it now!'

(*above*) Mark and Columbus turning to the last fence in the showjumping phase – Badminton 1974 (*John Topham Picture Library*); (*below*) The only way to drain his boots after an encounter with The Lake at Badminton 1976 when riding Brazil (*BBC*)

(*above*) Training Great Ovation on the airfield at Catterick thanks to inter-Services cooperation (*Rupert Ridgeway*); (*right*) Badminton 1971 – the first of two consecutive wins on Cheers. Note that Mark has lost the silk off his helmet; the silk has been 'lost' twice, but always returned and has become one of Mark's lucky talismans (*Mark Fiennes*)

Throughout that winter Mark had viewed Great Ovation very much as a second-string horse, one that would compete in open classes at a few one-day events, but definitely taking a back seat to Rock On and Chicago who would partner him in that year's major national and international three-day events. Bertie Hill had agreed to make Chicago available for Mark to compete, but in January it became clear that the economics of keeping a three-day-event horse for someone else to ride were impossible for a man who basically made his living as a farmer, and reluctantly Bertie offered the horse for sale.

A British syndicate put up the money, agreeing that it would be wrong to lose a horse of such potential to a foreign buyer, but on the day the British team vet, Peter Scott-Dunn, went to look at him, Chicago was lame after being 'pricked' by the blacksmith. As a precaution the horse had his feet X-rayed and subsequently Peter Scott-Dunn advised the syndicate against buying him. Instead Chicago went to Germany, and helped that country win a silver medal in the Munich Olympics, though Bertie Hill takes little pleasure in the horse's success. 'The horse wasn't really ridden. He did a pig's ear of a dressage test, and was taken across country so slow it was cruel.'

Understandably, Bertie Hill feels the decision not to keep the horse in Britain was 'a great mistake' as he believes that 'Mark stood the greatest chance he ever had of winning an individual gold – and it was taken away from him'.

Whether or not Mark and Chicago would have ultimately gone on to win European and Olympic honours is another of those hypothetical 'if onlys' that keep cropping up in the sport. The fact is that the horse and the opportunities were lost to Mark Phillips, but if it weren't for that disappointment, ironically, he might never have won his first Badminton that year.

As it was, Mark turned his attentions away from Chicago and Europe, and towards improving Great Ovation. He entered him in the intermediate at Rushall in early April, and won. Four days later the horse ran in the advance class at Liphook; Mary Gordon-Watson and Cornishman won the event, but Cheers came third. Badminton hadn't even been considered as a possibility that year, but suddenly everything clicked into place and with the minimum of fuss and preparation, Mark almost slipped into the conclusion that 'as he's going quite well – I might as well take him'.

So Great Ovation went to Badminton in 1971, 'on the off-chance' that he might get round, and it's still with a certain amount of disbelief that Mark says: 'The really extraordinary thing is that he led after the dressage. It was just one of those tests when everything went right.'

Not that he went into the crosscountry day confident that the name Mark Phillips would stay on top of the leader board as he didn't think he had any hope of finishing the course, and because of the sticky going had even considered withdrawing. For days before the competition it had rained steadily, and the water was lying on the surface in huge, shallow puddles. He knew Cheers wouldn't enjoy the conditions and that would make him even more difficult to ride. But in the six months since their disasterous round in Holland, Mark had found the key to getting Cheers safely over some of the more imposing obstacles: 'In laymans terms,' he says 'you just had to showjump him around.' In other words, there was none of the do-or-die launch at breakneck speed that he had with Rock On, and he couldn't ask him to 'stand off' the fences because he'd either stop, or fall. 'He didn't ever fill me with a lot of confidence,' admits Mark. 'I had to keep putting him to the bottom of the fences, and just let him pop over.'

So, using that steady approach, the pair safely negotiated The Coffin, the Luckington Lane and Tom Smiths Walls, which were in the first half of the course, when they were brought to an abrupt halt. An Irish rider had turned turtle at the Normandy Bank which held everything up for almost twenty minutes. A spectator draped his mackintosh over the horse's hindquarters to keep him warm and dry, while Mark considered his strategy for the rest of the round: 'The horse was as fresh as a daisy because we'd really only been hacking around, he was jumping well, and we'd had a twenty-minute rest – so I decided to go a little bit quicker.'

What they actually did was go quite a bit quicker, make nonsense of the times put up by some of the more fancied horses, and as they went clear as well, by the end of the day they'd extended their lead to such an extent that unless they knocked down every other fence in the showjumping-ring, they were unbeatable.

Mark and Cheers during their clear round in the showjumping ring which clinched the 1971 Badminton title (*Evening Post, Bristol*)

What happened on the Sunday is now part of the record books, though it's unlikely that any of them would use Mark's own description: 'To everyone's total amazement, Cheers jumped a clear round, and gave us a very easy win.'

If Rock On felt at all neglected while Great Ovation was getting all the attention at the beginning of the year, by mid-August he was fit and ready to tackle the course at Eridge which served as a final trial before the European Championships.

He came seventh overall, but once again honours went to Great Ovation who won the class and left the British selectors in no doubt that he should be included as a member of the official team. At the same time Princess Anne, who'd finished fifth at Badminton on Doublet and clocked up the equal fastest time of the day across country at Eridge — in spite of a fall at the water — was invited to compete as an individual. The Championships were to be held at Burghley during the first week in September and, as usual in the preceding weeks team members were required to train together at Ribblesdale Park, Ascot. And so the morning after the final trial, Cheers and Rock On were loaded into Mark's trailer and in company with his army groom, Toby Johansen, the quartet set off from Sussex planning to arrive in Ascot just after lunch. And, according to Mark's recollection, 'that's when things started to go wrong. I don't know if Cheers was a bit stiff from Eridge — but he just went bananas in the trailer.' On two occasions during the journey Mark got out to investigate after 'an enormous banging and clattering every time we went round a corner' and found that the horses were perfectly all right. But going down East Grinstead High Street 'to this day I don't know what happened. There was an almighty rumpus and when we looked, Cheers was down, and trying to climb up the side of the partition, which was being smashed like matchwood. Rock On was still standing, but he was squashed up against the side wall, and when I let the back of the trailer down he just shot out like a champagne cork.'

The town's mid-day traffic came to a grinding halt as Rock On careered down the main street and disappeared from view. Neither Mark nor Toby had any hope of catching him, and turned their attention instead to Great Ovation who was still down on the floor of the trailer, 'covered in blood — it was awful, I've never seen a mess like it. All the skin was scraped off the inside of his thighs, and on his hips there was a patch of red, raw skin the size of a magazine.' Eventually they got Cheers back on his feet, mended his head collar and then set off in pursuit of Rock On. They found him a quarter of a mile away, in a pub carpark, hemmed in by a crowd of rather nervous customers. The rest of the journey was uneventful, but they arrived at Ribblesdale hours late and 'with our tails definitely between our legs', only to be told by the vet, Peter Scott-Dunn, that although he was passed fit it might not be possible to run Great Ovation because of the sight of him.

All those red, raw patches would do little to enhance the reputation of the sport – let alone the rider!

When he talks about the incident now, Mark can afford to be flippant about it: 'Having won at Badminton and Eridge and been chosen to ride for the country – there was Britain's pride and joy without any hairs on his back.' But at the time there were ten anxious days before the competition when the horse showed no sign of pain or discomfort, but the skin was stubbornly slow to heal. Rock On was being held in reserve to run at the mini Olympics in Munich two weeks after the Championships, and could have been brought in as a spare horse, but on the day that the teams were finally announced, it was Great Ovation's name that appeared next to Mark's, and with the help

The dressage phase of the European Championship at Burghley in 1971; note the raw patch on Cheers' hip following the incident at East Grinstead (*Findlay Davidson*)

Princess Anne and Doublet, winners of the individual European title at Burghley in 1971 (*BBC*)

of a little cosmetic treatment the raw patches didn't look *too* alarming.

After the dressage Princess Anne and Doublet were 'streets ahead' of the rest of the field, and a fast, clear crosscountry round confirmed that she was almost uncatchable as the individual champion. For a while it looked as though Mark and Cheers would follow her into the arena in second place. The horse had done a reasonable dressage test and completed a faultless round over Bill Thompson's imposing course until he came to the second last – a V fence. Mark admits: 'Great Ovation wasn't the most generous person in his life, and the one thing I could never do in any Championship was jump a corner – because he'd always run out.'

When he'd walked the course Mark had considered it, but decided instead on the long way round – taking a stride in the middle. But as one of the last riders to go, he'd seen the rest of the field make the corner look desperately easy, so as he rode for home: 'My confidence was quite high, and I thought I'd give the corner a go – but sure as eggs is eggs he went straight past the red flag.' Without the stop he'd have maintained his second position; instead they dropped to fifth, 'and then, just to complete a week of misery, I had a foot in the water during the showjumping'.

Princess Anne rode an accurate, faultless round on Doublet to win the individual European title, while the British squad took the team award. In spite of Mark's own individual placing at fifth, he was still mad with himself for the mistake on the crosscountry: 'It was entirely my fault,' he says, 'no marks for the jockey on that one', adding that nowadays he hopes he wouldn't be so foolish as to fall into the same trap 'because the older and more experienced you get, the more you realise how easy it is to throw away a major competition because of a stupid mistake. If you have a chance to win a competition and you don't because you have a fence down, or a stupid stop, or you haven't gone fast enough, then nine times out of ten if you're really honest with yourself it's your fault – not the horse's. I've won a lot of competitions, but if I hadn't been doing stupid things like trying to jump corners, in the long run I'd probably have won a few more. So every time I enter a competition I try to concentrate on eliminating mistakes.'

But in 1971 he obviously wasn't concentrating hard enough, for just two weeks later, fate had another unpleasant lesson lined up for him at the mini Olympics in Munich. Four British riders, Mike Tucker, Lorna Sutherland, Mike Moffat and Mark, set off across the channel with their respective horses. Mark took Rock On, who had apparently become 'reasonably sensible at this stage of his life'.

A long delay at the German frontier while they waited for the local vet to sign their entry papers meant that by the time they arrived at the competition site on the racecourse just outside Munich, it was the small hours of the morning and there were no officials to receive them except the German army guards. It also seems that they'd caught the organisers on the hop by arriving a day earlier than expected because there were no proper stables for the horses – just a large marquee with stalls made from thin wooden battens – and nowhere for the competitors to sleep.

Eventually they settled the horses down for the night, borrowed camp beds from the soldiers, wrapped themselves in horse blankets, and snatched a few hours' sleep in a spare tent. It took a few days to get them and the rest of the competitors billeted in the official quarters, and by that time the four riders discovered that although they had gone to ride as individuals, the Germans were also running an 'unofficial' team competition, and the four immediately became Britain's unofficial representatives.

By day the team practised conscientiously, but by night the attractions of the Munich Beer Festival beckoned. A trip to the fairground and a ride on the big dipper left them all feeling 'rather sick', and after a particularly uproarious session in a bierkeller Mark's groom, Toby Johansen, found himself isolated in the middle of Munich without money or a word of German, and only got back to the stables after sneaking a ride on a succession of trolley cars and jumping clear before the conductor could ask for his fare!

The relaxed, almost carnival atmosphere amongst the riders when they were off-duty did nothing to remove the sharpness of the competition itself, and at the end of the second day the British 'team' were in the lead, with Mark and Rock On way out in front on the

individual scoreboard. And that was when the British observers
started taking an interest in them.

'Up to that point,' says Mark 'we didn't have a *chef d'equipe*, we'd
done all our own organising and were doing very nicely thank you on
our own. But as soon as we started doing rather well, we suddenly
became rather important.' During the evening, after the crosscountry
phase, the Germans had organised a party and at ten o'clock, the
British 'team' was told to 'go home to bed'.

As Mark says: 'Because no-one had paid any attention to us before
we rather objected to being told to go to bed just as the party was
warming up. There were a few harsh words exchanged, and eventually
we were carted off. But when we got back to the hotel we stayed up
until four o'clock in the morning, drinking beer, and complaining like
mad about these wretched people who'd come out from England and
upset the apple cart.'

The following day Mike Tucker, Lorna Sutherland and Mike
Moffat maintained their position after the showjumping phase, and
when Mark rode into the arena as the overnight leader with two fences
in hand, it looked as though Britain was all set to take both the team
and the individual gold.

The winning British team (*l to r*) Richard Meade on The Poacher, Mark on Cheers,
Debbie West on Baccarat and Mary Gordon-Watson on Cornishman, September 1971
at Burghley (*Findlay Davidson*)

As soon as Rock On began jumping it was clear that he was enjoying himself. 'He was spectacular,' says Mark. 'He didn't come within two feet of anything, and every time he jumped he just went higher and higher.'

The German crowd rose to the occasion and began cheering and clapping each time the horse sailed over another fence. Mark's parents were sitting in the grandstand with 'Babe' Mosley: 'The Germans do love a soldier,' says his mother, 'and I must admit he did look very glamorous in his uniform, and as he approached the last fence, they'd obviously decided that he'd won the competition, because they all started cheering.'

It was right then, when Mark practically had the championship in the bag, that fate decided to teach him another lesson in concentration. Mark knew the horse was getting stronger and stronger as he jumped towards the finish – and even if he had one fence down, he would still be the winner. As he approached the final fence – a triple – in his own words: 'Jo took off from God knows where, and landed in a heap right in the middle. We both went end over end – so that took care of that little win.'

He had incurred forty penalties and dropped from first down to fifth. The team still carried off the gold medal and the individual honours went to another British rider, Lorna Sutherland. Mark puts

Mark and Rock On during the steeplechase phase of the Munich mini Olympics; a mistake at the last showjumping fence prevented Mark winning (*Milan Czerny*)

the episode down to experience and with a shrug of the shoulders chalks it up as another occasion when 'there were no marks for the jockey'.

Having achieved a boyhood ambition to ride at Badminton and, moreover, carry off the winner's trophy with Great Ovation, it became a fairly logical consequence that Mark would want to go one better and win the trophy two years running on the same horse, a feat already achieved by Frank Weldon on Kilbarry and the great Sheila Wilcox – High and Mighty partnership.

Mark knew that Great Ovation had his limitations but, like any good jockey, with sensitive riding and a steady programme of training, he minimised the horse's weaknesses and capitalised on his strengths.

Mark had recognised, for instance, that Cheers always ran better in the spring competitions than those entered in the autumn, and put this down to the fact that he started the year full of enthusiasm after a winter's hunting, but found life very dull and boring after a summer at grass. So the first stage of his preparation for the Badminton 'double' was to get Cheers in top gear with a season following hounds and, by early March, he was showing the sort of spark and determination that had made him a winner the year before. Then, during a day with the Bedale – disaster! A strand of wire buried deep in a hedge slashed through Cheers' knee, and made a nine-inch gash down his foreleg diagonally across the knee onto the cannon bone. Mark's reaction was fairly predictable: 'I thought, that's it – the end of Badminton, the Olympic games, everything.' The wound was stitched, Cheers had two days' rest in his box, five days of gentle walking, and made such a miraculously quick recovery that within three weeks, by the end of March, Mark was able to enter him in the Ermington One-Day Event – which he won. A week later he came third at Rushall and in mid-April arrived at Badminton, ready to defend his title, looking none the worse for the accident.

Cheers may not have been the most generous of jumpers, but his temperament was ideally suited to the hothouse atmosphere of the dressage arena. 'He was never a difficult horse to relax,' says Mark, 'and when he went into the arena he'd see all the crowds, the stands, the flowers; and the atmosphere would give him just that extra bit of spark to turn in a good test.'

There's undoubtedly an 'art' to being able to ride a good dressage test, apart from the obvious ability of being able to do a basic walk, trot and canter. According to Mark part of the trouble is that 'nine people out of ten leave their test outside the arena because they try to do perfect dressage outside when they're warming up'. He admits that not everyone would agree on his own formula, but it's one that's brought him unquestioned success. 'I do all the hard work at home, making them concentrate, getting them obedient, and perfecting various movements. But I *never* do a complete dressage test. I'll practise the different movements to get the transitions from one to another, but I jumble them up – lose them – in a series of unrelated movements so that they never get too clever and learn the test – otherwise when you go in the arena they'll be anticipating every move instead of concentrating. And the nearer you get to a competition, the more devious you have to be – and the more patient. It's no good having a major confrontation or getting angry, because if they go into the ring and do something wrong they'll expect a wallop and then the whole test will go for a burton.' And on the day of the test, again, Mark doesn't believe in aiming for perfection until he actually performs the test in front of the judges. 'I try to hardly pick up the reins – just get the horse nice and floppy on a loose rein and then, when he's really relaxed, I start to ask for a bit of movement. It may take as much as two hours, but it's worth it. I find that I can really pick up the reins just a few minutes before I go into the arena, ask for a bit of trot, and lengthening, a few transitions, canter, halt and finish, then straight in. By then he should be relaxed in himself, not all bored with dressage because he's really only done a few minutes of concentrated work, so it's always a light relief to go into the ring and do some work.' To give him his due, having delivered this thesis of 'the perfect way to ride in a dressage test', Mark gives a lopsided grin and shrug, as if to say 'well, that's the theory', knowing that in practice it doesn't always work out

Mark and Cheers negotiating the drop in Huntsman's Close during the crosscountry phase at Badminton 1972 (*Clive Hiles*)

that way. But it was certainly a theory that bore fruit with Cheers – as by the end of the 1972 Badminton dressage test Lt Mark Phillips and Great Ovation were in the lead.

On crosscountry day Mark made an uncharacteristic error – he forgot to start his watch when he set off on the steeplechase course and had to time the section in his head. He crossed the finishing line three seconds over the optimum time – furious with himself for making such a blunder 'because we could so easily have corrected our speed and made sure that we finished inside the time'.

It meant that he started phase D – the crosscountry – with an unnecessary 2·4 penalties against him and the knowledge that Richard Meade, riding the brilliant young Laurieston for the first time, was chasing him hard.

Both riders steered their mounts to clear rounds across country but while, in Mark's words, Cheers 'went his normal way and hacked around', Laurieston clocked up a faster time and nudged into the lead by just half a mark.

After jumping a faultless round in the showjumping ring, Mark stood on the sidelines and watched Richard Meade also jump clear to clinch the title. 'I was standing at the entrance to the ring next to Laurieston's owner, Derek Allhusen, and as Richard cleared the last I shook Derek's hand, congratulated him, and went to get my horse.'

What Mark, and most of the spectators, had failed to realise was that in his effort to jump a meticulous round and hold onto the lead, Richard had erred on the side of caution and ridden so slowly that he'd incurred one-and-a-quarter time faults. That swung the balance back in Mark's favour – giving him the championship by the slimmest of margins – just threequarters of a point.

'So my long face suddenly turned into a broad grin,' and the names Lt Mark Phillips and Great Ovation went down in the Badminton record books for the second year running.

A few weeks later, when competing in the army horse trials at Tidworth, Bertie Hill remembers 'being woken up in the middle of the night when Mark got back from a party, so that he could tell us what a super girl Princess Anne was'. Mark had spent part of the evening dancing with the Princess and was clearly bowled over by her. But the incident was soon forgotten, as riders and trainers alike turned their attentions towards the Munich Olympics.

Although Mark's career in the top echelons of event riding had been comparatively short, he was already well embedded in the annual competitive routine which evolved round Burghley each autumn, a season's hunting during the winter, Badminton each spring, and a summer 'trial' for one of the major international competitions towards the end of the year. And during that summer of 1972, Mark had his ambitions firmly fixed on the ultimate goal of any amateur sportsman – to represent his country at the Olympic Games.

Badminton 1972 – Mark and Cheers completing a faultless showjumping round to clinch the title for the second consecutive year (*Clive Hiles*)

His inclusion on the Olympic short list with Richard Meade and Laurieston was a foregone conclusion after the Badminton win. But, as ever, the contenders had to provide absolute proof to the selectors that they were worthy of a team place by competing in the final Olympic trial – held once again at Eridge – which boasted a list of competitors that included the full strength of the United States team.

A succession of hot, sunny days had baked the Sussex clay on which the Eridge course was built into a solid brick, but just before the competitors set off across country a thunderstorm turned the surface into sludge, and transformed the whole course into a skating rink. No-one had a particularly pleasant round, but Great Ovation, who was a careful horse at the best of times 'absolutely hated it and went like a drain'. And Mark wasn't too enthralled either: 'I've never ridden in such slippery conditions as we faced that day. When Cheers found he couldn't keep his feet, he didn't go well at all.'

Nevertheless, Mark nursed him round the course and managed to go clear until fence twenty-three, just three from home. The fence was a fairly innocuous pole over a stream which had flooded with the rain and obliterated both the take-off and landing. 'To make matters worse there was a hole on the landing side and, needless to say, Cheers put his feet straight in it, and we both went under for a ducking.' The hole claimed a number of victims, including Richard Meade and Laurieston. But it's unlikely that any of the casualties were affected by the incident quite so severely as Great Ovation, who was by nature a careful and cautious animal. Mark rated the competition 'far from being a confidence booster before the Games, it totally shattered Cheers' and he believes that if he could have given the horse a few days' hunting 'just to get his confidence and enthusiasm back, he would have been fine', but in the middle of August there was no hope of such a rest cure – and Cheers flew off to Munich a disillusioned animal with his rider convinced that he no longer had the heart or enthusiasm to face an Olympic test.

Fortunately the rest of the team didn't share Mark's anxieties, and Richard Meade, Mary Gordon-Watson and Debbie West viewed the approaching competition with growing optimism as their horses Laurieston, Cornishman V and Baccarat completed the final stages of their training.

The atmosphere of the Olympic village was as always one of sporting admiration and international goodwill. All that was shattered on the night of 5 September when members of the Black September group of terrorists attacked and killed two of the Israeli team, holding nine more hostage. The world was stunned, and although the humanitarian and political consequences outweighed all other considerations, for a while it seemed as though the very foundations of the Olympic movement itself were beginning to

Princess Anne on Columbus at the Batsford Horse Trials in May 1972 when she came second in the Intermediate Class (*Findlay Davidson*)

crumble. There were suggestions that the Games should be cancelled, but Mark no doubt echoes the sentiments of most athletes who found themselves on the perimeter of that outrage when he says: 'We all felt desperately sorry for the Israelis and shocked by what had happened, but afterwards most of the athletes wanted to be left alone to get on with the Games.'

Mark rarely commits himself in public to any comment on matters of national debate – but on the question of sport and politics he's adamant: 'I've always believed that sport and politics should be kept apart. As far as politicians are concerned that may be a naive and impractical way of looking at it, but the most pathetic thing I think I have ever seen in my life was the African athletes at Montreal who sat on the steps in the village and cried when their countries decided to boycott the '76 Games. They were totally shattered, disillusioned, because everything they had dreamed of, all those hours and hours of training and preparation, had suddenly – at the flick of a politician's fingers – gone out of the window. The reason that people compete in sport is that they enjoy the competition of proving that *they* can jump further, run faster, or whatever, than the next one. In the case of the Olympics you're up against the best in the world – that's what sport is all about – not politics.'

But the politics of the Middle East had intruded on the Munich Olympics, and no-one associated with that festival of sport was left unmoved by the experience. In comparison, the individual tragedies of success and failure at the Games seemed insignificant – except to the people they involved. In the British equestrian team, Debbie West faced her own major disappointment when Baccarat went lame on the day before the start of the dressage phase, and her place in the team passed to Bridget Parker and Cornish Gold.

Mark had been convinced that Cheers was not properly settled to his dressage work, and the horse hadn't been helped by a plague of small black flies that crept inside his ears and bit into the soft, tender flesh, not unnaturally making him toss his head and lose concentration. A can of fly-repellant and a set of loose cotton earmuffs solved the fly problem, and a session in front of the video cameras finally convinced Mark that the horse wasn't moving quite as badly as he'd thought. In fact, Great Ovation produced the best dressage test of the British team, taking third place overall.

But Mark admits to having little confidence in his performance as they tackled the crosscountry course, which offered plenty of galloping between big, demanding fences. 'It wasn't really his sort of

(*above*) Burghley 1980 – Percy clearing the Zig-Zag two fences from home; (*below*) The final vets's inspection at Burghley. With Persian Holiday leading after the dressage and crosscountry – an anxious look to make sure that all is well!

course,' he says. 'He was much better at fiddly fences like coffins, and the sunken road. As soon as we started I knew that he wasn't going well – and sure enough, at the fourth fence from the start, over we went. It was a wide parallel and he just didn't have enough oomph to make the back rail. Perhaps if he had more confidence and had been attacking the course we would have made it.'

But the legacy of Eridge was obviously still clear in Cheers' mind, and to make matters worse, when Mark re-mounted: 'A most extraordinary thing happened. My right rein looped under his chin, round his nose, and back to my hand. I must have ridden twelve or thirteen fences with him like that, but he was always a bit wooden going across country and I really didn't notice any difference in what I'd got in my hands.' The rein righted itself at the sunken road when the horse stopped, and added a technical refusal to his tally. Then at fence twenty-three he had another stop and then another crashing fall five fences later. In fact, fence twenty-three turned out to be the bogey and claimed most of the day's casualties, including two more members of the British team, Mary Gordon-Watson and Bridget Parker. Towards the end of the day it was clear that the only way to jump the fence was on the left and not on the right as most people had done, so when Richard Meade set off as the last man, he had the benefit of his colleagues' advice, and turned in a magnificent clear round.

Great Ovation's disappointing performance meant that his was the discounted score when the points were totted up for the team award. But Richard's clear round, and a supreme effort by Mary and Bridget – who'd both cleared everything on the course with the exception of the notorious twenty-third – ensured that Britain was the overnight leader. All four horses completed a faultless showjumping round, and Britain achieved a memorable Olympic double, winning both the team gold and the individual gold medal which went to Richard Meade.

The thrill of winning an Olympic gold medal, coupled with the emotion generated within that huge stadium as the National Anthem was played, remain one of Mark's outstanding memories. 'It was a very moving occasion – something to bring a tear to anyone's eye. It gives you a marvellous feeling of pride.' But there is a hint of regret in his voice when he adds 'not that I contributed an awful lot to it'. Being there and competing was certainly one stage better than he'd attained in 1968 at Mexico, but he naturally regrets that it was his score that didn't count in the final tally, and he's never yet had another opportunity to satisfy his own standards and ambitions as an Olympic sportsman.

So near and yet so far – but at least we have a piece of silver to take home. Persian Holiday, second at Burghley in September 1980

Mark and Cheers on the Munich Olympics crosscountry course; note the rein looped under Cheers' chin (*Milan Czerny*)

The one positive thing to come out of the Munich Olympics was that Mark had taken the opportunity to renew his friendship with Princess Anne, who'd gone to the Games as a spectator. The two were still quite simply 'good friends', with a common interest in horses. In fact, at that stage the friendship was so low key that soon after returning from Munich, Mark took his mother completely by surprise when he casually asked one day if he could bring Princess Anne home for dinner. Mrs Phillips admits to being 'mildly surprised when I realised that he had Princess Anne's telephone number – but I never realised there was anything serious between them'. Though when she says that Mr Phillips gives a knowing smile which suggests that perhaps he'd already recognised what neither Princess Anne nor Mark Phillips had themselves identified as an interest beyond a mutual love of horses! Even when Princess Anne asked Mark to take on her bold, headstrong grey eventer, Columbus, she admits: 'It wasn't because I actually fancied him – I asked him because I thought he was the best person to ride him.'

Columbus was owned by Her Majesty the Queen and had proved to be a 17·1 handful for Princess Anne. He'd been placed at novice and intermediate level, and had won at Liphook during the spring. But Columbus was clearly not a 'lady's ride' and after the steering failed with Princess Anne on the steeplechase course at Burghley during the autumn of '72, Mark was asked to take him on. Many observers were convinced that the horse was totally wild and dangerous. But, while admitting that he was 'strong' and 'when presented with a big open space he liked to take off', Princess Anne was convinced that riding Columbus was not a question of 'brute force and ignorance. And having watched Mark ride, and made up my mind what I thought about the others, I really felt he showed more adaptability than most of the top-class jockeys. There didn't seem to be much he couldn't get on with.'

So in September Mark began making regular trips from his regiment in Catterick to Alison Oliver's training stable in Berkshire, to forge a partnership with Columbus that has lasted ever since.

To begin with the visits were fairly patchy; Mark was still nursing Great Ovation back to his old form though he admits that, after Munich, 'he was never the same again', and he was asked to ride two more horses – George and Laureate. George was the least complicated of the offers. He was owned by the Straker family who lived quite near to Catterick and as their son, Matthew, had gone abroad with his regiment, Mark was asked to take the promising young horse around the intermediate course at Chatsworth in October.

Olympic gold – Mark, Mary Gordon-Watson, Richard Meade and Bridget Parker celebrating their victory (*Daily Express*)

And 'much to everyone's surprise,' says Mark, 'he won – and
Princess Anne came second on Goodwill!' adding that 'considering
that we were quite friendly at that stage it wasn't the most popular
move I ever made'. But, with a win to his credit, George was returned
to the Strakers, and Mark began the long, tedious grind of getting
Laureate fit to ride. He'd gone to see the horse after his owner, Terry
Mills, wrote to say that they didn't want to sell him but they didn't
want to pay for his keep either – so would Mark be interested in taking
him on. Mark has always reckoned to have a good eye for a horse –
and he must have needed it when seeing Laureate for the first time. 'He
was so fat he looked just like a stallion, so I hacked him out, swathed in
mackintoshes and rugs, to sweat the fat off. If I'd stuck to just walking
in the ordinary way, we'd still have been going now.'

Within weeks of Laureate's arrival, there were two more additions
to the Phillips household – a black Labrador called Moriarty, and a
handsome five-year-old gelding by the name of Persian Holiday.
Percy, as he's universally known, was found by Flavia as a result of an
abortive horse-buying trip to Barbara Tatlow's stable near Chipping
Norton. 'Nothing at Barbara's took my fancy, but she knew that I was
always on the lookout for something decent for Mark, so she told me
about a nice-looking horse that one of her neighbours had for sale. I
saw him, liked him very much, and suggested that Anne and Peter
should take a look at him.'

He was owned by Roger Dancer at Chipping Norton and, although
the family coughed slightly at the asking price of £2,000, they
collectively fell in love with the horse, describing him as 'one of the
nicest people' and took him back to Great Somerford, where he spent
the winter hunting as a preliminary to the spring competitions.

Moriarty, on the other hand, made his presence felt immediately
Mark acquired him. He'd belonged to an army friend who left the
regiment to work in Africa; as he couldn't take the dog with him,
Mark agreed to have him as a replacement for his lovely greyhound
bitch, Precious Beat, who'd been killed in a road accident earlier that
year. Whenever Mark took the horses out for exercise, Beat was
always there, trotting beside him or eating up the ground with an
effortless, graceful stride that kept pace with the horses as they
galloped across the open ground. 'She was a super dog,' recalls Mark.
'So quiet and friendly and when she curled up on a chair and looked at
you with those soft brown eyes – everyone just turned to jelly.' For
more than a year she was Mark's constant companion, and she died
whilst travelling with him to Inverness.

'I'd driven through the night to join an exercise and stopped to have
a cup of coffee outside Edinburgh. It was dawn and I let her out to
stretch her legs and spend a penny, when suddenly she caught sight of
some rabbits on the other side of the road and was off like a rocket.
The rabbits saw her coming, and disappeared, so she trotted back

across the verge – just as a lorry came round the bend and bang, that was that.'

But where Beat had been sweet and loving, Moriarty quickly established himself as something of a bully. 'He was everybody's friend – especially when they gave him something to eat – and if he couldn't scrounge in the mess there were always the dustbins round the back. But the thing he couldn't stand were Yellow Dogs – especially yellow labradors' and on more than one occasion Mark's big black labrador was at the centre of a mess dog fight.

Whichever way you look at it, Mark had a busy and eventful end to the year. The army, not unnaturally, had the greatest claim on his time, but whenever he could snatch a few hours off or a day away from camp there was Cheers to hunt, Laureate to get fit, the new horse – Persian Holiday – to school and a partnership to make with Columbus. To the casual observer it would seem that Mark Phillips couldn't go wrong. He'd ridden in the winning teams at the European, World and Olympic three-day events, had won Badminton twice on the trot, and could look ahead to the 1973 season with a stable full of good horses. But there was one black ugly void in his life – Rock On was dead.

After the mini Olympics in Munich the year before, Jo had suffered another bout of leg trouble and, following a fairly inactive summer, they decided to operate on his tendons. While the operation itself was a success, as Rock On was coming round from the anaesthetic, he died. A post mortem later revealed that a small nodule had broken away from the aorta and blocked one of the valves in his heart. The family were heartbroken; 'Sloppy Jo' was much loved by them all and Mark admits unashamedly: 'I cried and cried and cried. And even now, just talking about him gives me a funny feeling.'

Together Mark Phillips and Rock On had established that rare thing in the horse world – a perfect partnership – and although other horses have brought Mark greater individual honours and fame than any he achieved with Rock On, that horse maintains a very special place in his affections. There are people who believe that riders are cruel to their horses, others who take the opposite view and scoff at the sentimentality shown towards them. But Mark's tribute to Rock On puts that special understanding that exists between man and horse into perspective.

'He was the bravest horse ever, and you have to really admire pure courage in a horse. He'd look at you with a big, wide brown eye, and I'd think, "Why should you be so brave, so courageous?" And if you ride a horse like that, it really starts to get to you, because you feel – who are you to ask such a proud beast to be so brave. Rock On always had his ears pricked, saying "come on dad – let's get on with it". He didn't know what it was to give up. He just didn't know the meaning of the word No.'

Chapter Five

Ask Mark Phillips nowadays how he rates the rangy 17-hand Columbus, and he'll tell you that he's 'one of the best horses I've ever ridden, and one of the all-time great horses of three-day eventing'. But in the autumn of 1972 when he was first asked to ride the horse, Mark admits to being 'not over-impressed' and frankly nervous at being asked to ride him, knowing how acutely embarrassing it would be if he couldn't manage the powerful grey. As a curtain-raiser he agreed to ride him at Chatsworth in October where he won on George, 'but I was left none the wiser about Columbus who went lame before the dressage test, and was returned to Alison Oliver's stables without even getting in to the arena'.

Another five months were to pass before the pair made their competition debut at Liphook on 28 March. The week before Mark had ridden the now fit, slim Laureate to victory in the novice class at Ermington, also coming third on Cheers in the open intermediate, with Princess Anne just nudging ahead into second place on Goodwill. At Liphook Laureate repeated his winning performance and took first place in the novice competition, and for a while it looked as though Columbus would make it a winning double for Mark – he was leading the open class until a run-out at a corner coming out of the coffin dropped him to sixth position. The jockey's verdict: 'He went quite well and pulled hard, but we still hadn't got the act together.'

In direct contrast to Mark's slow progress with Columbus, his friendship with Princess Anne had flourished. On several occasions during the previous autumn the Princess had been a guest of the family at Great Somerford, and Mrs Phillips recalls that 'they had about six weeks of comparative calm. They would go riding together, and the whole village said not a word. It wasn't until they went hunting in November that the media latched on. Then all hell was let loose, and after that they never had a moment's peace.'

Mark's frequent visits to Alison Oliver's stable to train with Columbus, the fact that he lent Princess Anne his new horse Persian Holiday during the spring of 1973, and was invited to Sandringham as a house guest during January, had the Fleet Steet 'gossips' and pundits gaily predicting a spring Royal Engagement as if the whole thing was a foregone conclusion. But as far as the two main characters in the proceedings were concerned, it was anything but; 'in fact' says Mark 'the more we kept reading in the press that we were going to get engaged, the more we were determined not to'. Publicly Her Royal

Highness continued to deny reports of a 'romance' between herself and Mark and, although undeniably they were being drawn closer together, 'romance' is definitely too strong a word to describe any feelings they may have had for each other at that time.

It can never be easy to sort out your emotions in the full glare of tabloid publicity, but clearly – in private – Princess Anne had started to come to terms with her own feelings on the subject. 'Mark never mentioned any idea of getting married,' she says, 'and I definitely got the impression that he thoroughly enjoyed his bachelor existence. Anyway, even if I thought there was anything really serious going on at the time, I don't think either of us would have been in the least bit intelligent if we'd decided (to get engaged) before going to something like Badminton because we were, after all, competitors in the same sport, and I think it would have been tantamount to irresponsibility because we might have been totally non-speaks by the end of it. Even if he had asked me I would have said "don't be ridiculous – this might be a disaster".'

Both riders were hoping to compete at Badminton, Princess Anne with Goodwill and Doublet, and Mark on Columbus, as well as Great Ovation in the hope of establishing a record – never yet achieved – of winning the event on the same horse for three years in succession. So while Fleet Street continued to speculate on their emotions, Mark and Princess Anne concentrated on their riding, though it was almost impossible for either of them to go anywhere without reporters and cameramen 'creeping about in bushes'.

On 1 April Mark took Columbus to the one-day event at Rushall in Wiltshire. He was still desperately trying to find the 'key' to unlock the potential that Princess Anne was convinced the horse possessed. But with characteristic flamboyance Columbus tried to jump an impossibly wide V fence, called Caroline's Corner, in one mighty leap instead of putting a bounce in the middle; he dumped Mark in a heap – then rolled on top of him. For a moment it looked as though Mark's head had been crushed under the full weight of the horse, but by chance the saddle formed a bridge across his shoulders and gave him some protection, but he was knocked out, and when he came round was 'frightened to death because I couldn't see out of my right eye. Everything was grey – it was just like looking through a smokey glass window. The doctor said it would be all right after a few days but I really thought I was going to be like a pirate for the rest of my life – with a black patch over one eye.' All through Sunday the 'blindness' continued but when he woke on Monday morning and put his contact lenses in, everything was back to normal, so Columbus and Cheers were loaded up and driven down to Bertie Hill's farm in Devon for a final concentrated effort before the Badminton test.

Bertie remembers Mark being very disheartened that year, needing not just help and advice with his headstrong partner Columbus, but moral support and confidence to tackle the course at all. Bertie's philosophy is simple and modest 'at an event, a trainer is nothing but a buffer. All you're there for is to recognise when the rider gets up-tight about things, and tell them it's all right – give them confidence.' And that year Mark needed the support and strength of friends like Bertie more than ever before, as the combined effects of competition nerves and non-stop press attention began to wear him down. At the best of times he admits that before a really important competition his nerves reduce him to 'a pathetic heap just curled up under a tree' but that year he carried the added pressures of attempting a new Badminton record on Cheers, of riding Columbus who still didn't fill him with confidence, and the uncomfortable knowledge that almost every move he made was being watched through the ever-prying eyes of an army of press cameramen.

To make matters worse, he'd been on a strict diet to get down to his 'fighting weight' under twelve stone. The regime of black coffee and no sugar, sweets, puddings or potatoes is a regular part of his training programme every spring and makes him, by his own admission, 'bad-tempered'. But even Princess Anne remembers that he was 'fairly crotchety – probably the worst he's ever been' during that competition.

And as the week progressed things didn't improve. Although Great Ovation took the lead at the end of the dressage section, any elation in the Phillips' camp soon evaporated on Saturday morning when the horse broke down on the steeplechase course and had to be retired. When Mark came to ride Columbus, he put him in a roller gag as that seemed to provide the most efficient steering and braking system, and Mark recalls that 'he gave me such a good ride over the steeplechase fences that I thought I'd ride him in the same bit across country'. But almost as soon as he started on the four-and-a-half-mile course he knew he'd made a great mistake. 'Instead of pulling into the fences, he was backing off – getting behind the bit and going slower and slower.' Columbus was making it clear to Mark that he objected to a mouthful of ironmongery and with barely ten fences jumped the pair took a crashing fall at the Second Luckington Lane Crossing, which that year consisted of a set of rails on the edge of a bank that fell away to a steep drop. Ironically that was the one fence on the course Bertie Hill had forecast as a bogey. 'Columbus was such a bold horse I knew he would probably jump in too far, and come out too deep to the second element – which is exactly what he did do.' So Bertie was there to pick up the pieces, and send him on his way to yet another tumble, and a ducking, in The Lake.

It would be fair to suppose that when the pair finally got back to the stable, wet and bedraggled after a disappointing round, Mark would be even more disheartened. In fact he was quite the reverse; somewhere between the traumas and the tumbles, horse and rider had

Badminton 1973 – Mark and Columbus clearing the second Normandy Bank following two earlier falls (*Findlay Davidson*)

finally reached an understanding, which would explain Mark's rather surprising comment in the circumstances that 'he gave me a super ride. At last I realised what a good horse he was – that he was *really* something special.'

Meanwhile Princess Anne had ridden a stylish round on Goodwill, marred only by a technical refusal for allegedly crossing her tracks at The Quarry, and was to finish the competition in eighth place after a clear showjumping round.

At the end of the trial on Sunday evening, Mark and Princess Anne returned to the Phillips' home at Great Somerford and, while Mrs Phillips prepared dinner, they went for a walk across the Wiltshire countryside in the early spring sunshine.

'I think that right then we were both probably on a down,' says Mark. 'I'd been eliminated on one horse, had two falls on another, and Princess Anne had been given a refusal with Goodwill. Whether being downhearted together we found consolation in each other, I don't know' but that was the moment he chose to propose, with the rider that 'it just seemed a good idea at the time'. And if that all seems just a bit too casual, even Princess Anne confirms that 'I think it was the first time he'd thought of it'. The Princess needed no time to consider a reply admitting that 'during the course of the competition I had thought about it, on the basis that if I got asked – which hadn't exactly been in the offing – what my answer was likely to be' which was of course 'yes'.

That evening watching the highlights of the day's competition on television they saw the Whitbread Trophy pass into the deserving hands of Lucinda Prior-Palmer. If at that moment the family felt at all depressed with their own result and cheated out of a victory celebration, their gloom was soon dispelled when Mark announced that Princess Anne had agreed to be his wife.

During the next few days Mark made an appointment to see Prince Philip at Windsor and formally ask permission to marry his daughter. The scene could so easily have been an uncomfortable one. As someone who's shy and easily lost for words, asking the Duke of Edinburgh if he – a commoner– could marry his daughter – a Royal Princess – might well have left Mark tongue-tied and nervous. He actually remembers very little of the interview, admits to being 'petrified' but adds with a grin 'at least I'm still alive to tell the tale – and that's the main thing'. But he certainly came away with the impression that 'it was all a bit of a shock to Prince Philip. He had been out of the country for some time and hadn't really appreciated what was happening – but I think the Queen already knew.' In retrospect it's clear that almost all their small circle of close friends and relatives

Mark jumping Laureate into the Bourne Coffin at Tidworth Trials in May 1973 (*Findlay Davidson*)

'knew what was happening' while the two main characters apparently refused to acknowledge the obvious, and instead buried their feelings under the weight of responsibility to the competition. For Princess Anne still states emphatically 'people gaily wrote that off and said we all knew – but we most assuredly didn't.'

Although Prince Philip had given his permission and everyone associated with the couple no doubt felt enormous relief – as well as happiness – that the matter had finally been resolved, Anne and Mark could not share their news with the world. Protocol demanded that Heads of State and Members of the Government, as well as individual members of the immediate families, should be told before any official announcement was made. It meant a delay of almost five weeks. Close friends and relatives were sworn to secrecy, though both Mark and the Princess admit that for them keeping their secret was no hardship; 'we'd already had such a hard time from the press – holding out for a few more weeks was no problem'. Choosing the engagement ring was done privately at Buckingham Palace when a man from Garrards arrived bringing a selection of rings to suit Princess Anne's taste, and Mark's army salary. They settled on a sparkling combination of two diamonds either side of a sapphire and chose a plain, slim band of gold – made from the ever-diminishing supply of Welsh gold – for the wedding ring.

While these discreet preparations were going ahead behind the scenes, both Mark and the Princess were still competing in horse trials and facing the inevitable questions from Fleet Street about a romance and possible engagement. But the secret remained secure, and the only positive thing journalists were able to report was that Mark Phillips was back on a winning streak.

Laureate was proving to be an exceptionally talented horse; he'd won every novice competition Mark had taken him to that year, and on his first outing as an intermediate competitor on 12 May he came second at the Batsford One-Day Event. Just six days later he carried off the Griffin Trophy by winning his first-ever three-day event at Tidworth. Immediately after the competition ended, Mark drove north to Scotland and spent a week at Craigowan on the Royal estate at Balmoral, where the Royal Family was enjoying a spring holiday. On the evening of Tuesday, 29 May, a Court circular issued from Buckingham Palace said simply: 'It is with the greatest pleasure that the Queen and the Duke of Edinburgh announce the betrothal of their beloved daughter, The Princess Anne, to Lieutenant Mark Phillips, The Queen's Dragoon Guards, son of Mr & Mrs Peter Phillips', finally confirming what so many had suspected for so long.

The following morning Mark travelled south with the Royal Family and, after a private lunch attended only by the engaged couple and their parents, Princess Anne and Lt Phillips walked out on to the lawns of Buckingham Palace to meet the press, accompanied by the eternal show-off Moriarty and Princess Anne's own black labrador, Flora. Although Mark had been interviewed many times as a successful sportsman and had almost grown accustomed to the audience of pressmen that had followed him for months, the prospect of a formal press call where his most private and personal emotions were being questioned was something quite new to him. Princess Anne coped with the easy professional calm of someone who's used to being in the spotlight, but Mark was visibly uncomfortable, and seemed to find the experience something of an ordeal. It was, by any standard, a very gentle introduction to what his life would be like in the future as a member of the most public family in the land. Although his riding achievements would always have made him a sports personality, his impending marriage undeniably established him as a public figure with the minimum claim to privacy, attracting the maximum interest in even the most mundane features of his life. Who would have blamed him if he'd stopped for just one moment to consider 'what on earth am I letting myself in for'. But with disarming frankness he admits that the question didn't even occur to him, adding simply 'if that thought had stopped me marrying the person I loved it wouldn't have been much of a relationship – we both loved each other' and that's all there was to it.

The morning after the official announcement, the early ferry from Dover took Mark back across the channel from where he drove to his regiment at Hohne. Behind the physical barrier of the camp perimeter and surrounded by the security of a British military unit overseas, Mark avoided any further immediate contact with the press and resumed his duties as assistant adjutant and troop leader. Even when Princess Anne arrived in Germany on an official visit just one week later, that same protective mantle from the military and close friends ensured that the couple had time together, away from the questions and the cameras.

Not so Mark's parents. Their house had been 'under surveillance' for months, with the men from Fleet Street apparently working a rota which left a cameraman and reporter outside the front gate in the hope of catching a glimpse of Mark and Princess Anne together, while the 'reserves' were drinking in the local. Telephone calls informing them that 'your son has left Germany' and demanding 'are you expecting Princess Anne' became quite common, and Anne Phillips found that 'whenever I went out to pick the sprouts, prune the roses or whatever, there would be a camera on the wall'. It all started to get a bit unnerving, but they both say philosophically 'the press were obviously very curious and were undoubtedly only trying to do their job. They bore us no ill-will, and we got to know some of them quite well.'

But if they were 'surprised' by the attention they got before the engagement, they were completely overwhelmed by what happened afterwards. Following the official announcement and press reception at Buckingham Palace the Phillips agreed, via the Royal Press Office,

The official engagement picture – Mark and Princess Anne with Flora on the lawns of Buckingham Palace, 30 May 1973 (*Press Association*)

to be interviewed at their home in Wiltshire. Says Mrs Phillips 'as we were driving down the M4 I said to Peter, I don't suppose there will be many people there, and he said no, I shouldn't think so, just a few'. What actually greeted them when they turned the last corner into Great Somerford village was a press reception worthy of a visiting President. 'There were cars all the way to the War Memorial, cars up the drive. A television crane parked in the stableyard and the lawn was solid with reporters from all nations of the world.' Peter Phillips handled most of the questions in his usual calm, unflappable way, while Anne Phillips says she was 'speechless'. American interviewer Barbra Walters arrived in a chauffeur-driven Rolls, wearing a thin sugar-pink dress, and as the Phillips had decided that none of the film crews would be allowed inside the house, all the interviews were done out on the lawn. After watching Miss Walters gradually turn blue with the cold Peter Phillips anxiously enquired 'are you all right – you look frozen stiff' to be told 'who's doing this interview – you or me'. She was followed by Douglas Fairbanks Junior who threw the whole household into confusion by arriving an hour early, then came Pete Murray from Radio 2 and a whole galaxy of well-known reporters from newspapers, magazines, radio and television. They didn't have to see them all, of course, but with a typical display of generosity and fair play, they felt that 'having said yes to one – we really felt we couldn't refuse the rest'.

Mark meanwhile had settled back into his old routine of combining professional soldiering with competitive riding. Preparations for the

Burghley Three-day Event, 1973 – Mark riding Bertie Hill's mare Maid Marion during the crosscountry phase

Mark and Maid Marion approaching the last fence of the showjumping section at Burghley, 1973

wedding which would be in Westminster Abbey on 14 November were in the capable hands of the Lord Chamberlain; all Mark had to do was nominate his best man and without hesitation he chose Capt Eric Grounds – the man who'd steered him through his first few weeks with the regiment and had become one of his closest friends.

Persian Holiday and Laureate were stabled at Hohne and Mark was able to ride them both at a number of local German shows as a warm-up to the autumn season of one- and three-day events in Britain. Percy had been placed at each of the events he'd entered in the spring, and made a good start to the second half of the year by coming second at Annick and Dauntsey Park and third at Everingham, all within the first three weeks of August. At his first three-day event at Wylye in October he picked up another third rosette and Mark admits with some chagrin 'I tried and tried to win a novice event with him that season – but we just couldn't make it.' Nevertheless Percy's consistent record of a fourth, two sixths, two seconds and two thirds ensured that by the end of the year he'd won enough points to be upgraded to intermediate level for the start of 1974.

The record books for 1973 show that in nine weeks from 15 August

Mark and Maid Marion at Ledyard for the American Three-Day Event which proved to be the end of the partnership (*Warren E. Patriquin*)

Mark rode four horses at seven competitions, in addition to his own Persian Holiday and Laureate who continued his run of good luck by coming second in the intermediate at Everingham. The Strakers asked him once again to ride George at Annick, where he won, and Osberton where he came second.

Then literally days before the start of the three-day event at Burghley, Bertie Hill offered him a ride on his latest top-class eventer, Maid Marion. Tony Hill, Bertie's son, had enjoyed a run of good results with the horse in junior competitions, but just before Burghley, at Osberton, his luck ran out. He had a disastrous fall in which he injured his back and neck so badly it became clear that he wouldn't be able to ride for some months. Mark had sat on the horse once or twice earlier that year when helping Tony with his dressage work – but he'd never jumped a fence with her. So when horse and rider came together for their first training ride on the Tuesday of the competition, it was by any stretch of the imagination an unorthodox and highly speculative arrangement. On Bertie's own admission Maid Marion was not an easy horse to ride. She had limited scope – refusing to 'stand off' at fences, needing instead to be taken right up to them and bounced over.

But Bertie has never doubted Mark's brilliant adaptability as a horseman, and watched with consummate pride as he rode her into the lead with an effortless display of dressage, and stayed there after unbeatable crosscountry and showjumping rounds. The result couldn't have been better, but according to Mark in order to achieve it horse and jockey had 'done a bit of a conjuring act together. She really wasn't over-enthusiastic about the job, and didn't want to know. At the start of the course she was just climbing over the fences, and needed a lot of strength, and a lot of coaxing. But to be fair, the further she went, the better she went and although we had some quite hairy moments, she did everything but stop – so we won.'

Five weeks later the winning pair flew to the American Three-Day Event at Ledyard – but the outing ended in disaster and Mark gamely admits 'once again it was my fault'. A silly mistake on the steeplechase course had cost them vital seconds and in trying to make up lost time Mark pushed her hard over the last few fences and she broke down. The mare went back to Devon where she's since proved to be an invaluable brood mare but has never competed again.

The upset at Ledyard came just weeks after an equally disastrous outing for Princess Anne who'd taken Goodwill to Kiev in September in defence of her European title. The Russian course-builders had produced a test worthy of the Championship but neither they, nor the competitors, appreciated the havoc that would be caused at the now notorious fence number two. It claimed thirty-five victims, fifteen of them being eliminated – including Princess Anne who retired after all but dislocating her collar bone in a spectacular fall and to this day has slightly uneven shoulders as a result.

For a while it looked as though the engaged couple were doomed to approach their wedding day on a run of bad luck in the equestrian field. But on 4 October, Laureate obligingly tipped the balance by winning the Midland Bank trophy at the Wylye Three-Day Event, and in his first international event at Boekelo in Holland on 28 October, he produced another brilliant performance to be just pipped into second place by Richard Meade riding Wayfarer, by ·8 of a mark. 'It was as if everything I rode turned to gold' is how Mark regards that stage in his career, but at the same time he has to admit in retrospect he was in too much of a hurry to get Laureate to the top 'and we paid the penalty. I really started to go off the rails after Wylye. That's when I should have stopped and turned him out to grass; instead we went to Holland where he gave himself a bang on the tendon and had to have a year off.' It affected the horse both physically and mentally, though just how badly he didn't discover for another two years.

As the date of the wedding drew nearer Mark took up almost permanent residence in London – posing for official photographs, going over last-minute details of the wedding ceremony and giving a pre-wedding interview to the BBC and ITV at Buckingham Palace. The meeting was timed for mid-morning, coinciding exactly with the changing of the guard. Andrew Gardner and Alastair Burnet worked their way through the list of questions that had been approved by the Palace Press Office and did their best to compete with the Band of the Irish Guards who could be heard playing non-stop through the conversation, providing the producers with a technical nightmare when they came to edit the interview for transmission.

Nor were they helped by the fact that Mark rarely delivers snap answers to interviewer's questions, taking time to consider his words before speaking, and then usually offering his answers with a halting delivery. On this occasion it left many observers thinking that while the newly promoted Captain Mark Phillips was undoubtedly a good sport, a charming fellow, and a highly likeable individual, from an interviewer's point of view he was a speechless non-starter. And when Alistair Burnett asked the totally unexpected question 'what will you say to the people you haven't invited to the wedding' the atmosphere stiffened visibly. Neither the interviewers, nor the interviewees, were particularly happy with the finished result, and Mark was left feeling that the exercise had in no way reflected any of the happiness of the occasion. For behind the pomp and ceremony that of necessity would turn his marriage into a state occasion, people close to Anne and Mark were left in no doubt that just like any other young couple approaching their wedding day, they were two people very much in love, wanting to share their happiness with everyone around them.

On the morning before the wedding, gossip columnists had a field day reporting Mark's 'raucous' stag party at the restaurant Julia's, and though his own memory of the evening is rather vague, he says with a

(*above*) Mark and Laureate in
the silage pit at Wylye, en route
to their third three-day event win
of 1973 (*Findlay Davidson*);
(*below*) at Boekelo in 1973, when
Mark and Laureate finished
second to Richard Meade by 0.8
points (*Benelux Press*)

reminiscent smile 'we certainly had a fair night. I drank champagne until it was coming out of my ears – ah, the good old days!' But after two decent nights' sleep at the Cavalry Club the groom faced the ceremony and the day without the traditional hangover, and no doubt many people echoed his mother's delight at waking up that November morning to find that the sun was shining.

'The first drama was making sure we got to the church on time', a sentiment that bridegrooms everywhere will appreciate, though it's unlikely many of them would have the added problem facing Mark that morning of negotiating a journey through central London when most roads around the route to Westminster Abbey had been closed. Travelling in an official car and wearing inconspicuous lounge suits, the groom and his best man were driven along an ingenious zigzag of roads that avoided the crowds and were deposited at a side door of the Abbey in plenty of time. In the Deanery they changed into the glamorous scarlet-and-gold regimental dress uniform of The Queen's Dragoon Guards, adjusted spurs and swords, made sure that Eric Grounds had the ring safely in his pocket and then 'feeling like death, crept in, rather like two naughty schoolboys, along one of the side aisles to where we had to sit and wait'.

Outside the Abbey, all along Whitehall, through Admiralty Arch and up the Mall, the crowds stood in their thousands in the bright November sunshine cheering and waving as members of the Royal Family processed in open carriages from the Palace, with the bride and her father driving out through the gates in the Glass Coach at precisely twelve minutes past eleven.

While the organist of the Chapel Royal, Harry Gabb, filled the Abbey with the glorious music of Bach, Brahms and Handel, the congregation which included many friends from the equestrian world watched the procession on television monitors that had been discreetly placed at vantage points throughout the building. But neither Mark nor his best man could see a monitor, and instead passed the time 'telling each other jokes – probably jokes in rather poor taste at that – anything to take our minds off the fact that we were both feeling so nervous. I had been in lots of parades and things, but it was the first time I had been involved in anything like that. There was so much pomp and ceremony – it was marvellous. But finding myself up the sharp end – I was a nervous wreck.'

A fanfare sounded by the trumpeters of his own regiment, 1st The Queen's Dragoon Guards, signalled the start of the bride's procession and the moment when Mark had to move out from his pew to stand at the foot of the sacrarium steps. To the strains of the hymn 'Glorious things of thee are spoken' Princess Anne made her way with smiling, graceful dignity down the long central aisle on the right arm of Prince Philip. A quick smile of encouragement passed between her and Mark when they saw each other for the first time that day, and as the Dean of

Westminster pronounced the words 'Dearly beloved, we are gathered here in the sight of God and in the face of this congregation to join this man and this woman in Holy Matrimony' Mark entered the most significant fifty minutes of his entire life.

The solemn vows, made before the Archbishop of Canterbury, and the poetic language of the James I Prayer Book brought a moving simplicity to the service which had been wrapped in so much colourful pageantry. But Mark remembers little of those precious moments; 'my one real regret is that I was so nervous, desperately trying to remember to say the right thing, and do the right thing at the right time, that I really don't remember a lot about it. I do remember signing the register and thinking what an extraordinary thing it was to have me and my family signing, with Princess Anne and her family – it didn't seem right somehow'.

To the soaring strains of Widor's 'Toccata' the couple walked down the aisle to the west door and out into the sunlight to acknowledge the cheers of the waiting crowds, cheers that followed them every inch of the way back to the Palace, and echoed round the lofty state rooms while half the crowned heads of Europe and the Phillips family from Wiltshire were cajoled and bullied into formal pictorial groups by photographer Norman Parkinson.

If Mark had thought it odd to see his parents' names beside those of Her Majesty the Queen and Prince Philip in the marriage register, it must have seemed totally bizarre to find that his wedding album included a group photograph containing three Queens, one King, eight Princes, eight Princesses, a Crown Prince, two Duchesses, one Duke, three Earls, a Viscount and a Lord. Not that he would have had time to consider the unique nature of the situation, for each section of the day had been timed with usual Royal precision, and at 1.30 pm in accordance with the timetable Mark and his bride, flanked by members of their families, walked out onto the balcony at the front of the Palace to be greeted by roars of delight and shouted con- gratulations from the thousands of wellwishers who'd crammed around the Victoria Memorial and were still scattered halfway along the Mall.

'It was unreal – quite extraordinary. Something that as a layman I found very difficult to take in. I just couldn't believe that so many people wanted to wish us well, and had gone to so much trouble to show pleasure in our happiness. It wasn't as if I had really done anything to deserve it – but it says so much for the Royal Family and Princess Anne that they wanted to be there.' It also says much for Mark's own unassuming nature that it obviously didn't occur to him that not only had his own charm and good looks left many young ladies weak at the knees, but the prospect of a Royal Marriage, which was so clearly a love match, had brought out the romantic spirit in an entire nation, and in the circumstances the cheers and good wishes

On the balcony acknowledging the cheers and good wishes of the crowd after their wedding (*Keystone Press Agency*)

were most certainly aimed at him as well. On the right of the balcony Mark's mother watched her son and new daughter-in-law with pride, remembering how in 1945 she had stood opposite the Palace gates on VJ night, as a young Wren, joining in the chant 'we want the King'. Now nearly thirty years later, she was herself standing on that very same balcony, looking down on the crowds with the thought that 'the millions and millions to one chance of people like us standing there was just amazing'. Just as on VJ night, after the Coronation, and at every major Royal event since, the crowds wouldn't let them leave. Each time the family disappeared behind the long glass doors into the corridor beyond, the chanting crowds drew them back for yet another glimpse of the Royal bride, her husband, the Queen and much-loved Queen Mother.

At last the doors were firmly closed, the curtains drawn, and the bridal party made their way to the ballroom at the rear of the Palace for the wedding breakfast – which was lunch. And once again Mark got an attack of nerves. By tradition the bride's father, a master at after-dinner speaking, made the first speech. 'Prince Philip got up and started off by saying "unaccustomed as I am" and there was a long pause "to speaking at breakfast" and the whole place absolutely fell apart. And I thought – O Lord what do I say now.' If Mark had followed his father-in-law's example and begun by stating 'unaccustomed as I am – to making after-dinner speeches' it would have been quite true, for he wasn't. Instead he 'took a deep breath, stood up, said thank you, and a few more appropriate words, then sat down again'.

When the formalities were finally over Captain Phillips and his bride drove in an open carriage to the Royal Chelsea Hospital, where they transferred to an official car and drove to Thatched House Lodge in Richmond Park, the home of Princess Alexandra and Angus Ogilvy. The crowds were still out in force which Mark found 'extraordinary' and the following afternoon there was more cheering and waving from wellwishers when they boarded the 1.15pm British Airways flight from Heathrow to Barbados where they would board the Royal Yacht *Britannia* at the start of their honeymoon. After such a fairytale wedding, a cruise in the West Indies seemed a suitably romantic way to begin married life 'but for the first four days we were both sea-sick' – a statement which slightly destroys the idea of love on the high seas; although Mark now tells the story with some relish, he went through misery at the time. 'After the wedding I was pole-axed and whenever I get *really* tired, even now, I get shivery and a bit feverish. And that's exactly what happened – so it wasn't a very good start.'

But then *Britannia* steamed into fine weather, and for two glorious

Mark and Princess Anne below the majestic 18,000ft Cotopaxi volcano after a picnic south of Quito, Ecuador – part of their South American tour following their honeymoon (*Associated Press*)

weeks they meandered through the sunlit islands. Each morning the honeymooners would be dropped off on a small island, from where they'd watch *Britannia* steam off as decoy taking the Fleet Street flotilla with her. 'Then she'd come back and pick us up in the evening, and steam on through the night, each day getting closer to Panama.' By 1 December they were through the canal, on their way to the Galapagos Islands for a memorable few days among Darwin's seabirds, mammals and reptiles. From there an Andover of The Queen's Flight collected them to begin an official two-week tour of Equador, Colombia and the West Indies. It was Mark's first taste of being a 'Royal' visitor and while Princess Anne took the whole thing in her stride to the manner born, the guards of honour, official speeches and receptions had Mark on tenterhooks, determined to make a good impression and 'not let the side down' but at the same time feeling totally out of his depth.

'At my first lunch I sat next to two ladies who couldn't speak a word of English – the only language they had was Spanish which I didn't know at all. All we could do was draw little pictures and make sounds to each other, which meant we ended up having quite a giggly lunch as a result.' Having survived the first fence, the rest of the visit didn't

Mark meeting officer cadets at Sandhurst when taking over his new job as a Platoon Instructor in 1974 (*Press Association*)

seem quite so daunting. The kindness of the people and the sight of a condor – that huge majestic bird of the South Americas gliding effortlessly beside their car as they sped along at sixty miles an hour – are his two lasting impressions of that country.

Bogota, the capital of Colombia, was next on the itinerary, and Mark realised that facing the official welcome, the guard of honour and all the pomp and ceremony afforded to a visiting member of the Royal Family 'wasn't quite so bad second time around'. Their visit began with a tour of the country's Gold Museum immediately before attending a lunch at the British Embassy. 'Just as we were heading for the car, I started to feel queasy. It was the most awful sensation, so I grabbed Princess Anne's Private Secretary's arm and said "don't go – because I'm off – I'm going".' They made it to the car, and he was bundled in, with more haste than Royal ceremony. The Embassy doctor offered no explanation as to the cause but suggested twenty-four hours' rest – after which he was completely recovered and ready to tackle the final stage of the tour which took in Jamaica, Antigua and Montserrat. Princess Anne had a crowded schedule that packed receptions and lunches, visits and gala dinners, into a series of fourteen-hour days. Shaking hundreds of hands, meeting dozens of strangers, and always, always smiling, Mark quickly discovered how very hard the 'Royals' work when they're on duty, and says that after that initiation he was 'totally, totally shattered'.

They left the Caribbean sunshine and flew back to the cold and damp of a British winter on 16 December, to join the Royal Family at Windsor for Christmas. The Queen had invited Anne and Peter Phillips and their daughter Sarah to join them, a thoughtful gesture which avoided divided loyalties and meant that both families could celebrate their first Christmas with the newlyweds together. At midnight on New Year's Eve people all over the world looked towards the New Year of 1974 with varying degrees of anticipation and optimism. Mark Phillips must have been more optimistic than most. He had a new job – as an Instructor at the Royal Military Academy, Sandhurst, a new home – Oak Grove in the grounds of the Academy, and was on the threshold of a whole new way of life – as the husband of Her Royal Highness The Princess Anne.

Chapter Six

Most people connected with the sport of eventing looked forward to the 1974 season with extra relish, knowing that Britain was to stage the World Championships that year and that, on current form, British riders and horses would provide the major challenge for team and individual honours.

For Mark and Princess Anne there was the added spice of competing against each other for the first time as husband and wife; a situation that could have been fraught with difficulties, for as Princess Anne admits: 'Training is all very well. You may yell at each other, and that can be quite helpful. But the business of actually riding in a competition is rather different, because you are actually competing *against* each other and whatever happens that's how it goes. It would be a pity if you both minded so much that you couldn't speak thereafter.'

Their experiences at Badminton had made it obvious that the fierce atmosphere of competition wasn't something that intruded on their relationship. If anything, the pair presented a formidable front of support and talent that's made them unique in a sport so geared to individual endeavour. From the very beginning they established an unwritten rule that, when training together, they would never comment on each other's riding. Instead, says Mark: 'We confine our comments to the way the horse is going, saying so-and-so is going nicely, or could do with a bit more bend, or whatever. It's very difficult for a husband or wife to say, "Sit up! Use your seat a bit more! Left foot back a bit!" and so on, because the answer is always "I am".' Not that either rider would suggest for one moment that they know it all, and regularly take instruction from some of the finest trainers in the country. But trying to instruct your wife or husband, whether it's in golf, driving, or riding, can be fraught with danger. Though occasionally Mark admits: 'Sometimes I don't know what the hell I'm doing wrong, and I ask Princess Anne to see if she can put her finger on the problem. But that's putting the boot on a different foot – because you ask for help, and hope it will be constructive.'

And, according to his wife, 'even if you do have a bit of a barney, by the time you get back to the stables, it's either made sense or it hasn't, and the chances are that you've probably translated it into being useful'.

As you'd expect, the two are quick to compliment each other's riding, with joint admiration based on an understanding of the sport's

94

Mark and Princess Anne riding Laureate and Flame Gun respectively at the Amberley Horse Show in 1974 (*Srdja Djukanovic*)

complex demands on both horse and rider. Princess Anne is convinced that Mark has improved her crosscountry riding and adds, rather modestly: 'I don't know that I've ever done anything for him – except that I occasionally save his horses from working too hard!' An observation that backs up her husband's own admission that at times he 'niggles at the horses', demanding too much perfection and too much obedience. Certainly, as an outsider, watching them ride together, the formula seems to work. And it demonstrates an interesting contrast in personalities. For while it's fair to assume that most people think of Mark Phillips as being fairly quiet and reserved, with Princess Anne, the more volatile member of the partnership, in training it's Mark who's more likely to show signs of tetchy impatience when things aren't going right, while Princess Anne treads a careful path between gentle persuasion and tactful suggestion. In fact, this apparent reversal of personalities from the public stereotype demonstrates just how little is really known about either Mark or Princess Anne, outside a small, discreet and highly protective group of friends.

Immediately before his wedding, Mark had gone through the embarrassing experience of seeing his past, present and future being analysed by feature writers in almost every national newspaper, and a crop of 'souvenir specials'. Former headmasters assessed him as 'a most useful member of the school' and 'a very popular chap'. Riding friends confirmed that he was a determined but sporting competitor with a great sense of humour, always guaranteed to be at the centre of any 'lark', and although journalists dug and probed for some clue to his character, most were left with the opinion that he was 'a pleasant young man and a jolly nice chap to know, with a wide, toothy smile and not prone to public utterances'. Apart from that he remained something of an enigma, a state undoubtedly cultivated by his own naturally reserved and shy nature. 'Shy' seems almost too gauche a word to use when describing someone who's excelled publicly at one of life's more dangerous sports, but it's a description he accepts, adding 'I haven't got a lot of confidence when I am talking to strangers. I'm always nervous of saying the wrong thing, of sounding stupid.' Which begs the question 'How on earth do you cope with the official side of being a member of the most public family in the land?' He answers without false modesty 'Not very well', a reply that gives no idea of the supreme effort he puts into public appearances to make them as comfortable as possible for himself and for the people he

Princess Anne and Mark at an official engagement, meeting Hinge and Bracket at a Gala Soiree in aid of Action Research for the Crippled Child (*Press Association*)

meets. Following the example set by the Royal Family, he makes sure he's always briefed before going to a function on its background, the people involved, who's done what and any nugget of information to keep the conversation going – but he never finds it easy, and always 'terribly, terribly tiring. Because you can never relax. To get over the initial tension, embarrassment, shyness, call it what you will, you ask an opening question, then you have to think of another, and another, always mentally jumping ahead so that there isn't a pregnant pause when you both just stand there looking at each other.'

Most people who are naturally shy can successfully avoid public confrontations with dozens of strangers by simply living their own private, secluded lives. Mark acknowledges that for him that's no longer possible, but certainly doesn't expect anyone to feel sorry for him. After all he chose the role of 'Royal' husband willingly and, according to Princess Anne: 'Although a lot of people thought he wasn't really suited to it, I think he copes very well.'

Before their wedding, Princess Anne did her best to prepare her fiancé for the public side of their life together by 'trying to point out that it was a funny sort of existence. Though there wasn't a lot I could do, to be honest. It's such a way of life, rather than a tangible thing, and not an easy thing to warn somebody about. You can only hope that they have observed what's gone on before.'

And the fact that Mark did 'observe' and fit in to that 'funny sort of existence' draws the compliment from his wife that: 'He's remarkable really, in the sense that now it doesn't seem to bother him. He comes on some of the trips abroad. But I'm sure it's right that he's in a position to have his own life and doesn't have to come on many more trips, because I think he'd hate that.' A sentiment that blows another widely-held public myth that Mark is firmly under Princess Anne's thumb and generally does what he's told.

On a number of occasions I've watched while various friends, employees and members of the family voice their opinions of what should be done in a situation, while the Captain listens patiently, and then ends all argument by announcing what *he* intends doing. Mark Phillips is very much master in his own house and at times, says his wife, 'very stubborn'. At the suggestion that it's usually herself who's regarded as the headstrong member of the family, she smiles indulgently, saying: 'People keep telling me that I've got better since I got married and had children. To me, that's a myth, invented by somebody who is single, or who hasn't really understood the point of getting married in the first place. When you're married you are no longer living on your own. You're living with another person, and you have to adapt to some degree. It's the same when you have children, the whole structure of your life changes. Really, if you didn't change as you went along, you'd be a bit of a disaster; that's what life is all about really – adapting to experiences.'

In Princess Anne's case that's clearly meant not just adapting to the role of wife and mother but also to the fact that, while she feels that she can usually be converted to another's point of view 'if they're cunning about it', her husband is rarely persuaded to change his mind once it's made up.

If being stubborn, strong-willed and determined to run his own life – with the proviso that there are times when Royal protocol must take precedence – doesn't exactly fit the image the public and press have moulded for Mark Phillips, there are other sides to his character they might find surprising too.

He can spot a social climber at a hundred yards and is fiercely loyal to friends, demanding equal loyalty in return. But if they let him down, or speak out of court, 'it always gets back – and they never have a second chance'. His temper is generally subued – 'slow to boil' is how Princess Anne describes him, indicating the warning rumbles that come before occasional stinging flashes that inflict maximum discomfort in one swift outburst – but pass, leaving neither rancour nor grudge.

He's most likely to be at his worst when he's in the middle of a diet. The beginning of October heralds the start of three months when he takes sugar in tea and coffee, eats potatoes, pudding and all the forbidden fattening foods, totally ignoring the reading on the bathroom scales. But on 1 January, he resumes the strict dieting

Princess Anne and Mark galloping together on Ascot Racecourse riding Arthur of Troy and Laureate respectively before the Ledyard event in 1975 (*Srdja Djukanovic*) see page 111

regime to bring him down to a riding weight of around eleven stone eleven. As someone who has little difficulty keeping her own weight in check, Princess Anne says, with some sympathy: 'Every year it gets more difficult. He's quite a big lad, and has got a big frame. So it was never easy, but the older you get the more difficult it is to shift the stuff that catches up with you in the off-season.'

Mark's staff reckon they can read him like an open book and when they see a storm brewing they ride it out, or run for cover!

His memory on certain things is impeccable – for instance he'll talk you stride-for-stride over a crosscountry course ridden ten years ago, but it's not unusual for him to forget a dinner engagement, or completely miss an appointment. His explanation is simple. 'I'm always trying to get too much into a day, and think I've got time to do this and that before I go off and do something else – it'll only take five minutes. But then it doesn't take five minutes, it takes ten, or fifteen or longer – and then I'm late.' He makes the distinction that 'I'm rarely late for something that's really important like an official engagement – that just wouldn't do.' Except that there was one Royal garden party that almost finished without him; he'd been showjumping at Wembley and left the arena in plenty of time, only to be stuck for three quarters of an hour in the garden party traffic jam at Hyde Park Corner. He covered his tardy arrival by creeping in a side entrance and slipping in amongst the crowd as though he'd been there all the time. Apart from that, there've been no 'public' disasters, though in line with most people who are bad timekeepers, he's maddeningly self-effacing about the habit, saying: 'The trouble is you've got to be consistent. If you're always ten minutes late, people can work to that, but if you suddenly arrive five minutes early, then it throws the system.'

In keeping with his association with animals, he's sentimental about the horses that have shared his career with him, but never sloppy to the point of idolatry; he demands total discipline when they're called on to work, and gives respect to their dignity and courage in return. He's sensitive to misinformed, unfair criticism, and the name 'Foggy' never fails to rankle.

Friends are quick to deny the description, but then you'd expect nothing less from anyone worthy of the name 'friend' in the first place. Frank Weldon is perhaps more objective, though no less dismissive of the label, when he admits that, in public and with strangers, 'Mark does have an unfortunate manner. He doesn't have a very good speaking voice.'

This combination has undoubtedly left most members of the public with the impression that he's slow and dim-witted. The Mark Phillips his friends see is one who is totally at ease in the company of people he knows and trusts. His conversation is without any suggestion of hesitation, and when he's teaching or talking to other riders according to Col Weldon: 'They soak it all up – because he talks such sense.

Make no mistake about it, he's not stupid. What he says is well understood by riders, and that's all that matters if you're a horseman.' But the name sticks, carrying with it the cruel and totally inaccurate assumption that, like fog, he's both wet and thick. The events of Wednesday, 21 March, 1974 should have been enough to prove that he was neither, though it's unlikely that either Mark or Princess Anne would have chosen such a dramatic demonstration to make the point.

In what's now generally referred to as The Mall Incident, four men were shot and seriously wounded when Ian Ball attempted to kidnap Princess Anne and hold her to ransom.

The evening started quietly enough. As Patron of the Riding for the Disabled Association, Princess Anne, accompanied by Mark, had gone to Sudbury House in Newgate Street to see a a new film about the Association called 'Riding Towards Freedom'. After the showing, at about 8.30 pm, the couple had settled into the back of one of the official Royal cars to be driven by chauffeur Alex Callender around Trafalgar Square, under Admiralty Arch, along The Mall, and back to Buckingham Palace. With the Victoria Memorial in sight, and just a few yards from the Queen Mother's front door, a white Ford Escort swerved in front of the Royal limousine, forced it to stop – and then the shooting began.

At first it looked as though just another lunatic motorist had tried to 'cut them up' and even when Princess Anne's personal bodyguard, Detective Inspector James Beaton, got out of the car to challenge the driver, no-one in the car suspected that they were dealing with anything more serious than a Bolshy motorist. But as Jim Beaton walked towards the other car, the driver pulled a gun and shot him in the stomach. From the back of the car it seemed as though they were suddenly being forced to take part in a badly-made gangster movie as the detective slumped to the ground, and another shot found its mark as the chauffeur opened the door to go to the detective's aid. Deciding that they were safer inside the car than out, Mark and Princess Anne stayed where they were, but as the gunman advanced on them, the Lady-in-Waiting, Rowena Brassey, opened the rear door and scrambled out. The opposite door was thrown open and Mark and Princess Anne found themselves face to face with a potential killer.

As a professional soldier, the prospect of being killed in the service of his country was one of the less attractive unwritten clauses he had accepted and come to terms with in his army contract. But somehow facing a maniac with a gun in the middle of a crowded capital city presented a situation that was both terrifying and unreal. They both tried to stay calm and talk their way out of the bizarre, frightening mess around them.

'It may sound funny, but we were saying to him, "Look, go away, we aren't coming with you, so get in your car and forget about it." We just kept talking and talking, trying to keep things on a reasonably sane level, knowing that sooner or later the police would arrive. After a few minutes, Jim Beaton got back in the car, even though he was badly injured, but because his gun had jammed he couldn't do very much, so he tried to put himself between Princess Anne and the gunman, and was shot again. At that point the gunman stopped being passively reasonable, and started to get desperate.

'He grabbed at Princess Anne and tried to pull her out of the car. But I hung on to her, so for a while, she was in the middle of a tug-of-war. Then another policeman turned up, effectively said "What's going on here, then" and the chap turned round and shot him in the stomach.' In that split second, he loosened his grip on the Princess and Mark was able to drag her back inside the car and slam the door shut. 'Both of us were hanging on to the door, still talking and talking, saying over and over, "Go away, get in your car and no-one will say anything".'

It must have seemed a lifetime; in fact it took more than fifteen agonising minutes before help finally arrived, and from Mark's point of view: 'That was the most frightening moment. I really thought that was it. Up until then he'd been waving the gun about and threatening us, but while we'd been talking and arguing we'd managed to keep things on a reasonable level. But then, suddenly, we were surrounded by police cars and flashing blue lights, and it was a bit like cornering an animal – there was no escape for him and at that moment I really thought we might have been shot.'

Princess Anne visiting James Beaton, her personal bodyguard, in hospital recovering from bullet wounds received during the Mall Incident (*Keystone Press Agency*)

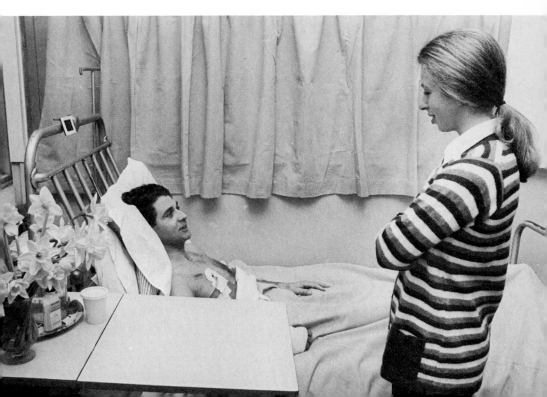

But there was no more shooting; as the gunman tried to run off through St James' Park, Constable Peter Edwards floored him with a classic rugby tackle and the drama was over.

Even to this day, Mark finds it amazing that the episode lasted so long. 'People were driving past, walking along the pavement, standing on the other side of the road, watching while there were men lying half-dead in the middle of the road – but nobody actually called the police.' As it happened a passing taxi driver had been the first to raise the alarm, but most people just stood and watched the whole drama, assuming that 'someone else' had done the obvious thing and called the police.

Since that night, every Royal engagement, however informal or close to home, has always been accompanied by a back-up car, for as Mark points out: 'Everyone realised that if there had been more than one person involved they would have succeeded without any shadow of doubt.'

Princess Anne had remained calm throughout the episode, and Mark pays tribute to his wife's courage by saying, 'I don't think it had ever occurred to me that something like that would happen. But Princess Anne *had* thought about it, and had got clearly in her mind what she would or wouldn't do in the circumstances. That's why she was so marvellous at the time.' Mark is honest enough to admit that afterwards it did occur to him that 'perhaps I should have put one between the chap's eyes and tried to disarm him – done a sort of John Wayne or James Bond', but in the circumstances it wouldn't have been a practical solution. Three men had already been gunned down at point-blank range, and with Captain Phillips injured, there would have been no-one between the gunman and the Princess. 'So, as it was, I didn't panic, I don't feel as though I did anything particularly brave – but I didn't do anything particularly stupid either which might have made things worse.'

A stiff whisky at the Palace, and reassuring telephone calls to the Queen and Prince Philip who were in Indonesia on an official tour, gave Mark and Princess Anne valuable breathing space to get over the shock of their ordeal, before driving back to their home at Oak Grove.

Not unnaturally, the possibility of a repeat performance has occurred to Mark many times since, 'and I'm still slightly nervous in traffic or a crowd if someone does something unusual or unexpected. It probably doesn't mean anything – but the possibility just flashes across my mind.'

Discreet but effective security is an aspect of public life that some people might find oppressive, but it's one which Mark accepts with equanimity, as he accepts the unwritten, unspoken knowledge that it exists only because his wife and young family need its protection.

———————

Columbus is not the most endearing horse in the Phillips' yard. His stable name of Monster describes his bared teeth, flattened ears and bad temper perfectly, and when Mark says 'if you went into the stables and put your arms round him, he'd pick you up by the seat of the pants and shake you' believe me, he means it!

Affection is not an emotion you'll find in Mark's vocabulary when he's describing his feeling for the horse. It's trust, respect and admiration that have forged the bond between horse and jockey through almost ten years of glorious success and heartbreaking failure.

At Ledyard in 1973, Mark had found himself at the centre of a bragging match with his close friend, Mike Tucker.

'We had been talking about the prospects for 1974, and Mike said he'd bet me £10 that Columbus wouldn't get into the first three at Badminton. I said something outlandish like "He'll do better than that, he'll win!" So Mike said, "Put your money where your mouth is." Let's face it, he must have thought he was on to a good thing because I hadn't had a very good track record, with a stop and two falls on a horse that many people thought was a rogue, and not very safe. But I really believed he could to it.'

At Oak Grove there were six stables, so when Mark and Princess Anne moved into their new home most of the horses went too. Columbus was stabled with Alison Oliver a short drive away, so Mark could ride him seven days a week. Sometimes he managed an hour before breakfast; at other times he would dash home at lunchtime, throw leather chaps over his trousers to protect his uniform, ride for half an hour, and then drive back to the college for afternoon lectures. This 'snatch and grab' routine wasn't ideal, but it achieved the regular contact with the horse that was essential if Mark was ever going to come to terms with his wayward, brilliant mount.

The gag snaffle bit was discarded in favour of a mild linked Waterford snaffle and there were compromises on both sides as horse and rider stamped their characters in the slow, patient process of getting to know each other. By April, Mark was optimistic that he'd found the formula to unlock the grey's potential, and Columbus met the challenge by winning the advanced section of the Downlands One-Day Event. Within a week mere optimism matured into trust as the pair finished third at Windsor, so that Mark approached the Badminton Three-Day Event, not only having supreme faith in the horse's ability to finish well, but also fairly confident that Mike Tucker was about to lose £10.

Aficionados of the sport couldn't have asked for a better result at the end of the dressage, which showed Princess Anne in the lead on her European Championship winner Doublet, with Mark second on Great Ovation whose legs were now fully recovered after a year's careful nursing, and equal third on Columbus. Goodwill, Princess Anne's second horse at that stage, featured well down the placings at a disappointing twenty-seventh. But, as always, it was crosscountry day that provided the real drama, bringing its usual crop of surprises and disappointments and alterations to the overnight scoreboard. Doublet was withdrawn after ploughing into the open ditch on the steeplechase course, and Great Ovation topped an uncomfortable round that included a near-disaster at the Normandy Bank by coming to a grinding halt at the bullfinch. Mark's assessment was that 'He just wasn't in love with it any more – so we retired him and Flavia's been hunting him ever since.'

With the two overnight leaders out of the competition, Columbus had everything to ride for. Says Mark: 'We were holding all the aces. He made the course look easy, and never made the semblance of a mistake. At the big fences he stood off, where they were trappy he could bounce and hop his way through.'

It was a virtuoso display of balance and skill, courage and style, matched by an equally brilliant round by Princess Anne on Goodwill, which left husband and wife in first and fifth places respectively by the end of the speed and endurance phase. A clear round in the showjumping ring moved Goodwill up one notch to finish fourth and, although Mark found that Columbus was 'a bit long and flat over the show jumps' he went clear, and that was good enough to give him his third Badminton win on a horse that had confounded his critics and was being hailed as one of the stars of '74.

In a minor league Persian Holiday was making steady progress by crowning a third at Stocklands and a second at Batsford by winning the Griffin Trophy for intermediate horses at the Tidworth Three-Day Event in May. In the previous twelve months Mark had the unique distinction of having won every three-day event in the country.

After a well-earned post-Badminton rest, Columbus was quickly back on form, working towards an almost guaranteed place in Britain's World Championship team that would line up against nine other countries at Burghley in September. As a 'warm-up' to the championships, Columbus was loaded into the Phillips' horse lorry along with Percy, Goodwill, and Princess Anne's promising newcomer, Arthur of Troy, and driven north to complete the early Scottish circuit at Annick, Lockerbie and Eglinton. For the Princess it was a successful trip as she came third at Annick and Lockerbie where she rode Columbus. Mark was less fortunate; a recurrence of back trouble left him 'crippled' for the first week of the tour. Jean Cooper, a physiotherapist from London, went to Scotland with him and got him fit enough to ride Columbus at the last competition of the circuit at Eglinton. Although Columbus won at Eglinton, he bruised his foot and was unfit to ride in the final championship trial at Osberton.

Fortunately the selectors were prepared to judge him on the record he'd already established and ultimately included him in the team without seeing him at Osberton. Not that his absence prevented Mark from riding in the competition, as once again the Strakers offered the redoubtable George as a possible reserve for the Championships, and Mark admits that he would like to have ridden him at Burghley. But their joint names didn't appear in the Championship catalogue, and the partnership ended unhappily after a fall during the Osberton trial at the third fence. 'We came over a rise either to a biggish corner or rail at which you jumped the first part, landed in a dip, then turned to jump out. But as you were landing on a drop, that turn wasn't as easy as it sounds – especially on George who tended to pull a bit. So I gave him the chance to get motoring, jumped the corner, and got it as wrong as I could ever hope to get anything wrong. We hit the deck and that was that. I never rode him again that year.'

The sequel to the story is heavy with irony. Towards the end of the year, Mark received a telephone call from Lucinda Prior-Palmer, saying she'd been offered George as a ride the following year and asking 'Shall I take him on? Is he any good?' – obviously concerned by the fact that Mark had fallen with him. 'I told her that I thought she should take him because he was a hell of a good horse, and what happened at Osberton wasn't his fault, and that apart from that I'd never come unstuck with him.'

Mark on Columbus clearing the Park Wall en route to victory at Badminton in 1974
(*Findlay Davidson*)

So Lucinda took the ride, and in 1977 she achieved the enviable double of winning the Badminton Three-day Event in the spring, and the European Championship at Burghley five months later. In contrast it was five years before Mark and Columbus were to make any impression on the record tables in spite of two days in September, when for a while they'd had the world at their feet.

Britains' challenge for the team World Championship rested with the combined talents of Richard Meade on Wayfarer, Chris Collins riding Smokey VI, Bridget Parker on Cornish Gold and Mark Phillips on Her Majesty the Queen's Columbus, while Princess Anne partnered Goodwill as one of eight British individual competitors. Dressage had never been one of Columbus' strengths, but Mark was still slightly disappointed to find himself in tenth position at the end of the first phase; on crosscountry day he gave full rein to his brilliance, achieved maximum bonus on the steeplechase and attacked Bill Thompson's massive championship fences with a steady, faultless stride.

'After the trout hatchery I pushed on a bit, and at the second last, a big log over a ditch, he jumped beautifully, but as he landed and accelerated away it felt as if one of the bandages on a hind leg started to slip off. He was still galloping and jumped the last well, but I was convinced that something was wrong.'

An anxious backward glance from Mark as he crossed over the finishing-line indicated his concern to those watching. But as he walked the horse slowly back to the stables there was little to indicate a major problem, and most spectators were more concerned with celebrating the fact that Columbus had achieved a blistering pace across country, clocking up the fastest time of the day which put him a clear nine points in the lead. Although the rest of the team had fared less well, and collectively could only hope to come second to the outstanding four-man combination from America, it looked as though Mark was about to achieve a career first by winning a major individual title.

In the stableyard, premature jubilation was held in check as two vets examined the suspect hindleg. They agreed that a tendon had slipped off the hock, but they couldn't agree about how to treat it. One recommended hot compresses – the other cold. At regular intervals throughout the night the compresses were changed and the leg treated, so that by morning the grooms were exhausted and bleary-eyed – but Columbus was sound. Peter Scott-Dunn, the British team vet, called into the stables for a last check just before the public veterinary inspection. As he walked into the box, Columbus lashed out with his hind foot – and was back on three legs! None of the vets had been faced with exactly that type of injury before. Usually the tendon slips completely off the hock, and in those circumstances there is no question that the horse is unfit to work. But in this case it was neither one thing nor the other and no-one could say categorically whether or not it would be safe to showjump him.

'He might have got away with it,' is Princess Anne's cautious reaction, 'but it really didn't seem worth the risk.' And that was the bitterly disappointing decision that Mark came to. He was, after all, riding the Queen's horse and if the animal had broken down in front of millions of spectators in the seemingly selfish pursuit of individual glory, Mark would never have recovered from the outcry. But as a rider who has consistently put the welfare of his horse before personal ambition – although the decision was a painful one – it wasn't difficult.

Columbus did not jump on the final day of the World Championships and Mark watched instead, while individual honours went to the American Bruce Davidson riding Irish Cap. Everyone connected with the sport shared Mark's bitter disappointment; he rates the experience, along with that of losing Chicago, as being: 'The greatest blows of my life. Columbus had effectively won the World Championship – it was all over bar the shouting. He'd done the difficult bit, leaving just twelve showjumping fences on the last day. At that time there wasn't another horse in the world in the same class, he was head and shoulders above everything else.'

Burghley 1974 – Mark clears the water trough on Columbus and was in the lead at the end of the crosscountry phase but withdrew due to Columbus slipping the tendon off his hock at the penultimate fence (*Findlay Davidson*); (*overleaf*) Mark riding Favour in the showjumping phase at Downlands in 1976 (*Srdja Djukanovic*)

The Championship had been lost to Mark Phillips, the rider. But with the generosity of all successful three-day-eventers who believe in partnerships, Mark speaks of luck running out for the horses – not himself. 'Chicago and Columbus – they were two giants – it's unfair that a twist of fate robbed them both of the chance to go farther.'

Mark Phillips is often described as 'a member of the Royal Family' but without either disrespect, or false modesty, that's not how he sees himself. He describes his situation as being: 'A member of the family – but not a Royal! I do recognise that I have a role to play, and have a very definite responsibility to attend certain functions, and to act and behave in a way that they would expect. But I'm not an HRH. I lead my own life – though, at the same time, do my best to perform my duties as far as the Royal Family is concerned.'

It is not an enviable role and certainly there can be few men who'd be willing, or even capable, of establishing a workable balance between private man and public husband, maintaining his own identity, and yet recognising that publicly his wife must always take precedence. Many would resent sacrificing part of their independence and individuality to live a semi-Royal life, with all the restrictions that implies. But Mark has none of these hang-ups. People close to him observe that he's 'matured but not changed, he's still very much his own man'. He savours the benefits of his undeniably advantaged and at times privileged life-style, rarely even considering the disadvantages, contributing his own measure of duty and responsibility to The Family without being overawed by it. Few national or local organisations boast his name as a patron or representative. 'I don't see the point,' he says 'in just being a name on a letterhead. Who's Mark Phillips anyway? How much better for them to have someone who really can work for them, and do something constructive.' So he confines his 'name' and energies to the local county boys' club and sports committees, where he tries to make a positive contribution. 'Official' visits get the same, practical appraisal.

When the demands of his working life as a soldier, and more recently a farmer, make it impossible to take days off, Princess Anne fulfills her engagements alone. 'After all' says Mark, 'it is Princess Anne they want to see – not me.'

But evening engagements and important state occasions find him at his wife's side, as support and escort, a role he now fulfils comfortably and with charm, having had plenty of practice during the first twelve months of married life. Her Majesty the Queen accompanied by Prince Philip had agreed to preside over the Commonwealth Games in New Zealand, and then go on to an official tour of New Guinea, and the paradise islands of the Solomons and New Hebrides. Captain Phillips and Princess Anne were invited to join them and, after a brief visit to Canada, joined the Queen for her visit to the Cook Islands before joining up the Royal Yacht in New Zealand.

Having been married just three months, Mark was still new to the rigours of Royal life on tour, and although the South American trip after his honeymoon had given him some idea of what to expect, his first official reception in Roratonga uncovered another trap for the uninitiated. After a superb dinner the couple were invited to watch a display of national dancing performed by local schoolchildren. Garlands of exotic flowers, heady with tropical perfume, were draped round their necks, and then the performance began.

'It was marvellous music and super dancing, but after a while the time change from Ottowa started to catch up with me; what with that, and the music, and the sweet, scented smell from the garlands, I fell sound asleep.' If he'd been sitting next to Princess Anne, no doubt an unobtrusive Royal dig in the ribs would have kept him alert, but he wasn't and, 'when Princess Anne got up, I was left there, kipping. It was only the sound of the chairs scraping as everyone else stood up that finally woke me – it was all very embarrassing.'

The rest of the trip passed without incident, and left them both with breathtaking memories of the suicidal 'vine' jumpers on Pentecost Island, and exotically painted tribesmen in Papua, New Guinea, as well as watching the Commonwealth's greatest athletes in action at the Games.

Back in England, they both picked up the threads of their own competitive careers, and although Columbus no longer figured in their immediate plans, Badminton 1975 was the goal for Goodwill – making his third appearance there with Princess Anne – while Mark anticipated giving Persian Holiday his first crack at the course in company with Laureate, who seemed to have benefited from his year off and looked particularly fit and well.

Early mornings, long, tedious hours of walking the horses back to fitness, getting soaked to the skin in the unpredictable weather of January and February, and nursing the inevitable chilblains, are the miserable aspects of working with horses that melt into insignificance when once their grooms and riders finally reach their goal. But that year the backbreaking work and effort were for nothing. The week before the competition, Percy developed 'leg trouble' and was withdrawn; then, after two soggy days of dressage, the entire event was cancelled as the Gloucestershire countryside succumbed to a week of endless rain.

For Percy there would be other years, but his stable companions sorely missed the test of a major competition in the spring as Laureate was destined for the American Classic at Ledyard, Massachusetts. Mark was left with no opportunity to convince the selectors of his right to a place at the European Championships at Luhmühlen in September. Princess Anne was also in the running with Goodwill for a place in the Championship team. Laureate failed to get a placing at any of the competitions before his American trial. Instead it was the name 'Favour' that appeared throughout beside Mark's in the result sheets.

The mare belonged to Helen Carpendale who lived in Somerset and had had her trained at Bertie Hill's. Recognising a spark of 'something special' in the horse Helen asked jockey John Kersley to partner Favour at Rushall and Chagford in 1974 where they won the novice sections in both competitions. When Mark accepted the ride, Favour had been upgraded to intermediate level, and lived up to the promotion by finishing second at Batsford and Tidworth. It's always satisfying to be in the ribbons, but Mark would have been happier if Laureate had shown some of his old sparkle. As it was, he flew to America with a horse that looked fit to run for its life, but psychologically wasn't prepared to accept the challenge of competition.

For some inexplicable reason, the start of the roads and tracks phase at Ledyard was quite a distance from the stables, and horses had to be tacked up, then loaded into horseboxes six at a time, and driven to the starting-box. Laureate was the last horse to go in his group of six, which meant standing in the lorry for just over an hour and watching his companions being taken out one at a time until he was left alone.

'What with watching all his friends go, and having the loudspeaker blaring out all the time, he worked himself up into a right state and got his tongue over the bit. Anyway, we sorted him out, and he went well over the steeplechase course, and through the roads and tracks. But on the crosscountry he just dropped me altogether. He got his tongue

The British team for the Ledyard Three-day Event (*l to r*) Lucinda Prior-Palmer, Sue Hatherly, Mike Tucker, Janet Hodgson, Mark and Princess Anne (*Warren E. Patriquin*)

back over the bit so that either I had nothing in my hands at all, or I couldn't stop. The whole thing was a disaster.'

So perhaps it's not surprising that it was fence 13, the appropriately-named coffin, that finally proved their downfall and had them eliminated from the contest. After Ledyard, Laureate never regained his old enthusiasm. 'If I took him to a competition, he would just stand in the box shaking, literally dripping with sweat. Basically, he couldn't stand the pressure any more.'

In many ways, despite a string of wins and rosettes, Laureate ranks as one of Mark's disappointments. He'd taken him on in 1972 when he didn't have a top horse of his own, and admits that he attempted 'too much too soon', lured on by the heady success of so many brilliant outings. But once the horse made it clear that he'd lost his appetite for the big competitions, Mark offered him to his sister Sarah as a hunter.

In the early days, when Flavia had been getting the horse fit for competitions, she recalls how on one occasion, when the girl groom who was riding him made a move to open a five-bar metal gate, Laureate was too impatient to wait and cleared the obstacle almost from a standstill. He never again displayed that degree of style and unpredictable brilliance after Ledyard – but he regularly followed hounds up to the winter of 1981 with a dash and enthusiasm which proved his zest for life.

Chapter Seven

The idea that eventing was a man's sport not suited to 'little girls on big horses' had been aired frequently in the late '60s, mostly by men themselves who certainly dominated the results and regarded the steady inroads being made by successful women jockeys like Sheila Wilcox, Anneli Drummond-Hay and Jane Bullen as startling exceptions that would never become the rule. However, lady riders have made nonsense of that patronising attitude over the past ten years by consistently demonstrating their courage and skill with a series of results that have left them just ahead on honours from the two major three-day-events at Badminton and Burghley – with Lucinda Prior-Palmer holding an accumulated six firsts to Mark's five.

But when the British team selectors announced that they were sending an all-female team to Luhmühlen in 1975 to represent us at the European Championships, enough of the old prejudices were still in evidence to make chauvinist diehards in the equestrian fraternity believe that the selectors had taken leave of their senses. As it was Lucinda on Be Fair, Janet Hodgson with Larkspur, Sue Hatherly on Harley and Princess Anne on Goodwill, represented such a formidable line-up of talent that they were immediately dubbed the Britischen Amazonen by the German press, for apart from a lone woman in the Irish team they faced an all-male European challenge.

Mike Tucker was Britain's only individual competitor, and while Mike was never one to regret finding himself the thorn among four roses, he no doubt welcomed the company of male camp followers like Mark who turned up to support the team and act as cheer leaders and general dogsbodies.

And there was plenty for them to cheer about. The four girls embarked on crosscountry day as leaders after the dressage. Janet Hodgson was first to go and had two disappointing falls on Larkspur, but the rest of the team galloped home in fine style. Mark was too caught up in the excitement of his wife's impeccable crosscountry round to feel any frustration at being a spectator rather than a competitor and, in a rare display of public emotion, demonstrated his relief and pride with a hug and a kiss when the Princess emerged from the weighing scales. With the stage set for Britain's 'Amazons' to carry off the team and individual gold medals, Sue Hatherly had a fall in the showjumping ring which dropped them eight penalties behind Russia into the silver medal position, but Lucinda maintained her lead to win the individual gold, followed by Princess Anne as individual silver

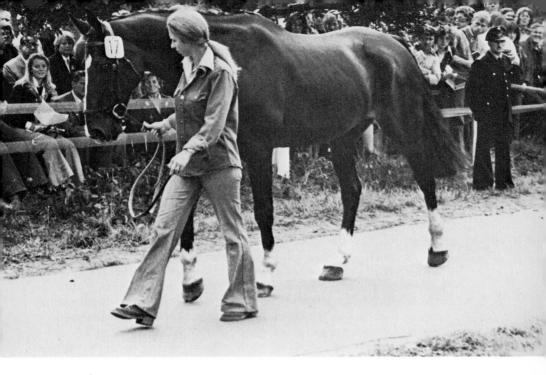

Princess Anne walks Goodwill out for the final veterinary inspection (*above*) at the European Championships at Luhmühlen in 1975 where she gained the individual silver medal and the British girls the team silver medal; (*below*) the team (*l to r*) Lucinda Prior-Palmer on Be Fair, Princess Anne on Goodwill and Sue Hatherly on Harley (*Findlay Davidson*)

medallist. Mike Tucker was the next best placed Briton at seventh on Ben Wyvis, and although celebratory parties were destined to go far into the night, Mark was already packing his bags to fly back to England where the Burghley championship was due to start in three days' time. With his own advanced horses, Columbus, Laureate and Persian Holiday all out of the running, Mark had assumed he'd be giving the competition a miss in 1975, but Janet Hodgson was so badly concussed from her falls at Luhmühlen there was no way she could ride her other highly successful horse, Gretna Green, so she offered the ride to Mark.

Two days before the competition opened, Mark sat on the horse for the first time; six days later, after demonstrating yet again his extraordinary sensitivity as a horseman and his ability to get on any horse at any time and coax the best out of it, he collected the rosette, prize money and trophy awarded to the runner-up in the competition, after coming second to Aly Pattinson on Carawich. It brought the season to a close on a high note, for in many ways 1975 had figured as one of Mark's less successful years.

In contrast, Princess Anne could be well pleased not only with her European silver medal, but also with the consistent performances of her up-and-coming horses, Arthur of Troy and Mardi Gras. The only disappointment husband and wife shared together was a death in the family. Not the sort that makes national newspaper headlines, but one that leaves a genuine gap when an old friend dies. Flora, Princess Anne's black labrador, had mellowed from wild youth to dignified old age. Then, one morning, after following the Princess up the stairs in their home at Sandhurst, she keeled over with a heart attack and died.

For a while Flora wasn't replaced and Moriarty ruled the roost. His strength was phenomenal – as Princess Anne found to her cost on a few early shooting trips. While the beaters were at work, the dog had to be anchored 'and I started off by anchoring him to my good wife. But having been dragged horizontally across numerous fields, she retired from that occupation.' Instead, Moriarty had his lead attached to a large screw which was sunk in the ground, a device which successfully pins most gundogs to the spot, but he managed to burst two choke chains and rip the anchor out of the ground. It wasn't the sort of behaviour likely to endear him to his hosts, so at the end of the season Moriarty was demoted from the position of gundog, and a year later was replaced by one of Flora's Sandringham puppies, Fox, whose field manners were a definite improvement. Moriarty disliked the usurper on sight, so was moved to Great Somerford for his retirement with Mark's parents. However, he had already spent some months living in solitary splendour – until Pleasure arrived.

Lincoln coming over the drop fence at Shelswell in 1981 on his way to victory

On one of her trips north, Princess Anne had admired the Dumfriesshire foxhounds of Sir Rupert Buchanan-Jardine. Later she received a telephone call from Sir Rupert, offering her one of the bitches from the pack who refused to hunt. Pleasure was two and according to Mark: 'One of the most intelligent dogs I've ever had the misfortune to meet. Her low cunning was unbelievable. When we moved to Gatcombe she became a great visitor – her round took in most of the neighbourhood. We'd try to stop her going off, but she'd wander out in front of the house, as if she was only going to spend a penny, and pretend to be sniffing about, doing nothing in particular, then she'd get to the corner – and be gone like a lamplighter. A few hours later we'd get a phone call saying, "We've got Pleasure – would you mind coming to pick her up." And there she'd be, curled up in front of the fire being fed biscuits. She was so sweet, no-one could bear to throw her out so, of course, she always went back there again.'

In Moriarty she found a soul companion, and soon it wasn't just one dog that went missing – but two! Moriarty's only redeeming feature was that at least he would come to heel if called, so Mark hit on the solution of harnessing the dogs together with binder twine whenever they were out; if Pleasure took off, a quick whistle brought Moriarty back, dragging an unwilling Pleasure with him.

The dogs were the greatest of friends and soon became two of the 'characters' to be seen regularly at competitions early in the 1976 season. And in addition to the new 'doggy' face in the Phillips' camp, there was a new arrival in the stable line-up, too. Favour had been ridden at Burghley in the capable hands of her former jockey, John Kersley, but in January the mare was offered to Mark in joint ownership. He'd been impressed with her performance at Batsford and Tidworth the year before, and with Laureate retired and Columbus still taking life easy, Favour looked a good prospect for the year ahead.

The year 1976 was a major turning point in Mark's life. It was a year that brought all the drama and upset, elation, anticipation and bottomless depression that makes the competitive horse world such a masochistic existence. All the outward signposts by which others judge the progress of a career were there suggesting that once again Mark Phillips was enjoying a fairly successful, satisfactory year, but it was the changes that took place privately in Mark's ideas and attitudes to life in general and eventing in particular that, before the year was out, were to have far more impact on his future than anything that appeared in the cold, unemotional print of the record books.

(*above*) Mark and young son Peter playing at Gatcombe and (*below*) with Princess Anne and baby Zara

Mark on Gretna Green at Burghley in September 1975; he took over the horse after its owner, Janet Hodgson, was severely concussed in a fall at Luhmühlen a week earlier but even with their short aquaintance they still finished second; note that horse and rider are beginning to turn in the air (*Findlay Davidson*)

1976 was Olympic year, and all successful three-day-event riders in the country had their ambitions firmly set on winning a place in the national team that would ride at Bromont – the site of the equestrian section of the Montreal Olympics in July.

As always the equestrian press was drawing up its own lists of 'possibles' early in the season, looking with an experienced eye and anticipating the likely performance of the most fancied horses and riders. Not unnaturally the lists included the names of HRH Princess Anne and Captain Mark Phillips, but for once the popular press joined in the speculation, as they considered the prospect of a British Olympic squad of four people containing a husband-and-wife team of which the wife also just happened to be a Royal Princess. The combination of the Olympics, a touch of romance, rivalry and Royalty had all the makings of the best 'sports' news story for years.

No rider would ever presume to voice his or her expectation of an Olympic place in public, whatever their track record and credentials, but if ever anyone deserved the right to privately believe they were in with a near-certain chance of being included in the team when the official short list was drawn up in June, it was Mark Phillips. He'd actually started the year with an empty stable as far as fit, open, international horses were concerned and for a while it looked as though he'd even have to give Badminton a miss altogether. Any other year it wouldn't have mattered – but Badminton was the major showcase for aspiring Olympians, and anyone who failed to impress the selectors there would have to make up a lot of ground in the relatively few weeks left between April and June.

Then out of the blue he was offered a horse called Brazil. 'I was that desperate, I'd have taken anything,' recalls Mark – a statement that isn't quite as condescending as it sounds, for Brazil's career was one that had occasionally twinkled rather than dazzled, but Mark summed him up as: 'A good, honest horse. Without the ability of some of the ones I have now, but certainly able to make a monkey out of most of what was about at the time.' So Brazil was taken into the Phillips' yard and began the long, arduous, lone preparation for Badminton. But within weeks Mark had accepted part-ownership of Favour, and at the same time Persian Holiday came good, displaying all the temperament and ability to make him a potential winner. Suddenly Mark found himself organising a training programme for three horses that took on the proportions of an equestrian juggling act.

All three horses qualified for the competition, and when he checked with the organisers he was told that he would be allowed to ride all three horses. Mark's feelings were that 'Brazil was the least talented of the three, while I thought I had my best chance on Percy'. So he entered

Mark during the showjumping phase at Downlands in 1976 in partnership with Favour (*Srdja Djukanovic*)

them in reverse order of merit, Brazil first, Favour second, and Percy last. Unfortunately what the Badminton Office hadn't told him was that only the first two rides would count in the scoring, and the third horse would have to compete *hors concours* – meaning that whatever he achieved his score wouldn't be counted in the final analysis. Mark was furious. The entries had already been logged and couldn't be changed, so there was no way of putting Brazil last in place of Percy; and he couldn't enter the first horse *hors concours*, as that would be like having a practice ride round the course, and would be totally unfair to the other competitors. There was nothing to be done. Percy was ready to tackle Badminton but, because of an administrative muddle, whatever he achieved – even if he demolished the opposition and won – it wouldn't count.

Brazil was the competition pathfinder. Drawn Number 1 he was first to go on crosscountry day and provided the huge crowds of spectators and cameramen at The Lake with their best picture of the day. Frank Weldon had built a course befitting an Olympic year – a course that would leave the Olympic selectors in no doubt about the ability and scope of the horses worthy of a place on their short list. It included quite a few innovations – like a log in the middle of The Lake. Brazil approached The Lake having already had a minor upset at the Pardubice Taxis – a huge brush fence with a terrifying drop on the landing side – where he'd lost a shoe. From then on he was slipping and sliding all over the place, losing his feet and his confidence with every step. At The Lake he jumped in cleanly enough, but Brazil lost his hind legs on landing, and so with balance and momentum gone was only able to slither over the pole and took a nose dive that had horse and rider totally submerged. Mark's riding boots took in water like a leaky tin. There was no way that he could get them off to empty them out – it takes a boot jack and a strong willing pair of hands to remove

The Ski Jump at Badminton, 1976, when Mark finished third riding Favour (*Marston Photographics*)

them at the best of times. Filled with water, they were jammed fast; but equally, it would be impossible for him to complete the ride with two pints of water sloshing around inside them, so he lay on the grass bank on his back, stuck his feet in the air and let the water drain out.

Everyone was greatly amused – except Brazil. His head had gone under, the water had poured into his ears, and he hated it. Mark remounted and rode on across half a dozen more fences, until he reached the sunken road. A less sensitive rider might have pushed on regardless, but Mark recognised that the horse was defeated. 'He just wasn't interested and said "I've had enough", so I withdrew him, which was very sad. I still think that if he hadn't pulled a shoe off at the third fence he would have gone well and surprised everybody.' But it had been an unpleasant experience, one that Brazil never forgot, so after the event Mark returned him to his owners, Marguerite and Rex Boucher, and a life of one-day events where he could enjoy himself without the heady pressures of international competition.

Mark prepared for his second round of the day on Favour, and the mare turned in a by now characteristically sound performance to clinch third place by the end of the week.

In spite of the fact that Percy's round wouldn't – however it went – count in the official placings, Mark knew that he couldn't just go on a 'jolly' over the fences regardless of the consequences. Badminton was still the competition at which Percy would show off his new-found confidence and ability to the selectors, and Mark was determined that the horse would give a good account of himself. In fact he almost followed Brazil's example by having a stop at the pole in The Lake, but this time neither horse nor rider got a ducking and finished the course in fine style with a score that left them in sixth place. The following morning he showed slight signs of a soreness in one foot on a 'corn' and as Mark was convinced that the horse had already done more than enough to prove himself, he decided to withdraw him from the show-jumping phase.

The gamble paid off. When the selectors published their short list of possible contenders it included both Persian Holiday and Favour, and

Mark and Persian Holiday about to negotiate The Lake at Badminton, 1976 (*John Topham Picture Library*)

Princess Anne with Goodwill, who had been excused Badminton but had rightfully earned a place on the short list after clinching the silver medal at the European Games the previous year. Mark's Aunt Flavia had no doubt that Percy would ride at the Olympics. When she'd been getting the horse fit as a youngster and people asked her his name, she would say,'His real name is Persian Holiday – but I'm calling him Montreal.'

Three weeks before the team were due to leave for Canada they assembled at Osberton for the final trial. Favour was notoriously temperamental in front of large crowds and, in the hope of avoiding the 'packed houses' that would watch the dressage later in the day, Mark elected to ride Favour first, with the result that the mare 'did quite a nice test', while Percy lived up to Mark's expectations and earned a score that placed them third.

So far – so good. But Mark admits that 'Favour was always very difficult at one-day events – she was so strong that she was quite difficult to settle' and before Mark had even reached the second fence she started playing up. 'As I came round the corner to the fence, which was a log pile in the wood, there were people all over the place. That – combined with her being a bit difficult – was enough to make her put in a stop. But she jumped the fence at the second attempt, and went perfectly well after that.'

As for Percy, the big-striding chestnut never put a foot wrong and his fluid, faultless performance put him into the lead – where he stayed.

Mark allowed himself to believe that both horses had done more than enough to impress the selectors, and that at least one of them would make it to the final draw. In the event 'I took them both to Montreal for a holiday'; the statement is flippant – but those who know him realise it's a camouflage for a deep and bitter disappointment. After their customary huddle, the selectors announced that Britain's hopes for Olympic honours would be carried by Hugh Thomas riding Playmar, Lucinda Prior-Palmer with Be Fair, Richard Meade on Jacob Jones, and Princess Anne on Goodwill. Captain Mark Phillips was to be the reserve rider with two spare horses Persian Holiday and Favour. Being reserve meant that he would go to Montreal, stand on the sidelines and watch, but not ride – unless, that is, a miracle or a disaster occurred.

At the time Mark kept his feelings to himself. After all he'd been down this path before – eight years before at Mexico. Then he was 'thrilled' just to be there, albeit as reserve. But this time, who would blame him if he felt cheated, especially as his preparation, and even his competition performance, had been aimed at that one major goal. Even his attitude to Badminton had been different. He explains: 'That was the first time ever when I wasn't really out to win. It may sound a stupid thing to say now but because I realised that there wasn't very long between Badminton and the Olympics I didn't want to give the horses such a hard run that they'd be overworked by July, so I didn't extend either of them at all. I gave them quite a steady round. You could argue now that it was a mistake – but at the time I thought I was doing the right thing. They both had a good preparation and after Osberton I thought I had a real chance.'

Because the Olympics offer such an important and prestigious arena for sporting talent, they're equally a hotbed of emotions, and although Mark himself refuses even now to comment on or be drawn into the arguments, there are many people in the horse world who still feel strongly that neither Playmar nor Be Fair should have been selected to ride. Those of a generous disposition say simply that 'their fitness was suspect', while others, more outspoken, assert that 'we sent two lame horses to Montreal and even members of the American team were thanking us for handing them the gold medal on a plate'.

It's even been suggested to me that, while Mark's horses stood fit and clean-limbed in their stables, it was only the regular administration of the pain-killing drug Buteozolegin (Bute) that got others through the vets' inspection. But such is the nature of the horse world – where things whispered in private are rarely said out loud for fear that someone should be offended – that the selectors, and vets, were not persuaded to change their minds.

Reserve rider in action! Mark and Princess Anne at Bromont where the three-day event of the 1976 Montreal Olympics was held (*Cappy Jackson*)

Mark would have no part in the controversy that bubbled below the surface. Instead he maintained a fitness programme with his two horses that would enable them to compete in the autumn schedule of competitions on returning home and, more importantly, he diverted his energies and encouragement to his wife, and admits 'it certainly took my mind off the fact that I wasn't competing myself'. But it must have taken a strong will and sporting instinct not to register bitter irony when Playmar broke down on the crosscountry course, and Be Fair was withdrawn after slipping a tendon as Columbus had done at the World Championships. This robbed Britain of any chance in the team competition and left just two riders, Richard Meade and Princess Anne, to ride on for individual honours.

Demonstrating all the skill and ability that have made him so successful as an Olympic competitor, Richard finished individual fourth on Jacob Jones, adding yet another satisfying result to an already impressive list. Princess Anne's round earned the headlines after a spectacular fall at Fence 18. Goodwill was winded and lost a shoe, but the Princess lay on the ground – dazed and slightly concussed – for several minutes, with Bertie Hill, who had sprinted through the crowd, kneeling beside her. Bertie advised retirement, but Princess Anne insisted on being remounted and continued the course in something of an amnesic haze. Newspapers around the world carried photographs of Her Majesty the Queen – who was a guest at the Games – clad in headscarf and mackintosh, her hand covering her mouth, and her face bearing all the grey anguish of uncertainty as the tannoy announced that her daughter had fallen. No one recorded the look on Mark Phillips' face as he waited in the starting-box with the rest of the team of grooms and heard the news of his wife's accident booming over the crowds; it would have shown a controlled mixture of concern and disappointment – a public face registering only a shadow of emotion, while inside panic struggled to take over.

After the initial announcement there was a long gap and then the news that the Princess had retired. Mark remembers thinking 'that we ought to get our things packed up and try to get to where she had fallen – then came another announcement saying that she was setting off again – so all we could do was sit back and wait'.

Anyone who has close emotional ties with a competitor will tell you that the uncertainty of waiting, the dread of a really bad accident, make the role of spectator and supporter almost worse than that of competitor. Parents are particularly susceptible, husbands and wives equally so. As a competitor Mark knows all the risks; as a husband it doesn't stop him going through a private agony whenever anything looks like developing into a potential disaster. But both he and Princess Anne have come to terms with the dangerous possibilities of the sport. Mark's philosophy is simple: 'I've got confidence in her as a jockey and the horse she rides – so I just hope that the two of them can put it all together on the day. If every time she went off round the crosscountry course I became a shivering wreck of nerves, not only wouldn't it achieve very much, but I probably wouldn't live to see tomorrow. When you start thinking about falling off and breaking arms, or necks and backs – that's the time to give up. But I must admit I'm always glad when she comes back in one piece!'

On that occasion, as on many before and since, both horse and wife did return in one piece – if slightly battered – and went on to complete a slow but sure showjumping round on the final day to finish in twenty-fourth place.

Before the final Osberton trial Princess Anne had been quoted as saying 'being on the short list I consider to be an achievement, if I get to Montreal I will consider that to be another achievement, and if I actually get around that will be quite something'. Well, she'd gone, she'd ridden and she'd finished. And although there were no highly-prized Olympic medals to add to her two European medals, with a display of skill and courage she had once again proved to the cynics that she wasn't in the team just because she was the Queen's daughter but because she was, and is, one of the country's finest horsewomen.

After the Three-Day Event there was time to relax and enjoy the rest of the Olympic competition in the main Montreal stadium. Mark was keen to see the finals of the main field and track events – and he also had in mind a little 'sport' of his own.

Apart from winning an actual Olympic medal one of the great trophies to claim on these occasions is an Olympic flag. At Bromont they flew from tall flagpoles all along the route into the main stadium. The roads were floodlit and busy – hooking one off its pole was not going to be easy! Mark planned the assault like a mini-military exercise – and enlisted the help of some of the Canadian security men who'd been detailed to shadow Princess Anne during her stay. 'They were brilliant at their jobs and the most unpolicemanlike policemen we've ever come across,' says Mark, while Princess Anne remembers them as the only undercover men who've ever turned up wearing jeans and sweatshirts looking as if they belonged in them. Apparently most overseas policemen aren't used to tailing such informal 'Royals' as the Princess and her husband and usually turn up at competitions in the middle of crowds of casual 'horsey' people trying to look inconspicuous in stiff, beautifully-laundered jeans and brand new wellingtons managing only to look uncomfortable and out of place. But not the Canadians. They melted into the scenery of well-worn jeans and frayed shirts, and found the British team's off-duty escapades light relief from the usual undercover round of following the heroin trail and tracking down criminals.

On a quiet stretch of road a flagpole was shinned, and the flag unhooked. But just as it was being bundled into the boot, a police car came along full of uniformed police. There was no way that the security men were going to be caught red-handed by the uniformed branch – so they dived back into the car and according to Mark: 'We took off at the rate of knots, out into the countryside, parked up in a wood somewhere, and hid the flag in some bushes, then drove back to the Olympic village. Later on, when things quietened down a bit, we went back to retrieve it.' The flag is one of the trophies that the Phillips' *don't* have on display at their home. It's folded away in the tackroom of the stable and Mark says 'I'll hang it up in the school one day.' 'For what?' I asked. 'An incentive?' Mark gives a sidelong look, grins and says with a hint of irony 'You could say that.'

Chapter Eight

Unlike the rest of the Olympic horses who were put out to grass on their return from Canada, either for a well-earned rest or to recover from their injuries, Percy and Favour were keen, fit and raring to go. Mark had philosophically used his month's 'holiday' in Canada as a continuation of their training programme. Just three weeks after her flight across the Atlantic, Favour was crossing the channel for the three-day event at Luhmühlen in Germany. The mare gave a creditable performance and, in spite of a stupid mistake on one of the banks, finished in eighth place. But it was the last major competition at which she ever appeared. Mark started preparing her for the 1977 Badminton 'but I gave up in mid-flight. She started to become more and more impossible. Just like Laureate she couldn't settle to competitive work, she would get uptight and jazzy. It wasn't physical – just mental, as if she was worrying about it,' so the mare was retired to stud at Windsor. But even the quiet days of maternal rest don't seem to suit her as she's slipped every one of the foals she's conceived, and there's regret in Mark's voice, as if he feels she has never really fulfilled her potential, when he says: 'It's a shame – she's such a sweet-natured mare – when she's not competing!'

Mark approached the Burghley competition in September with an even stronger desire to win than usual. Here was an opportunity to show the selectors how wrong they'd been to under-estimate Persian Holiday's ability. After the dressage he was in the lead, and although he took three seconds over the optimum time to complete the steeplechase course, the soggy going slowed everyone down and Percy's was the fastest time of the day. On the crosscountry course the big chestnut chewed up the ground, and flowed effortlessly over the fences. Flying towards fence 7, looking like champions, Mark made what he describes as 'one of the most idiotic, crazy, stupid mistakes ever. When we went across country I put my foot to the floor and we were going like hell. When we got to the coffin I knew we were going much too fast, but he was so brilliant at coffins that there was never any problem. He jumped in, down the bank, over the ditch and up, but we were going so fast that instead of putting in another stride before the jump out, he tried to do it in one. The rail was an awful long way up, and he just made a nonsense of it.' Mark's explanation for the mistake is simple – and understandable. 'Because I was so angry at being left out of the Olympic team, I wanted to prove to everyone else how wrong they'd been not to let Percy run in Montreal. I was just

(*above*) Mark and Persian Holiday in the crosscountry phase of the 1976 Burghley Three-day Event (*Findlay Davidson*); (*right*) wading through a swollen stream during an army exercise with student officers from Sandhurst (*Press Association*)

trying too hard – and going too fast.' Without that one mistake Percy would have been a clear winner that year at Burghley as on showjumping day he went clear, and in spite of the 60 penalties for a fall at the Coffin, he still finished in eighth place.

With the eventing season over and his leave over, Mark went back to work for the army. His two years as an instructor had come to an end, and instead he was to be deskbound at the Ministry of Defence in Whitehall as a GSO 3 in Army Training – the department which dealt with overseas training in twenty-two countries around the world. Mark describes the job as 'gratifying and frustrating'. Gratifying because he could see an end product to his work. He had special responsibility for the battle group training area at Suffield in Canada and would send seven battle groups a year on full-scale exercises using live ammunition. Everything connected with the exercise, the transport, the equipment, the finer details of organisation, passed across his desk. 'I would go to watch occasionally as the "observer" from the great Ministry. It was very realistic, and Suffield is probably still the best military training area in the world. It was always very rewarding as people enjoyed going there, and usually managed to have good fun too.' The frustration came from dealing with the minutia of administration, mountains of paperwork, and the infuriating habit of many government departments to ruin the ship for a ha'p'orth of tar because someone somewhere didn't think the exercise through. But if nothing else, Mark Phillips is an optimist. He made the most of his job, introduced new systems and fresh ideas as far as his rank would allow, and outwardly appeared to be the very model of an efficient career soldier.

But Mark had not joined the army to push paper. He enjoyed the active life of regimental soldiering, and felt disillusioned with being a staff officer and divorced from his regiment as they completed a tour of Northern Ireland and prepared to return to Germany. Being married to the Queen's daughter, there was no question of allowing him anywhere near Northern Ireland; even Germany would have been difficult and, as Mark saw nothing but a deskbound career looming before him, he reluctantly decided that he must break with the army and find a more active, rewarding career in some other sphere.

But doing what? Mark admits that his life had revolved around horses and the army and that he was in no way equipped to tackle a job in civilian life. 'I decided that as the one thing I did know about was horses I could do a "Bertie Hill" and become a teacher and trainer, and at least earn myself a living and do something that I'm reasonably competent at.' The principle was sound, but there were two major drawbacks. Firstly, they would have to find another home. While he remained in the army, home was Oak Grove at Sandhurst, but once he became a civilian he would have to find a house with enough land to accommodate stabling, schooling and grazing facilities for the horses.

Secondly, once he became a fee-earning, professional trainer, he would lose his amateur status. And that would be the biggest blow of all. He would not be allowed to compete in European, World or Olympic trials and the opportunity of winning that elusive individual title would be lost to him for ever.

But Mark wasn't just disillusioned with the army. He'd become disillusioned with much that was going on in the eventing world as well. Much of the old camaraderie and team spirit had gone out of the sport and the fiasco of the Montreal team had been the last straw. He admits: 'From that moment on I had a different attitude to the sport. Before Montreal all I'd ever wanted to do was compete. The only thing that ever mattered to me was to have a horse in the European, World or Olympic Championships, and for ten years I'd done everything I could to have a horse available for the team – and then I'd been kicked in the teeth. After that I decided to hell with it – I've had enough. I couldn't compete any more with the attitude that this is for the team or my country – I decided that I was going to do it for myself.'

The hypocrisy of those who said one thing to his face, and another behind his back, finally got to him. He looked on the sport with less rosy, more dispassionate eyes and decided that the old team spirit that had been such a vital part of Britain's equestrian strength had disappeared. 'I think it just became a bunch of individuals, riding for themselves, pretending to be a team.' It also seemed to him that the trainers and selectors had got their priorities out of proportion by putting so much emphasis on good dressage marks and less on the performance across the country and says: 'In my humble opinion it's one of the reasons why we haven't been so successful in the past few years as a team. When we were winning gold medals, all the while we were going for three clear rounds across country. Hang the dressage, you can be twenty or thirty or even forty marks down on dressage – it doesn't matter. If you go through the international results you'll see that the Americans had to count Bruce Davidson's fall at Montreal, and they still won the gold medal, even with his 60 penalties – so what does a little bit of dressage matter. A good, safe clear is what wins international competitions, and medals.'

Mark's ideas may sound like heresy to those riders and trainers who spend hours perfecting the finer movements of dressage, and indeed it would be wrong to discount the importance of the phase altogether. But it's interesting to note that since Munich the only gold medals to come Britain's way were won in the 1977 European Championships at Burghley, and at Horstens in Denmark in 1981, and on both occasions Britain's team riders had fast, safe, clear rounds across country!

As 1976 mellowed into the golden days of autumn, Mark's new attitudes hardened into positive action. He would leave the army, give up the image of good old dependable team member Mark and, even though it meant sacrificing his amateur status, become a professional trainer. Princess Anne shared much of her husband's disappointment, especially over his decision to leave the army. Her reaction was that 'it was a pity, but it was more or less forced on him I think. If he'd been able to do what he wanted to which was basically stay and command a squadron and then possibly the regiment, I would have been very happy, though I don't suppose I would have made a very good colonel's wife. There was no question of going to live in Germany, which in a way was a pity, because then I would have had to be an army wife, so to speak. But he was really never going to be in a position to do that, and there wouldn't have been much point in him spending the rest of his life behind a desk in Whitehall.'

So the search for a house became fundamental to Mark's new life and new ideals. The couple had been looking at property in a half-hearted sort of way for some time. What they had in mind was a comfortable family house with about a hundred acres in the area around Oxford and Newbury. Somewhere that was in the country, but still close enough to London for Princess Anne to be able to continue her official duties and work from Buckingham Palace.

Their early forays were a waste of time. Everything they looked at failed in some way to meet their specification, and it didn't take long for the couple to realise that in several cases the price took a dramatic upward leap once the vendor realised exactly who it was that was interested. They even ventured as far as Gloucestershire – a good fifty miles further than the imaginary boundary line they'd drawn – and looked at a house just outside the village of Tetbury. It was called Highgrove and had recently been renovated 'so we could have moved in without any hassle' recalls Mark. But the land was expensive, the house a little too close to the road, therefore very public, too big, and in Mark's opinion it didn't have as much charm or as many possibilities as Gatcombe. Four years later Prince Charles was to alter the inside considerably, no doubt to give it some of the 'charm' that both Mark and Princess Anne had found lacking.

Lord Butler ended their search. He'd heard on the grapevine that Mark and Anne were looking for a home in the area, and wrote suggesting that they might be interested in his old home at Gatcombe Park. They drove down to Gloucestershire, turned off the Minchinhampton road and bumped down the steep, potted driveway that curved through ragged laurels, past an old crumbling coach house, and ended in a thinly-gravelled sweep in front of a delapidated Georgian house. The steps up to the front door, the pillared entrance, long graceful windows, and beautifully-proportioned façade broadcast that this had once been an elegant family home. But it was shabby from neglect, and inside was a disaster. Nevertheless, that one visit convinced Mark that Gatcombe would be his home, and speaking with the pride of a man who is settled in the place where he knows he belongs, he says: 'We stood on the front steps and looked out at the view; it was quiet, it was secluded, it was peaceful with woods down each side of the long valley. I thought to myself – well, whatever is inside we can change, given time. But this we can never change. This is just what we've been looking for.'

Michaelmas is a day on which country people traditionally settle the quarterly rent on land and property and when new tenancies are agreed. It falls on 29 September and it was on that date in 1976 that Captain Mark Phillips officially became Master of Gatcombe Park in Gloucestershire. But it wasn't he who signed the cheque for the purchase price. His army pay of just over four-and-a-half thousand pounds a year would probably have run to a semi on a housing estate, but certainly not a period residence *and* an estate.

Gatcombe was bought by Her Majesty the Queen as a gift to the couple for an undisclosed sum. Fleet Street pitched their guesstimate at around £750,000. 'It didn't cost anything like that,' claims Mark while still politely declining any discussion of private, family financial matters. Whatever the price, it secured not only the eighteenth-century house, but also a collection of ramshackle outbuildings, two sheds, a small farm complex, and five hundred acres of arable farmland, grazing and woodland. What the gift did not include was the total sum needed to completely renovate and refurbish the house to make it habitable.

His description of the house being 'a mess' may seem a harsh and indelicate choice of words considering that it had been the home of Lord and Lady Butler, but the couple had stayed there only occasionally, using just a few rooms at one end of the house. The plumbing and electrics were a maze of pipes and wires that meandered through the building ending in a jungle of connections in the pantry which was, to quote Mark, 'a dingy dark hole', and although the rooms at the front of the house on the first floor command a stunning view down across the valley, these were taken up with bathrooms, while the bedrooms were relegated to the back of the house – overlooking a tangle of woodland and crumbling stone wall.

What Mark and Princess Anne had in mind was to create a home that would do credit to the requirements of a Royal residence, while losing none of the warmth and comfort of a real family home. To achieve this would take more than just a few rolls of wallpaper and a lick of paint. What was called for was major surgery and to cover the cost of that operation Mark joined the queue of borrowers and took out a mortgage.

In January the builders moved in, and within weeks had ripped out the old kitchen and pantry and reduced the first floor to a shell. The

The family relaxing at home during the summer of 1981

men from Rentokil removed the worms, the whole place was rewired and replumbed, the bathrooms were returned to the back of the house, and a set of beautifully-proportioned bedrooms, each enjoying a stunning view of the park, built at the front. A nursery complex with its own bedrooms, bathroom, sitting-room and kitchen was made on the top floor of the house in the attics, while the kitchen and pantry became two enormous, high-ceilinged, light and airy rooms, lined with fitted units and modern equipment.

Designer David Hicks planned the decorations and colour schemes for the ground floor and bedrooms – including lavish wall coverings and carpets, most of which proved far too expensive for the cost-conscious Phillips. At this stage, early in 1977, Gatcombe was not the official residence of Her Royal Highness – her home was still Oak Grove at Sandhurst – and so none of the fifty thousand a year she received from the Civil List could be spent on the house. Instead Mark and Princess Anne spent their savings and the mortgage loan. David Hicks' colour scheme was retained – but with cheaper materials on the ground floor and Princess Anne chose different designs for all but one of the bedrooms. Pale peach in the hall and across the landing, a bold rust in Mark's study, warm red in the dining-room, and a soft apple-green toned with cream and white in the formal drawing-room and the sitting-room at the far end of the house which now doubles as Princess Anne's office.

Throughout the spring and summer the workmen transformed the house, though Mark's visits to monitor and savour the progress were rare and rushed. Living at Sandhurst, working in London and devoting most of his spare time to working and competing his horses left precious little time for driving down to Gloucestershire, so it was almost inevitable that one of his mad dashes down the M4 would eventually lead to him being caught for speeding. He'd arranged to meet the architect at Gatcombe, and phoned Princess Anne from his office in Whitehall to organise a rendezvous at one of the motorway junctions near Maidenhead. Princess Anne was out, so he left a message at Oak Grove and set off through the London traffic. Threequarters of an hour later he arrived at the meeting point but there was no sign of his wife; a telephone call confirmed that she hadn't received his original message and when she finally arrived they were almost an hour late for the appointment.

Mark isn't a reckless driver – but he is fast. As he swung across into the outside lane and pushed his Rover up to 90mph, he and the Princess were caught up with what in the circumstances was a fairly typical exchange between husband and wife of 'I left you a message', 'I know but I didn't get it', 'Why didn't you get it?', 'I don't know', and

(*above*) Mark trying to demonstrate a point to his Range Rover Bursary scheme pupils; (*below*) A big fence, whichever way you look at it even if Laura is not impressed – the Cirencester Rails at Badminton

Mark riding Princess Anne's Goodwill in the jumping phase at Badminton 1977 when he finished thirteenth; Princess Anne could not ride herself as she was expecting their first child

so on, for a mile down the road. When Mark finally looked in his mirror, he saw that he was being tailed by a police motorcyclist. He was eventually fined £25 and had his licence endorsed.

The press recorded the occasion in full, but the episode was a minor ripple compared to the storm that broke a year later when he was 'done' for speeding at 60mph in Whitehall. A modest fine of £15 led to accusations of privileged treatment because of his Royal connections, and Mrs Vera Bray, a Lancashire magistrate, was so disgusted that she resigned in protest. Mark, as usual, kept his head down while the storm raged, but clearly on reflection feels that people over-reacted because it was *his* name on the charge sheet and because of the misleading way in which the case was reported. 'All I'd done was accelerate past a tourist who was ambling along in his car taking in the sights and looking at the birds and the bees,' says Mark. 'I had only travelled 300 yards from start to finish. I obviously went over 30mph but it was reported as though I'd been doing 60 down the length of Whitehall – in which case they could have taken my licence from me.'

Gatcombe Park – the end of the search for a home (*Srdja Djukanovic*)

As it was the £15 fine was accompanied by an endorsement – but since then he's managed to keep his licence clean.

In contrast to Mark's high-speed performance on the roads that spring of '77, his record in the horse trials world was definitely low-geared. After starting the year with both Favour and Persian Holiday as Badminton possibilities, Favour was retired and Percy hit a spectacular run of bad luck. In the weeks before the event he'd come second at Brigstock and won at Rushall – results that made him one of fancied horses for the 1977 title. He repaid the punters' optimism by lying second at the end of the dressage to Karl Schultz on Madrigal, with George – now partnered by Lucinda Prior-Palmer – lying third.

Crosscountry day was one of the wettest on record and on tackling the steeplechase course at the end of the day Mark was riding 'into the teeth of a thunderstorm. Going over the fences I couldn't see a thing; I kept my head bowed into this wall of water, and kept having a peep to see when a fence was coming up, holding on to his head like mad, and hoping he could see more than I could.' More by luck than judgement, they completed the steeplechase clear, then set off across country 'going like a bomb'. Just three fences into the course they entered Huntsman's Close, Percy pecked slightly ·on landing after jumping the drop fence, and Mark remembers: 'It wasn't a bad peck – he didn't fall or anything, but I tightened the reins slightly to help him and make sure he didn't go down on his knees – and suddenly "ping" everything came up in my hands.' The reins had snapped, and Mark came out of the cluster of fences with no way of holding, steering or stopping the huge powerful chestnut, who galloped on past the Elephant Trap and off the course towards the carparks.

No top-class rider ever goes into a competition without making a minute and detailed check on his equipment. Mark is no exception. The bridle had been examined that morning, and shown no signs of wear. It was a totally unexpected, unexplained fluke – and one that knocked him right out of the competition. Winning at Sherborne and Batsford two weeks later was little consolation, if anything it only confirmed Mark's belief that Percy would have proved a formidable Badminton contender.

If it occurred to him at all to brood over the fact that his much-loved leggy chestnut gelding seemed doomed to a career punctuated with bad luck and missed opportunities, there was soon another, altogether far more important matter to occupy his emotions. Princess Anne was pregnant. The baby was due in November, and Mark could not have been happier. Things may not have been going to plan in the eventing world, but in other spheres life was definitely looking rosy.

Gatcombe was being transformed slowly but surely into the comfortable, elegant house he and his wife had dreamed of. Before the end of the year they'd be able to move in, and the nursery – planned in hope rather than expectation – would have its first occupant. But

(*above*) The old stableyard at Gatcombe, no longer suitable for keeping horses in today (*Srdja Djukanovíc*); the new stables – less attractive but more functional (*Jim Bennett*)

although the family would be well-housed, there was still the problem of what to do with the horses. There were eight of them altogether and Gatcombe had no stable accommodation, something that Mark would have to remedy if he intended to earn his living as an instructor and continue riding as a professional competitor. But the coach house would have cost a fortune to renovate, and even then would have been too small, and the elderly farm sheds would only serve as temporary accommodation.

Mark considered his options and decided that the only solution was to build a new block of looseboxes. The fairly flat land at the side of the farmyard offered an ideal site. He could build a model complex based on those he'd seen in eventing stables in Germany and America, where everything was under cover and served from a central aisle large enough to take a small tractor. It wasn't an ambitious or lavish scheme – just highly practical with a £35,000 price tag. The money raised by the mortgage was already fully committed to pay for work being done to the house, and Mark's own savings and resources had reached rock bottom.

They decided that the only solution was to sell Bull and Willy. Bull was really called Cassette, but his chestnut and white colouring made him look just like a Hereford bull, while Willy was the shortened form of Dumwhill. Both horses were relative newcomers to the Phillips' yard, but had made an impressive start to their respective careers. On his two outings as an intermediate Cassette had come third at Henstridge and first at Rudding Park, while Drumwhill had been third at Brigstock, second at Downlands and Hensridge and had won the intermediate class at Wramplingham. Both horses went to Switzerland, and when he added the collective profit from the sales to the insurance money Princess Anne had received after the death of Doublet, they had enough to go ahead with the building.

The plan incorporated fifteen looseboxes and what has been rather grandly described as a 'swimming pool' for the horses – in fact nothing more than a loosebox with a sunken floor. The horses are led down a shallow ramp, and the water is pumped in through ducts in the walls. It hardly rates as a children's paddling pool, let alone a swimming pool, and is more usually filled with bales of hay rather than water. Considering the amount of trouble Mark had gone to to raise the money and keep costs to a minimum, he was understandably niggled by stories circulating at the time that he was building a '£100,000 stable complex with a swimming pool for equine comfort'. But these days he takes an obvious delight in walking visitors through the low-roofed, L-shaped building with its basic amenities and workmanlike atmosphere, pausing at the door of the fifth box on the left announcing 'that's the famous swimming pool' and watching the expressions on their faces.

All through the summer the house and stables continued to take shape, and Mark turned his attention to what would probably be his last autumn season of competitions as an amateur, and therefore his last opportunity to win an individual championship, for he had high hopes of Persian Holiday making an impression on the European Championships at Burghley. With Princess Anne unable to ride, he shared the role of jockey on her horses with one of his closest friends, Captain Malcolm Wallace, and for Malcolm it was a doubly happy association. Not only did he ride the talented Flame Gun and Inchiquin into the ribbons at five one-day events that year, he also lost his heart to Caroline Doyne-Ditmus who had earlier been Princess Anne's groom.

Mark also seemed to be hitting a lucky streak with Persian Holiday who won his first outing of the season at Eglinton, and went on to clinch the Midland Bank championship at Locko Park at the end of August. He was also pleased to be back in the saddle on his old friend Columbus. The big talented grey had been given over a year to recover from the injury to his hock at the 1974 World Championships.

Mark and Persian Holiday competing in the Franklin Mint Dressage Championship; they came first in 1977 and equal first in 1978

Towards the end of 1976 Mark had entered him in a few team crosscountry races with Demi Douzaine ridden by Princess Anne, Felday Checkpoint with Toby Sturgis and Mike Tucker on Ben Wyvis. They'd won the Cock o' the North trophy, and gone on to compete at the beginning of the following spring season. The old horse's hocks looked fine with no hint of any recurring trouble, but there was no question of returning him to top-class eventing at that stage, and so throughout that late summer and early autumn Columbus just enjoyed himself dashing across fields and clearing relatively simple fences in the company of three other really great event horses.

Percy looked a picture of health and fiery enthusiasm, having galloped away with the lead at the final trial before the European Championships. On his past form Percy looked more than capable of giving Mark a real crack at an individual European medal, but with just days to go the horse developed a virus infection and had to be withdrawn.

Is it any wonder that Mark accepts so much in his life philosophically knowing that whenever he gets to within a fingertip of success, one of the fates knocks him back down the ladder and makes him start all over again.

The climb back on Percy came just a few weeks after the Championships, which were won by the now well-established partnership of Lucinda Prior-Palmer and George.

Mark took Percy to Knowlton in Kent where they finished in the lead, with Princess Anne's Flame Gun third. It meant that Percy finished the season with a win, but it gave Mark little satisfaction to know that in a year when his horse had won the Franklin Mint Dressage Championship at the Royal International Horse Show, the Spillers Combined Championship at the Horse of the Year Show, and the Midland Bank Championship – a unique treble – and deserved to crown that consistent performance with at least a placing from Badminton or Burghley, he'd missed the opportunity at both competitions through nothing more than a double attack of misfortune. The one good piece of news to emerge by the end of the season was that Mark wouldn't after all have to give up his amateur status by becoming a trainer.

On one of his trips down to Gatcombe he'd approached his farming neighbour on the subject of buying adjoining fields which seemed geographically to fit better with Mark's farm than his neighbour's. The reply shook him somewhat. Instead of agreeing to sell just the two fields, he was offered the entire farm – some 500 acres. As Mark says: 'It caused a considerable turmoil. There was no way I could afford to buy the whole lot, but I did approach a few institutions and insurance companies with a view to them purchasing the farm, and me leasing it back.' His discussions with the 'institutions' looked fairly hopeful until one evening at the end of September when he and Princess Anne

Mark and Persian Holiday, winners of the Midland Bank championship at Locko
Park in August 1977 (*Kit Houghton Photography*)

were having dinner with the Queen. 'I told her what we were planning and she said "why can't I be the institution – why can't I buy it, and rent it to you in the same way". It was a very kind and generous offer – and that's what happened.'

In October Her Majesty began negotiations to buy the 500-acre Aston Farm. Faced with the prospect of becoming the Queen's tenant and having a 1000-acre farm on his doorstep from the combined acreage of Gatcombe and Aston, Mark was able to approach his future from an entirely different angle. Instead of limiting his land to horses and his energies to training, he would become a professional farmer. It was the perfect solution. He could leave the army, go into a profession that he already understood having spent his childhood on a farm and most of his life in the country, earn a living that gave him self respect and independence from State support through Princess Anne's Civil List allowance, and continue riding as an amateur competitor.

On 14 November Mark and his wife celebrated their fourth wedding anniversary together quietly at Buckingham Palace. In the small hours of the fifteenth she woke Mark to tell him that her contractions had started. At four o'clock Mark drove her to the private Lindo wing of St Mary's Hospital in Paddington. Mark stayed with his wife throughout her labour, and then faced the vexed question of whether or not to stay for the birth. He admits 'it wasn't something I particularly wanted to do' and Princess Anne had already made her feelings clear by declaring, 'If you feel like coming fair enough; if not, I'm not going to create a scene if you are not there.' He stayed, quietly convinced that whatever his wife *said*, she would be happier knowing he was there.

At 10.46am Peter Mark Andrew Phillips was born, a healthy 7lb 9oz baby boy. The moment of birth has been variously described by fathers as magical and spiritual and a time of great joy; while Mark would agree that all those emotions were present, his lasting impression is that it was 'quite a frightening experience'.

Released from the delivery room he telephoned the Queen to tell her that she was a grandmother and that both mother and son 'were fine'. A call to his parents at Great Somerford had the champagne corks popping and, while the customary official notice of the birth was pinned to the railings outside Buckingham Palace, inside the Queen made her own delighted announcement to the men and women who'd crowded into the Throne Room for an investiture ceremony. 'I apologise for being late, but I have just had a message from the hospital. My daughter has given birth to a son, and I am now a grandmother.'

It was a smiling Captain Mark Phillips who faced newsmen when he left the hospital later that day. In reply to the shouted 'congratulations' he quipped, 'It's nice to think I've done something right for a change.' It was delivered with genuine good humour, but the remark had been prompted by the fact that, in the weeks leading up to the birth, Mark had once again been the whipping boy of the gossip columnists and feature writers who'd been taking swipes at him over the purchase of Gatcombe and Aston, and the supposed £100,000 stable-block. It seemed that every time he picked up the papers, they couldn't find a good thing to say about him. And now, here he was, on 15 November, everyone's favourite father!

A few days later, when he collected his wife and son from the hospital and drove them back to Buckingham Palace, another storm burst over their heads. This time they'd annoyed the safety-conscious who were 'appalled' to see Princess Anne sit in the front seat with the baby in her arms – 'didn't she know that she and the baby should be in the back where they'd be protected if the car was in a collision' screamed the objectors, declaring that Princess Anne and her husband were setting a bad example to other parents. They were right, of course, and legislation now makes it illegal for children to travel in the front seat of a car. But the whole episode soured what was otherwise a happy occasion, and Mark couldn't wait to get out of London.

Ten days later he swung out of the huge black-and-gold gates of Buckingham Palace, drove through the fumes and the jangle of London traffic and down the M4 to Gloucestershire. He turned into an inconspicuous drive off a minor road. The wooden gate was off its hinges and propped against the hedge, the surface of the drive was uneven and potholed, but Mark Phillips had brought his wife and baby son home – to Gatcombe Park.

Chapter Nine

'The most unroyal of Royal households' is how Mark describes his home at Gatcombe. And certainly you have to constantly remind yourself that this *is* a Royal residence, and not just the country home of a well-heeled Cotswold farmer when you're greeted by a handful of free-range chickens who wander around the lawns scratching for tasty titbits, and find that the dominant thing at the foot of the stairs in the large, pillared, stone-flagged entrance hall is a rocking horse. At least one of the two family hounds will be curled up in a chair or sprawled across the floor, and when the butler, Mark, opens the front door to you, he's more likely to be wearing jeans and an open-necked shirt with the sleeves rolled up than the regulation pin stripes and tails.

There's a comfortable relaxed atmosphere about the house. It's reflected in the way people dress – in fact just about everyone in the household wears the ubiquitous blue jeans including the cook, the dresser, the personal detective and the Princess herself.

The long narrow hall table that takes up almost the whole of one wall, under a vast gilt-edged mirror, is always laden with the day's post, assorted hats and car keys and parcels that have been 'dumped' after a morning's shopping. A dog's water bowl occupies one corner, a collection of walking sticks another, and assorted soft toys and toy cars (Master Peter Phillips' property) are stacked under the stairs.

The formal drawing room on the left of the hall contains the most 'Royal' reminders in the shape of silver-framed photographs of regal relatives. In the room beyond squashy, comfortable, chintz-covered chairs and a settee are grouped around the open fire and a colour television set. Princess Anne's desk is always piled high with a mass of correspondence, and the display cabinets around the walls are filled with an astonishing variety of objects, from priceless porcelain to inexpensive china horses, and dolls made from sea shells. Every gift they've ever received finds a place somewhere in the Phillips' home.

The dining room is off the right-hand side of the hall, a long elegant room dominated by a mahogany table that will seat twelve in comfort. The oil paintings around the walls are of race horses 'borrowed from the Windsor vaults' admits Mark, while the long sideboard groans under the weight of silver trophies won by Mark and Princess Anne in the eventing world.

Meals are usually serve-yourself affairs from a piping hot serving tray placed on top of a second sideboard near the entrance to the kitchen. And unless they're giving a formal dinner party, the Phillips

Mark in his study at Gatcombe with Random, Princess Anne's Dumfriesshire hound (*Jim Bennett*)

never 'dress' for dinner – something that would have been unheard of in Royal households not so very long ago. From the dining room, a heavy mahogany door leads through to Mark's study – a warm, lived-in room, lined with books and full of clutter. On cold days a log fire burns cheerily in the grate, and it's in this room that husband and wife spend most of their winter evenings at home watching television.

It's very much Mark's room. The colours and textures are stronger than elsewhere in the house. Black and white houndstooth check for the easy chairs, dark green leather for the long sofa, a coffee table always overloaded with daily papers and old copies of *Horse and Hound* and *Farming* magazines. Piles of paper spill over from his desk onto the floor – information about horse trials, endless reams of correspondence, a booklet with the gripping title of *The Cereal Disease Treatment Guide*. Odd photographs are stuffed behind ornaments on the mantlepiece, and the tall white fitted shelves that line three walls are crammed with books. Though predominantly about horses, you'll also find the *Art of Embroidery*, books by Gerald Durrell, an autobiography of Liberace, art, music and history, in fact a whole range of subjects that would do credit to Smiths, though it's unlikely that Mark has ever read more than a dozen of them. He finds little time for 'leisure' reading, preferring to relax by watching television at the end of the day. Thriller writer Dick Francis has trapped him once or twice – but his required reading is usually confined to the *Farmers Weekly* and the sports section of the *Telegraph, Mail* and *Express*.

The ornaments reflect a mixture of achievement, memorabilia and sentiment. Among the awards from the Hunter Improvement Society and the beautifully-carved soapstone figures that were a gift from the Eskimos after a tour of Northern Canada, there's a cheap china beer mug, and an empty chocolate box with an ornately-decorated lid – put on a shelf because it was too pretty to throw away!

When Mark Phillips talks about his home, it's impossible for him to conceal his feelings for the place. His expression becomes benign, his attitude that of a man who takes pride in creating something worthwhile, not as a memorial to himself, but as a gift to those who come after him. And it isn't chauvinism so much as respect for heritage that makes him reflect with relief that his first child was a son. He clearly hopes that Peter will inherit not just the property, but also his father's deep and genuine love of the land, whereas a daughter 'might marry a fellow who hasn't the slightest interest in the place, and then all this would be for nothing'. His arm sweeps a small circle in his study, but it's a gesture that takes in the whole estate.

Mark would be the last to claim that even now the house is in perfect order. At the back of the building the retaining wall that holds

The elegant conservatory at Gatcombe; the shutters to the windows have since been removed (*Srdja Djukanovic*)

up the steep bank and paths leading to the farm is a mass of broken masonry and gaping holes, the distinctive dry-stone walling of the Cotswolds that surrounds the estate needs the attention of a craftsman, and the tall, elegant windows of the conservatory at the far end of the house look fine from a distance, but their rotting wooden frames don't bear too close an inspection. It's a state of affairs that doesn't please the Master of Gatcombe Park. 'I hate seeing things scruffy and untidy, whether it's the horses, the stable-yard, the barn, or parts of the house', a maxim he enforces rigidly, which is why the stables are always a picture of military neatness.

Although the house doesn't yet come up to Mark's precise expectations, his intentions are clear when he says: 'Things may still be in a bit of a state now, but in ten years' time it will be a lot better, and I hope that, as a result of all the work, at the end of the day I'll have something nice to hand over to the next generation.' But work is slow – the pace determined by the availability of cash, though these days it doesn't all come out of Mark's pocket. Gatcombe Park is now the official residence of Her Royal Highness The Princess Anne, and as such a proportion of the maintenance can be paid for out of the Princess's income from the Civil List recently increased to £100,000 a year. That figure sounds like a healthy fortune if you're out of work, but it isn't 'pocket money'. It has to cover some of the running costs of the house, the wages of a cook, butler, dresser and cleaners, and all Princess Anne's expenses as a working Royal travelling thousands of miles and attending hundreds of engagements throughout the country every year. None of the Civil List is spent on the farm and its staff, nor the horses and their maintenance. Buckingham Palace are quick to confirm that the books are very carefully scrutinised and *no* public money supports either the farm or Princess Anne and Mark's riding – *they* must support themselves.

Like her husband, Princess Anne has succumbed to the charm of Gatcombe and the Gloucestershire countryside. And although admitting that 'given a complete choice I don't know that I would have settled this far out of London', she obviously loves her home, describing it as 'a nicely-designed house, not nearly as large as people think, and in the most lovely situation'.

Gatcombe became 'home' on 25 November, just ten days after Peter was born. 'We did the thing you should never do,' says Princess Anne, 'have a baby and move house at the same time.' But the operation went ahead without too many hiccups, and as far as the 'human' occupants were concerned, it was just a case of moving from one comfortable location to another. For the horses, life wasn't quite so simple. The new stable-block was still being built, so as a temporary measure they were housed in various sheds and buildings around the farm – even the great Columbus had to make do with a bed in the cowshed!

But apart from the fact that his creature comforts were a bit sparse,

Columbus' general condition and wellbeing continued to suggest that he'd fully recovered from his hock injury. He even survived a hair-raising incident when being loaded into a trailer to go off on a morning's hunting. The front of the trailer hadn't been secured properly and as the big grey walked up the ramp, Mark felt the floor sag beneath them and suddenly the trailer started to roll down the hill on its own. Mark jumped clear, and the horse shot out backwards, his weight on the tailboard stopping the trailer. However, there was no sign of any damage or strain, and the horse went on to enjoy a day's hunting. Columbus had always been a strong ride, and on the hunting field he excelled himself. Mark found him 'quite difficult to settle and very hot to ride. He would go flat out over a bit of grass, and if he saw a hedge coming up he'd get that old glint in his eyes.'

Although the horse seemed fit, Mark never took his soundness for granted, always checking the right hock that he had injured in the World Championships. So it came as a shock after jumping a hedge whilst out with the Beaufort pack to feel the *left* hock go, a carbon copy of the incident at the Championships. Once again Columbus was turned out for six months, with nothing to do but eat, relax and recover. But the converted cowshed didn't stand empty for long. Mark bought two new youngsters, a handsome 16.3, four-year-old, dark brown gelding from Devon called Persian Minstrel – who was immediately christened Smudge because of the cream blob across the bottom of his nose, and a newly-broken three-year-old – Frog Prince.

Mark heard about Frog Prince when he was at Burghley in September, and during the competition he'd dropped in on the stable where the horse was being broken. He admits that when he saw him being worked on a lunge rein in the indoor school: 'I thought he looked a very ordinary, very expensive horse. He moved nicely, and was quite good-looking, but he didn't really do anything to particularly catch the eye. Certainly nothing to persuade me to spend a vast amount of money on him. But eventually they turned him loose in the school, in order to jump over a couple of cavalettis at about 2ft 6in. He came round the end of the building, pricked his ears and just took off. He sailed through the air, and from take-off to landing must have covered a good twenty feet in one leap.' It was an impressive performance, but still Mark didn't buy the horse there and then because of the price. It was several weeks later that the owner Major Tim Hellyer rang up and they agreed on 'a figure I've never paid before or since for an untried three-year-old'.

When the horse arrived at Gatcombe it wasn't his potential brilliance that made an impression on everyone, so much as his stubborn, wilful temperament, which quickly earned him the stable name of Toad! The title was lived up to on the first day that Mark tried to school him on the end of a lungeing rein. 'He gave a mighty buck and a kick, then took off, flat out, round the field. I had to let go the

Mark practising at Gatcombe with Classic Lines, originally named Frog Prince and with the well-earned stable name of Toad (*Jim Bennett*)

rein because I couldn't stop him. Whereupon he jumped straight over the metal-barred gate at the top of the field – reins trailing behind him – and galloped straight back into the stable. At least it proved again that he could jump, but it wasn't what you'd call a very auspicious start to the proceedings!'

Mark quickly realised that Toad was not going to be an easy horse to ride, but, as with all Mark's young horses, there was no pressure in those early months, and no rush to get everything right overnight. There would be years of patient, regulated work to develop his promising potential and at least eighteen months before even thinking of taking him to the most modest of one-day events.

As the 1978 spring season got under way it was Persian Holiday that set out once again on the path to Badminton. Mark's time with the horse was limited. During the week he lived in London and still worked at an army desk in Whitehall, only dashing home to Gloucestershire at weekends to pick up the reins himself. But on Friday, 24 March, he closed the door on his office for the last time and walked out of the Ministry of Defence into a new life as a civilian. The following day he rode Percy in the one-day event at Kinlet,

Worcestershire, and won, but the horse had banged one of his forelegs during the crosscountry phase and, on 5 April, failed to satisfy the vet and was withdrawn from the Badminton entries. Mark's other Badminton hopes, Favour and George, had been declared non-runners earlier in the season. Favour had lost all heart for the sport and retired; George – after his spectacular year in 1977 with Lucinda, winning Badminton and Burghley – had been offered back to Mark, who found him 'not the horse he'd been before'. Winning two major three-day events in one year had been a supreme effort, and Mark didn't think it would be fair to spoil that achievement with a second best performance. So for the first time in years the Badminton programme for 1978 had no mention of the name Mark Phillips. In fact there was a notable absence of his name from the record books during that eventing year as a whole. They log the win at Kinlet on Persian Holiday, another at Rushall on 1 April riding Bertie Hill's Sherpa, and then nothing until 9 August when Mark rode Persian Holiday and Persian Minstrel at Annick in Scotland and won their respective classes. For eventing it was a barren year – but only because Mark was chalking up an impressive string of achievements in another sphere of competition, as a showjumper.

During the winter of 1976 Mark had snatched a few days' holiday to go shooting in Yorkshire with Trevor Banks, the showjumping dealer. On the Sunday morning Trevor watched Mark riding some of his horses. Eventually the conversation came around to an idea Trevor had been toying with for some time. How would Mark like to ride some of Trevor's showjumpers as a change from eventing. Mark didn't need time to consider the suggestion, but said 'yes' there and then because 'I always had a hankering to try – simply because it was something I'd never done'. But Trevor hadn't made the suggestion just to offer Mark a diversion from his eventers. He believes, like so many others, that Mark is 'one of the best – a good, natural horseman, and I didn't see any reason why he shouldn't be just as successful at showjumping as he is with eventing. In fact I'm convinced that if he could devote enough time to it he'd be brilliant.'

So a few weeks later Mark booked in for a week at Trevor's establishment on North Humberside where he spent seven days 'riding myself stupid over fences that weren't jumpable, but learning more about jumping in just one week than I had in the previous ten years'. Trevor put him up on just about every horse in his yard, from the greenest youngster to champions like Hideaway, working on the principle that 'the only way to learn to ride jumpers, racehorses, eventers or whatever, is to keep getting up on different horses. If you ride the same one all the time, you get into a pattern and start to press buttons for that particular horse instead of being fluid and open-minded.' Although Mark has jumped a formidable array of fences in his career and proved himself to be one of the best all-round horsemen in the country, he had to start by 'overcoming my fear of the sheer size of the fences. I had only been used to jumping obstacles of around four feet. Suddenly to approach a fence that was five foot, and a parallel bar at that, made me a bit nervous to say the least.'

Fortunately Trevor had in his yard a horse that Mark has described as 'the finest schoolmaster in all England', Hideaway, the horse that had ridden in three Olympic showjumping teams and had, to quote Trevor, 'never turned his head once'. 'He had tremendous ability', says Mark, 'and he was as honest as the day is long. You pointed him at a fence, and the only thing that was going through his mind was to get to the other side. The horse had a wealth of experience; he'd done it all before, therefore if anything went wrong, I knew it was my fault.'

And not unexpectedly to begin with things did go wrong. Although in basic terms showjumping and eventing are equestrian sports in which riders ask horses to jump over fences, when you examine the two in detail they are, in Mark's words, 'a totally different science. In eventing, if you're coming up to a relatively small fence and the horse had got hold of the bridle, you can almost chuck the reins at it and say "go on – jump it". But if you're coming up to a big showjumping fence and you tried that you'd be heading for a fall. With showjumping you have to keep rhythm, impulsion and balance. To approach a fence on an active, round, bouncy stride, keep your leg on the horse and keep coming at the fence. And it's not until you actually come down to a really big obstacle that the importance of it all suddenly crystallises. Because if you haven't got all those things, you'll find that the fence will be just too big for the horse to jump.'

When Mark talks about the 'science' of showjumping now, his words are backed with the practical experience of a man who rode at the top end of the sport for over two years. It isn't text-book waffle and untried theory, but the technique had to be learnt, and the skill came slowly. As far as Trevor Banks is concerned 'Mark has a nerve of iron', totally dismissing the claim that his pupil found the bigger fences 'frightening'. The thing he did have to overcome was Mark's natural tendency to stand off fences as he would on a crosscountry course 'and to convince him that you don't need speed to jump the big fences'. But Mark was a willing and talented pupil and Trevor watched him 'improve with every horse he rode'.

Mark related the experience to his early days with Bertie Hill. 'I used to ride with Bertie and say "I can't understand this" – how to do a half pass, or whatever – and Bertie would jump up on the horse and say "look – it's quite simple really", then I'd try to do all the things he said and it would drive me crazy because I still couldn't do it. But as I got older and more experienced I was able to work out in my mind what I was trying to do – I actually got the feel of what I was trying to do and how to achieve it. With showjumping, it wasn't until I started to tackle really big jumps that I began to analyse what were the

Showjumping with Chainbridge at the Royal Highland Show in Edinburgh where they won the Grade C class (*Findlay Davidson*)

important components of jumping fences successfully, and then I realised that for years I'd been getting away with murder. I'm a great believer in learning from your own mistakes; it's only when you've made a right mess of something that you can work out for yourself exactly what you've done wrong. If I came into a fence with the horse too flat, then the horse would stop, the poles would go everywhere, and sure as eggs are eggs I would get a bollocking from Trevor.' By the end of the week Mark had absorbed a tremendous amount, perhaps the most important lesson being that showjumping wasn't going to be easy, and that if he really wanted to make headway, he'd have to progress out of Trevor's training school and into the ring.

His first appearance as a showjumper was at a local show on Beverley racecourse. There were no rosettes but the experience whetted his appetite and, in the summer of 1977, Mark partnered Trevor's horses whenever he could steal a few days off. His first win was on Chainbridge in the Grade C class of the Royal Highland Show. And in July he came first in the Top Score Class on Hideaway, and in the Lancome Speed Stakes on Strongbow at the Royal International Horse

Show. On dozens of occasions he left the ring empty-handed, but his steady progress and consistent form impressed the British Show Jumping Association. He was included in the team at La Baule in France with Hideaway, and again in the team that went to Calgary in September, where Mark won the opening class on Trevor Banks' Strongbow.

Many observers were surprised not only that Mark had shown an interest in showjumping in the first place when he was so closely associated with eventing, but that, having taken it on, he was so proficient. Mark found it less remarkable because he has a theory that 'if you have natural ability and the balance and feel it takes to be a good horseman, then you can be successful in whichever sphere of riding you care to dedicate your time to. If Harvey Smith or David Broome had wanted to ride eventers, or Lester Piggott had wanted to showjump, then I'm sure they would have been equally successful as they are at jumping and racing.' His own example proved the point.

At the end of the summer when he went back to eventing, many colleagues were sceptical of the effect that four months' showjumping would have on his riding. Mark recalls that the reaction was almost unanimous. 'Everybody said to me – it'll ruin your riding. When you go across country you'll be hooking and pulling and the whole thing will be a disaster. But I really sincerely believe that nothing could be further from the truth. I think I ride a lot better now across country than I did before. Having got involved and worked at it I found I could come back to my own horses and apply the same principles – not in terms of the style of jumping, but in terms of the approach to a fence. I give the horse more of a chance, which is all any rider can ever hope to do. But more than that, I discovered how much easier it was for the horse to jump well because I was doing the job properly. I hope my horses go a lot better for me having had that experience, they certainly *seem* to jump better, and we go quicker across country as a result.'

But there was little opportunity for Mark to demonstrate his theories to the more sceptical among the eventers as, by April of 1978, he was reduced to just one international standard horse – Persian Holiday – and Percy wouldn't be running in the classic showcase at Badminton. Instead Mark planned his summer around another session of showjumping, and on the home front concentrated on gaining as much practical experience of farming as possible from the very able farm manager and staff who were already installed at Gatcombe. In October he would start a year's agricultural course at Cirencester College, but meanwhile he became familiar with the day-to-day running of the farm, and began to adjust his own life style away from the nine-to-five office routine he'd known for two years, and into the seasonal demands of planting and calving, haymaking and harvest.

The fact that Mark was able to make such an immediate impression on the showjumping circuit is due largely to the fact that he was able to

(*above*) Mark showjumping on Trevor Banks' Hideaway in Amsterdam, October 1977 (*Findlay Davidson*); (*right*) riding Hideaway at Wembley in the King George V Gold Cup where he finished fourth (*Srdja Djukanovic*)

start virtually on the top rung of the ladder with some of the finest showjumping horses in the country. Not for him the years of anonymously plodding around county shows gaining experience and credibility, and to his credit he acknowledges the simple truth that 'by virtue of having the chance to ride Hideaway, which was a great honour and a great privilege, it meant that I was in the very fortunate situation of being able to go straight in at the top end of the sport.' Obviously it had its advantages, but there must have been disadvantages too, like the reaction of a public who undoubtedly expected the Queen's son-in-law and international horseman of repute to be as brilliant at showjumping as he'd been at eventing. Not to mention the attitude of a crowd of commercially-motivated professional riders, the most outspoken of whom had always regarded the showjumping phase of a three-day event as 'laughable'.

Where the public reaction was concerned Mark is phlegmatic. 'I wasn't particularly fussed about that; obviously I didn't want to go in the ring and look an idiot, but providing I was doing adequately well, and wasn't losing face, I was satisfied. Every clear round I jumped was a major achievement to me, and I got more satisfaction out of jumping a clear round in a Grand Prix than I would in winning a one-day event down the road, because I know on past form that I'm capable of winning a one-day event, but I don't know that I could go and jump a clear round in a Grand Prix.'

As for the professional riders, Mark felt they quickly accepted him as 'one of them'. 'They made me feel at home,' he says, explaining that 'I believe sportsmen the world over share the same bond, and kindred spirits, people within the same sport, are closer still – we're on common ground. So to begin with perhaps I was an outsider coming in, but very quickly I felt that I was accepted.' What helped, of course, was the fact that he proved for the second year running that he had the ability to make him worthy of a place in their ranks. On Hideaway he earned Trevor Banks over a thousand pounds in prize money and in July put up an impressive performance at the Royal International in the prestigious King George V Gold Cup, coming fourth.

The King George is to showjumping what Badminton is to eventing. It's the title all men riders want to win (women showjumpers have their equivalent in the Queen Elizabeth Cup) and, as he waited in the collecting-ring at the Wembley arena, Mark considered the extraordinary fluke of being there. 'I just couldn't believe that I was getting so close to a million-to-one chance. No rider had ever won Badminton and the King George.' It would certainly have been a remarkable achievement, but although Mark got through to the jump-off, he was still relatively inexperienced compared with the rest of the finalists and it was that which let him down. The course was shortened for the jump-off and what had been fence number four was now the first obstacle. 'I hadn't looked to see how big the first fence in the jump-off was. I'd already jumped it in the previous round when it was the fourth fence on the course, but didn't really appreciate what a difference it would make having it at number one. It was a bloody great big brown-and-yellow parallel bar. I just came hacking into the ring, rode at the fence and chipped the back bar off, because I didn't have enough umph to jump it clearly. It was damned stupid, and looking back I could kick myself. None of the experienced riders who are showjumping all the time would get caught out by it, but that's what experience is. By making mistakes like that, you learn the hard way.' Mark is game enough to admit that, even without that 'stupid' mistake, it's highly unlikely that he would have won anyway. Instead honours went to Jeff McVean on Claret, with David Bowen second and Geoff Glazzard third. Mark came a creditable fourth.

Throughout the season, at shows all over the country, his name appeared in the ribbons beside those of great horses like Chainbridge, Anglesarke, Strongbow and of course Hideaway. Mark wasn't able to ride the great showjumper every day and build the sort of close relationship that he enjoyed with his own event horses, but Hideaway had carried such a variety of jockeys on his back that another pair of hands on the driving wheel probably didn't make much difference to him one way or the other. Nevertheless, the pair achieved a working harmony that gave Mark a successful and satisfying season which culminated in being chosen to ride for Britain for the second year running in the Nations Cup team at Calgary, in company with Graham Fletcher on Buttevant Boy, Caroline Bradley on Tigre and Mike Saywell riding another of Trevor Banks' horses, Chainbridge.

In the first round of the competition Mark had one fence down, and two in the second round. But another member of the team accumulated even more faults, so both of his rounds were counted in the final scoring which showed that the British team had streaked ahead of their international rivals to win the Nations Cup. 'That meant a lot to me', says Mark, 'because for once I wasn't the fourth man!' Mark's return to England signalled the end of his showjumping with Trevor Banks' horses for that year, and the end of the eventing season, which had almost completely passed him by.

Persian Holiday still wasn't completely fit and hadn't made an appearance at Burghley or even been considered for the team to represent Britain in the World Championships in Lexington during early September. However, there was some compensation for Mark in the fact that Columbus was once again bouncing back, and proving himself to be quite as versatile as his jockey. He'd been given a six months' rest cure for the second slipped tendon, and in May began a daily programme of walking up and down the hills around Gatcombe to strengthen his legs and get him fit. As Mark was himself deeply involved with showjumping by the middle of the summer, he decided that Columbus would probably find a few showjumping rounds less

Mark riding to hounds with Columbus in 1977 as part of his fitness programme (*Srdja Djukanovic*)

strenuous than the demands of a one-day event, and entered him in a Grade 'C' showjumping class at Tetbury – which he won. In August a trip to Devizes was rewarded with a third place in a qualifying round for the Elizabeth Anne Championships, and October found them at the Horse of the Year Show in the finals. Columbus went clear in the first round, but had one fence down in the jump-off which gave him eighth place overall. Mark was delighted. Neither hock showed any sign of strain, and Columbus himself 'took to showjumping rather well', which left Mark thinking 'if he can do this, there's no reason why we shouldn't at least think about another Badminton'. At that stage, it *was* only a thought. A winter's hunting would test his fitness, and there would be time for serious consideration in January.

One other horse occupied Mark's mind that autumn – an eight-year-old black gelding called Lincoln. Mark had gone to Burghley as a spectator, and when the conversation and gossip had got round to which horses were doing what and where, Lincoln's name cropped up as a useful horse that had qualified for open classes at the end of 1977, but had spent the whole of 1978 in a field while his owner/rider, Pru Filner of Kent, took time out to have a baby. He'd never competed as an advanced horse, but Mark liked the sound and eventually the look of him, and bought him that autumn. He was independent and aloof, a difficult horse to get to know, and his huge head and inelegant Roman nose persuaded some members of the family to call him The Camel. But Mark ignored his looks; assessing instead what he believed to be enormous potential, he declared him 'a nice stamp of horse' and earmarked some of the early spring competitions as a testing-ground for 'the good horse Lincoln' to prove his worth. Mark's own timetable for the following twelve months was clearly going to be another feat of juggling with maximum commitment and minimum time.

His major commitment for the year was to Cirencester Agricultural College, where in October 1978 he began a five-day-a-week course in practical farming. In retrospect, it was a year earmarked by him as twelve months 'when my feet didn't touch the ground. I would get up at dawn – whenever dawn was – to ride the horses, be back on the farm at eight to get things started for the day, then scurry round the house, have a bite of breakfast, get changed and be at college, twelve miles away, by nine. Lunch was from 12.30 till 2pm and some days I'd dash back here to see to something on the farm, or in the house, or with the horses. Classes finished at 4.0pm, so I'd be home again at 4.30 to work on the farm, get through the paper work, or go to a function with Princess Anne. There really weren't enough hours in the day, and I didn't ever know whether it was Monday or Friday.'

With a commitment to Cirencester, another year's showjumping for Trevor Banks, and a stable full of horses ready to make an impact on the eventing schedules, Mark was about to embark on one of the busiest years of his life – providing he could stand the pace!

Chapter Ten

'The one thing I was terrified of was that something would go wrong with his hocks – and if that happened I would never be forgiven.' That was the dilemma facing Mark Phillips at the beginning of 1979. The subject of his concern was Columbus, Her Majesty the Queen's great three-day-event horse who had survived two injuries to his hocks and, at fourteen years of age, was as fit and strong as he'd ever been, looking every inch a Badminton contender. Mark desperately wanted to give the horse an opportunity to demonstrate his brilliance as a three-day-eventer at least once more in his career, but could he really trust those suspect hocks?

'I was determined not to put the horse at risk' he says, 'and while I was still trying to decide one way or the other, two opportunities came our way that were ideal tests for his soundness.' The first was the Melton Hunt crosscountry race which Columbus was unlucky not to win after taking an early 100yd lead and staying there for three miles. At least one of the fences had very boggy ground on the landing side, which put extra strain on the hocks, but when Mark crossed the finishing-line Columbus was as sound as a bell.

A few weeks later Fred Viner of the BBC's Outside Broadcast Department suggested – not too seriously – that Mark should challenge commentator and former National Hunt jockey Richard Pitman to a ride round the Grand National course. Both riders took up the challenge, Ladbrokes offered 10 to 1 against a clear round, and on 29 March two days before the big race itself, both riders lined up at the start for a two-man race. Mark decided that of all the horses in his stables it was the big-striding, fearless Columbus who would enjoy the ride most.

They set off at a steady pace to jump fourteen of the National 'classics', only The Chair being out of bounds. Columbus took the first two fences literally in his stride, and sailed over the third, while Richard's mount refused and horse and rider parted company. Mark sportingly pulled up and waited while he remounted, and then the two set off again. At the infamous Bechers Brook, Mark admits that 'my heart was in my mouth when we took off', but those watching the race were impressed by the effortless way that Columbus met each fence, sailed over and cantered off without ever once pecking or missing a stride. He didn't make a single mistake and gave Mark the impression that 'the old devil was really enjoying himself'.

Two days later he took him to a one-day event at Rushall where his

The ride round the Grand National course at Aintree on Columbus with former National Hunt jockey Richard Pitman (*Sport & General Press Agency*)

dressage was something of a disaster. His rider put that down to the fact that 'he didn't want to know about walk, trot and canter, because he was still thinking about jumping the fences at Aintree'. But across country he was his old brilliant self. Columbus could not have had a more testing run up to the competition, and he had emerged strong enough, fit enough and, most importantly, sound enough, to run for his life. Mark was finally convinced that the horse should and could run at Badminton. He was entered as a contender for the title and with ten days to go was taken down to Bertie Hill's Devon farm where, as usual, Mark spent a week putting the final polish on his own, and the horse's, performance.

Everything about the horse's entry and preparation for the event was unconventional. At fourteen he was something of a 'senior citizen' in a sport where few international horses compete beyond the age of twelve, and since the ill-fated World Championship year in 1974 he hadn't been entered in a single one- or three-day event until he'd qualified at Rushall, a few weeks earlier. As Mark Phillips says: 'No-one had ever done anything like the Badminton trial on a horse with two slipped hocks before. We'd taken Columbus hunting, to Aintree and the Rushall One-Day Event – given every opportunity for some weakness to show up – but he was totally sound. It was amazing.'

They had however paid two penalties for this 'unconventional' preparation. In Mark's words: 'Columbus looked like a greyhound. Very fit, but very rangy – more like a hat-rack than a well-muscled event horse. And also we hadn't really bothered with his dressage. All he'd had in mind for the past six months had been jumping and galloping, and ten days just wasn't going to be long enough to get him settled to the job.' His misgivings about the horse's attitude to the dressage test bore fruit on the first day of the trial. Columbus scored 66. 'He should have got at least 10 marks less,' says Mark. 'He was certainly capable of a better test, but he was still all lit up inside.' That flame burned just as brightly on crosscountry day when all the pent-up energy and fire in the old horse took him storming around the sixteen-mile course. 'He made it look easy' was the verdict, 'and didn't make a single mistake. In fact for the first time in my life I hit exactly the right time set for the steeplechase and the crosscountry phase to gain maximum bonus. It was pure fluke, because we'd covered the ground so easily I actually eased up over the last mile' – which gives some indication of the speed Columbus was capable of and the easy way he covered the ground. A clear round on showjumping day brought the whole extraordinary week to a most satisfying conclusion with Columbus finishing third.

Badminton 1979 – Mark and Columbus jumping on to the Normandy Bank at the First Luckington Lane crossing, when they finished third, completing a unique hat-trick of rounds at Badminton without time penalties (*Findlay Davidson*)

It left Mark wondering that if he hadn't been so concerned about the hocks, and had concentrated on a more conventional training period, whether or not the horse would have done even better. But that was the reaction of a perfectionist and in no way diminished the general joy and amazement of the overall achievement of a fourteen-year-old horse, with both hocks off, finishing third in the premier three-day event of the season – that was some comeback.

'But after that', says Mark, 'things started to get out of hand. He was shortlisted for the European Championship team, which hadn't been in my mind at all. We'd taken him to Badminton so that he could have some fun – not to qualify him for the National Team.'

They were spared the embarrassment of an outright refusal when Columbus developed a swelling on one joint. The vet recommended that Columbus should be blistered, and so Mark was able to decline the invitation to compete in the European Trials on 'medical grounds', while considering that 'we must have been in a rum state for them to think of putting a fourteen-year-old in the team'. Whether or not Columbus would actually have gone to Luhmühlen is unanswerable, but the team we did send of Merry Sovereign, Monacle, Killaire and Gurgle the Greek partnered by Clissy Strachan, Sue Hatherly, Lucinda Prior-Palmer and Rachel Bayliss won the silver medal, with Rachel and Gurgle claiming individual honours by coming second overall.

With Columbus out of commission Mark was able to test the quality of his two newcomers, Frog Prince (or Toad) and Lincoln. The early suggestion that Frog Prince had something of a temper was confirmed on several occasions. Once when Mark was loading him, with three other horses, to go off to a competition, he was last to be led up the ramp; because he was left standing on his own 'he just refused to move in any direction, like a child throwing a tantrum'. Earlier he'd got an infection in his foot which had to be poulticed out. Mark tried to get him to keep his foot in a bucket of hot water and Epsom Salts – but Toad refused to co-operate. 'In desperation, I thought "I'll fix you" so just as I got the bad foot in the bucket, I quickly picked up the other front leg and tied it up. It left him on three legs, so he had to stand still, otherwise he'd have fallen over. And do you know for six months after that he wouldn't let me near him in the box. The girls could go in, but if I tried to he'd come at me backwards.'

Fortunately for Toad, his potential brilliance outweighed any frustration at his appalling manners and he rewarded Mark's confidence in him by coming second at both Everdon and Wilton in his first season as a novice. Toad also learned that in spite of his own wilful temper and strength, Mark was the boss and always had the last word. 'I've always adopted the same principle of being desperately careful never to get into an argument with him that I might lose, because I think if he ever discovers he can beat me, that would be the end.'

Boekelo Three-day Event, Holland, October 1979; Mark and Lincoln finished second to Olivier Depagne by 0.4 points (*Findlay Davidson*)

Lincoln also posed a few problems that first season – not in his temperament, which was uniformly cool and aristocratic, but in his performance, which was wildly erratic. At Downlands in April the pair had virtually clinched second place when they were eliminated for 'outside assistance'. Mark had been warned that the rails over a ditch couldn't be jumped the way he'd planned so, as he approached it, he took a wide sweep to give himself time and space to work out an alternative route. Princess Anne thought he was going off course and shouted to him 'where are you going?' – and that was enough for the judges to declare them out of the competition.

It was some consolation to come second at the Windsor Three-Day Event in May. 'But then', says Mark, 'we had a series of disasters. He stopped twice in the championships and at Taunton Vale in September, and did exactly the same thing two weeks later at Tetbury.' During that first year with Lincoln Mark couldn't quite find the key that would settle the horse to a consistent performance. He describes him as 'a very difficult horse to ride. He would gallop on between the fences, and then start to back himself off a few strides away from the obstacle. I spent most of the season trying to get him under my control for those last few strides and it just didn't work.' It wasn't until Mark tried a totally unorthodox approach that the whole thing fell into place. Schooling over the fences at home, he took a gamble and left the horse alone to 'back off' the fence and find his own stride. He didn't stop once. Lincoln was obviously a horse that liked to find his own stride into a fence. It took courage and confidence from his rider to let him do it – but it paid off.

In October they won the Batsford One-Day Event, and ten days later Lincoln came second in his first international three-day event in Boekelo in Holland. It had taken almost twelve months for Mark to unravel the problem but although by the end of the year he was confident of Lincoln's ability, many observers had stamped the horse as unreliable, and that tag stuck for well over a year.

Throughout that summer Mark had once again turned his attentions to showjumping and, in partnership with Hideaway, won the Continental Class at Brabham in June. After two seasons as a showjumper his initial 'fear' of the bigger fences had obviously been conquered as, during the Royal International in July, the combination tackled the mighty wall of the Puissance competition and finished third. In October at the Horse of the Year Show they faced the imposing Puissance fences again and finished second, clearing just under seven feet. It was a spectacular way to end the season and – as it turned out – his career as a showjumper. Within a few months Trevor Banks sold his showjumpers and Mark decided that it was time to call it a day. He'd enjoyed the experience and the opportunity enormously but, taking a totally practical view of the situation, he knew he couldn't continue what was rapidly becoming a lunatic schedule.

Mark's reasoning was simple, and objective. 'Showjumping goes on for twelve months of the year with outdoor shows in the summer, indoors in the winter, while one of the major attractions of the eventing season is that it's confined to March, April and May, then August, September and half of October – two periods when I know I'm going to be very busy, do a lot of travelling and be away. But it is only just over five months when you have to organise your life around competitions – the rest of the year is your own. When I was jumping for Trevor I was dead pushed for time trying to fit the showjumping into the summer in between the two eventing seasons. I had limited success and it was great fun, but really I was only playing at it. I would go to a county show for three days, then I'd be away and wouldn't see the horse for a week, then I'd ride him in another show, and then be off again. That's no good. Not in top-flight showjumping. The full-time jumpers will ride at a show, then get into the box and drive straight to another show. Then perhaps have a couple of days at home to correct a fault or school the horses on, then they'll be off somewhere else. But I was riding by remote control, which is hopeless. If you're going to get to the top, and stay at the top in showjumping you have to be prepared to be totally commited – which I couldn't do.'

One of the main obstacles to that total commitment was that he had already embarked on another equally time-consuming and absorbing profession – as a farmer. Once his agriculture course at Cirencester College had finished in the autumn, Mark had been able to devote every working day to running his own farm, adjusting a year's classroom theory to grass roots practicality.

More than one person has suggested to me that Gatcombe 'farm' and the title 'farmer' are just a front and that, far from being a real farmer of the calloused hands and wellies boots variety, Mark Phillips is just another country landowner who plays at farming, and actually spends most of his time 'swanning off on his horses'. They couldn't be more wrong. No one would pretend that Mark Phillips is chained to his acres for 365 days of the year. He's not. His horses *do* take a lot of his time – but then he's not playing at being an international event rider either. Because our country looks for World, European and Olympic sporting honours from amateur sportsmen, without providing the massive financial support that makes so many Europeans virtually 'state-employed', our athletes train, compete, and win only by making enormous personal sacrifices, and adjusting their sporting ambitions and achievements to their own professional lives. Mark Phillips is no exception.

Throughout his career as a soldier in Germany, at Sandhurst and in Whitehall, he maintained his professional credibility by ensuring that his achievements as a sportsman were never earned at the expense of shirking responsibility to his job. He follows the same credo now that he's a farmer. But in order to make any impression at all as a competitor, there are times when the horses must come first for, as he says, 'if you are going to compete internationally, in any sport, it means a tremendous amount of hard work. I mean real hard graft. Not only to be fit, but to have mental dedication to get to grips with that total commitment to your sport. So for the period when you're actually doing it you've got to eat, live and sleep it. Also in equestrian sports, you have an added element – the horse. Because horses aren't machines, they can have moods, the same as humans, so riders have to devote extra time to establishing a very special relationship between themselves and the animal, and keeping that relationship on an even keel. If you only have half the relationship, you only do half the job, and come up with half the result at the end of the day.'

Mark's own impressive list of achievements prove that he's never been satisfied with doing just 'half the job', which is why for five months of the year his horses' health, fitness, ability and competitive achievements are a major concern. The farm has always demanded his attention as an administrator, but now that farm manager Geoff Stevens has left to be replaced by a tractor driver, Mark will become

Mark Phillips the farmer at work at Gatcombe – with an interested Lincoln looking on (*Jim Bennett*)

even more involved in the day-to-day graft. The farm team is completed by tractor driver Chris Excell, and the stockman Jack Russell, who are backed up by woodman Eric Hanchett, and the keeper John Stubbs. Collectively they're like a well-oiled machine, each man an expert in his own sphere and much respected by their 'boss'. In his absence it's they who run the Gatcombe farm and estate, but once the eventing season is over Mark falls in beside his men, working with them from dawn till dusk – from planting to harvest.

It's a large farm for such a small staff with 1250 acres in all. An established woodland covers around 250 acres and a further 300 acres are so steep that they're only suitable as grazing for the 150-strong beef herd. What's left is 700 acres of flat, exposed, arable land in one of the particularly cold corners of England on which 'farmer' Phillips grows a succession of cereals, mostly wheat and barley, with a few acres producing oats and hay for the cows, calves and horses. The seasons and the weather determine the pace of life on the farm, and the pattern hardly changes from one year to the next.

Woven into that pattern are the threads of Mark's competitive life, and his official role as a member of the Royal Family. The result is a timetable that would make a workaholic look idle. In January, after Christmas at Windsor and the New Year at Sandringham, Mark returns to Gatcombe to get ready for the spring work. From February onwards, the land is top-dressed and sprayed, the cattle are prepared for market, and the horses begin their spring training schedule. By March the one-day events have started, and on the farm they're beginning to be really busy with the cows starting to calve. Badminton is over in mid-April, there is still more spraying and top-dressing to do followed by silage and haymaking going on to the start of harvest in July – just when Princess Anne's diary is brimming with engagements. Whenever possible Mark accompanies her, but his days are more usually filled with stacking bales, moving stock and taking over the tractor and combine from Chris Excell at mealtimes, and working by headlights to bring in the harvest to beat the weather when necessary.

September means Burghley and barley – competing at one and planting the other – while in November the cows are moved off the grass and housed under cover. Every day there's something screaming for attention. A machine that won't work, food to be bought, animals to be sold, horses to ride, forms to be filled, stock to be moved, people to meet, problems to unravel. It's no idle boast when Mark Phillips says he 'leads a life of permanent exhaustion', and when asked what he'd do given a full day off, he replies with feeling 'I'd sleep'. In fact what he does do on rare days off at the end of the winter when things quieten down is go shooting, which he finds both relaxing and challenging. Challenging because 'to hit something that is flying high through the air is quite a feat, and if you're successful there's the satisfaction of having done the thing properly. Then you work with the dogs – either Fox, my Labrador from Sandringham, or Lottie, a youngster bred by Trevor Banks and trained at home by John Stubbs. I enjoy watching them retrieve and again there's satisfaction in seeing them work well.' There's the simple pleasure too for someone who really loves country life of just being out in the open and enjoying 'the peace, the quiet and the beauty of the place. We encourage pheasants and partridges on the estate – not for me to shoot but just because I enjoy seeing them around. When we go out walking around the corn or cattle and put up some partridges or a pheasant, I think it's a marvellous sight. I just feel at home in the country. London is great fun to go to the cinema, the theatre or whatever, but I couldn't live there. I was born and bred in the country and feel like a fish out of water in cities.' A winter's day spent shooting, with a dog at his side and the wooded beauty of Yorkshire or the Scottish moors all round him, is also a rare day of total release from the horses. 'I don't even think about them. Whether they're eating, if they've had enough work, why one wouldn't do a half pass, or whatever. I just forget all about them – until January, and then I start to get itchy feet.'

But the farm and its management need his daily attention whatever the other demands on his life, for he admits that 'if the farm doesn't make a profit – then we're in dead trouble'. Any suggestion that 'the Queen could always pick up the tab in a bad year' is met with a hardened jawline and swift reply 'why should she?'. Why indeed – though the situation is hardly likely to arise. Mark is too much his own man, too fiercely independent to allow Gatcombe to fail. It isn't just self-respect, it's a natural, stubborn determination to succeed at whatever job he takes on, and an equally firm determination not to be financially dependent on his mother-in-law. So far the fourteen-hour days and grinding workload have paid off. Apart from the first year, when most of his capital was sunk into stock and equipment to get started, the farm has managed to cover its costs and even show a small profit.

In contrast, towards the end of 1979 the horses were becoming a crippling drain on his resources. Unlike showjumping or racing, eventing doesn't reward its winners with handsome cheques. Prize money is in the tens rather than the hundreds, and you have to win Badminton or Burghley to count your winnings in four figures. Even now £3,000 for the Badminton winner after emerging victorious after three days of gruelling competition is small beer to the £11,000 paid to the winner of the Hickstead Derby. More importantly, it will barely cover the expenses of keeping a top-class eventer for six months, so the cost of competing can never be covered by the winnings. In other words, for thirteen years, just like the rest of his amateur colleagues, Mark had been paying thousands of pounds out of his own pocket (and his parents before him) to indulge his interest in a hobby which, by way of a bonus, had brought the nation a string of equestrian honours and him international fame – but no financial support. Eventing is an expensive hobby, and Mark is not a wealthy man. He wasn't, of course, the only one with cash problems.

In February of 1978 European Champion Lucinda Prior-Palmer, had accepted sponsorship of nearly £100,000 spread over three years from Overseas Containers Limited, and Olympic horseman Richard Meade later negotiated a sponsorship deal with the builders, George Wimpey. Both deals enabled the riders to stay in first-class competition, and maintain a yard of potential international eventers. Mark's position wasn't so straightforward. No member of the Royal Family had ever been involved with commercial sponsorship before, but clearly Mark was going to have to look for some kind of outside assistance to meet the ever-increasing cost of buying and maintaining quality horses if he wanted to stay on the top deck of the sport, without risking bankruptcy. Mark didn't exactly advertise his financial problems 'but I remember talking to Raymond Brooks-Ward at the Royal Cornwall Show when I was jumping Hideaway, and telling him that our finances were beginning to creak a bit, and that in order to carry on eventing I would have to find a sponsor, or cut back on the horses'. The idea of commercial sponsorship for individuals was still frowned on by many people associated with eventing, but in Mark's opinion 'it's vital and I don't think the sport can survive without it on two levels – in providing prize money and helping riders to go on competing at the highest standard with really good horses'.

At about the same time Land-Rover Limited were considering the possibility of promoting the sales of their Range Rovers by linking

Fieldsman, the promising young member of the Range Rover Team, out hacking at Gatcombe (*Jim Bennett*)

their name to some aspect of equestrian competition, so it didn't take very long for the promoters of the sport, British Equestrian Promotions, to bring the rider and the company together. After months of negotiation and some finely-detailed accounting to discover exactly how much it cost to keep a good event horse, Land-Rover Limited agreed to pay Mark £20,000 a year for three years to cover the cost of maintaining a string of six event horses to be called The Range Rover Team, with a further £5,000 each year to buy new horses. As an amateur Mark couldn't receive any of the money himself, instead it would go to the British Equestrian Federation who would pay the relevant bills as they came in. It seemed an ideal arrangement. One that would give Range Rover a certain amount of publicity, and relieve Mark's immediate financial problems.

But in addition to his own contract and unlike any of the commercial deals that had been agreed before, Mark insisted on a further commitment from Land-Rover which they were very happy to enter into. He felt that they should also finance a scheme to help young riders with their training, explaining that 'I genuinely believe it is wrong that companies just sponsor the big fish without putting something worthwhile back into the sport', and so a Bursary scheme was devised through which Land-Rover would award £100 to riders between 16 and 21 in selected Advanced Classes, to be spent on training fees. They also agreed to meet the expenses for eighteen riders

The Range Rover horsebox which can accommodate six horses and provide living accommodation for up to four people; the Range Rover Team horses in 1980 were (*l to r*) Lincoln, Town and County, Fieldsman, Classic Lines, Highwayman X and Rough and Tough (*Range Rover*)

a year to go to Gatcombe and receive specialised tuition with Mark, and also give a £1,500 Scholarship towards the expenses of the most promising young rider who visits Gatcombe each year. All round it seemed to be a worthwhile proposition. 'As far as I could see', says Mark, 'everybody was benefiting from it. I wasn't making any money out of the deal, because the Federation went to a lot of trouble to make sure that I didn't by paying me only what I spent, but Land-Rover are a highly profitable company, they are British and theirs is a vehicle that I can readily be identified with, both in the military and agricultural sense. We'd be giving British Leyland a boost as well as making a positive contribution to the future of the sport through the Bursary scheme.'

By October the final details had been agreed, and at the Chatsworth Horse Trials on 13 October, Land-Rover announced their new partnership with Captain Mark Phillips. The effect was explosive. Alan McLeod, Land-Rover's Marketing Manager, expected the story to be picked up by the media 'as a piece of general news'. What he discovered on his breakfast table the following morning was front-page coverage in every national newspaper backed up by major coverage on both BBC and commercial radio and television. In one day Range Rover cars got almost a million pounds worth of publicity – just thirty seconds of advertising during peak viewing hours has a £30,000 price tag and a single-page advertisement in any one of the 'popular' dailies would cost over £20,000 to buy, and here they were being splashed across the main TV news and the front page – for free! It made their £60,000 outlay for three years look like chicken feed.

Needless to say there was a sting in the tail. At the time of the announcement, British Leyland was millions of pounds in debt to the Government and, although the deal was not with BL but the highly profitable and separate division of Land-Rover Limited, few papers could resist the temptation of linking the fortunes of an ailing nationalised car giant to what looked like a personal £60,000 deal with Mark Phillips. Some Labour MPs threatened to bring the matter up in Parliament, Willie Hamilton described the deal as 'sheer bloody nonsense', Denis Skinner was 'staggered', and BL workers interviewed by the *Birmingham Post* said it was 'diabolical', 'disgusting', 'a waste of money' and hinted at an official Union protest. To make matters worse, when Mark had been interviewed about the deal and asked 'why do you need the money' he joked that 'like other young couples we've got a mortgage too'. It was said in fun and not meant to be taken seriously, but that sparked off a whole new 'controversy' over exactly what the money was going to be spent on, and the old chestnut of the hundred-thousand-pound stable-block and equine swimming pool reared its head again.

What Alan McLeod found galling was the apparent conflict between the editorial and commercial interest of the Press. 'There they were on the front page of some of the papers carrying stories saying how ridiculous it was for Leyland to put £25,000 a year into sponsorship, when inside they were carrying full-page adverts for the Allegro for which they themselves had charged us £20,000. The morality and hypocrisy of that was quite difficult to understand.' But when he weighed the good publicity in the industrial and equestrian press against the knockers in the popular dailies, he decided that on the whole there'd been more good reaction than bad, adding philosophically 'we knew that if one of our competitors had signed Mark, like BMW or Mercedes for example, exactly the same papers who were questioning the deal would be saying why the hell didn't Leyland do something clever like that. Leyland asleep again, and so on.' Mark is less magnanimous in his judgement of the affair. 'We really believed that I'd done something that would be good for me, good for Land-Rover and good for the sport. But I just got slated for it by the press, and ended up being disillusioned about the whole thing. The facts didn't matter, it was the untruths that made the story – taxpayers' money going to Phillips and his wife who're already being paid £80,000 a year from the Civil List. It's at times like that you wonder what do you have to do to do something right – apart from nothing, and then that too would be wrong!'

By the end of the week the story had died a natural death. But the personal attacks and inaccurate judgements made a deep impression on Mark Phillips and occasionally the scars still show. However, in spite of the sour reaction from some quarters, Mark knew he had a sound and honourable partnership with Land-Rover. So he put the unpleasantness behind him, lit the fire with the offending newspapers and started planning for the future with his exciting new 'team' of Range Rover horses.

Chapter Eleven

It didn't take long for the massive pale-blue horsebox, decked out in the black, green and yellow livery of the Range Rover Team, to become a familiar sight at the 1980 spring competitions. Nor for the citation 'Owned by the Range Rover Team' to appear regularly next to the name of horse and rider in the result tables. Effectively Mark had seven horses under the team banner; Lincoln, Classic Lines, formerly Frog Prince, and Persian Holiday were joined by two novices, Fieldsman and Going Places, the eight-year-old intermediate Town and County, formerly Persian Minstrel, and the newly-broken youngster Highwayman X, who as the 'baby' of the team made no impression on the scheme at all as he spent his first year being quietly schooled while the six remaining competitive horses clocked up an impressive list of achievements.

Town and County set the pace by winning the intermediate class on the team's first outing to Downlands in March. Classic Lines started out on what was to prove a brilliant year by coming second at Portman, then winning at Pebworth Vale with stablemate Fieldsman running into second place.

As Badminton loomed, Mark once again found himself in a quandary. There was no doubt in his mind that Lincoln should attempt the course, but what about Columbus? His fitness and general condition belied his age, and Mark was tempted to let the old man have one more ride. He took him to Downlands in March where he led after the dressage and showjumping, but dropped to fifth place after a technical stop on the crosscountry. Columbus then redeemed himself within two weeks by winning his advanced section at Brigstock, where Mark enjoyed a double win as Lincoln also won his section of the advanced class, so both horses secured their tickets to Badminton.

Everything was going so smoothly that Mark's pessimistic antennae should have warned him that something was about to flaw the proceedings, though what happened took everyone completely by surprise. Mark has always had such respect for his horses that the last thing he expected was to be charged with cruelty, but after an event at Sherston in March, Mrs Jean Pyke of Hayling Island accused Mark of kicking Highwayman and reported him to the police. Mrs Pyke hadn't been at the competition, but she'd seen photographs of Mark trying to load the horse into the lorry, and based her accusations on that. Mark was shattered. Highwayman had never been the easiest of horses to load, and on one occasion after nearly an hour had been spent trying to

Badminton 1980: (*above*) clearing the fourth fence on Columbus (*Jim Bennett*); (*right*) a mighty leap over the Keeper's Rails on Lincoln (*Hugo Czerny*)

coax the animal into the lorry after hunting in Badminton Park, the horse had to be walked home a good fifteen miles. At Sherston Highwayman had been his usual difficult self, and after the grooms gave up, Mark took over and was dragged down the ramp off balance. That's when the cameras clicked, and Mrs Pyke lodged her complaint. It was no good Mark launching into his theory about 'not being able to make a horse do what it won't do, working by reward not punishment, and achieving discipline through respect not cruelty'. He'd been branded 'the man who kicks horses' by someone who hadn't even witnessed the event, and although he declared publicly 'it just didn't happen, I've been falsely accused, the whole affair is ridiculous', he was interviewed by the police. His case went before the Director of Public Prosecutions for judgement. His conscience was clear, but as at a time when he wanted to give his full concentration to Columbus and Lincoln and their preparations for Badminton, it was a problem he could well do without.

When the draw was announced Mark found that he would top and tail the competition, going first of the field on Columbus, and last at number 88 on Lincoln.

As a trailblazer on crosscountry day Columbus was effectively a non-starter. He fell over his feet at the first fence and second, stopped at the third, and came to a grinding halt at the Luckington Lane. Mark didn't try to make him jump a second time. 'It just wasn't like him so I knew there was something wrong. I pulled him out of the competition, and when the vet looked at him we discovered a bruised foot – probably sustained on the roads and tracks.' With hindsight Mark says: 'It was a mistake to enter him. But anyone can be clever after the event, and on form Columbus had convinced everyone that he was going well, and capable of producing his old brilliance over the big fences. Fortunately no permanent damage was done and after a summer at grass Columbus was retired to the hunting field, where at seventeen he still commands attention as a "great old horse".'

Mark may have had a disastrous start to that crosscountry day, but it finished on a more satifactory note. Lincoln tackled his first Badminton with a display of confidence and agility in spite of two stops, both of which Mark says loyally 'were not his fault'. The first came at Fence 5, the Zig-Zag. 'Because we were last to go it meant we set off late in the day when the sun was low in the sky. We rode at the fence, straight into the sun. I had seen the peg on the ground marking the start of the penalty zone, but I couldn't see the fence at all, and it caught the horse completely by surprise. He just never saw it, and when we got to the take-off he just froze as if saying "what's that?". The stop gave him a chance to look at it, and when I rode at it again he sailed over another section of the fence not affected by the sun.

Seven fences from home, at The Quarry, came stop number two. 'This time it was fifty percent my fault. It wasn't an easy fence for him

to jump, and I wasn't as determined as I might have been; I just sat
quietly and left him to get on with it. Also I allowed my concentration
to wander, just for a second, as a spectator ran across in front of the
jump. I should have ignored him, and concentrated on the fence, but I
didn't so we stopped at the first rail. He jumped it the second time
without any problem, and overall had jumped the course beautifully.'

In spite of the two hiccups, they still finished sixth, and Mark found
himself in partnership with Lincoln on the short list for the 'alternative
games' in Fontainebleau after the BHS had agreed to boycott the
Olympics in Moscow. There was another piece of good news at the
end of the month. The Director of Public Prosecutions found there was
no evidence to suggest that Mark had been guilty of cruelty to
Highwayman, and the case was dropped.

In the same way that the football season seems to get longer each
year, in 1980 the eventing season rolled on from the spring right
through the summer with only a short break in July, and the Range
Rover Team added a few more rosettes to their collection. At
Wellesbourne in May, Fieldsman turned the tables on Classic Lines to
win his first novice event, while Toad cantered in at number four.

One of the most consistent horses in the stable proved to be Mark's
Devon-bred youngster Town and County. He followed up his win at
Downlands by coming first in the regional final for the Midland Bank
novice championship at Bicton, and looked like making it a hat-trick
at the Windsor Three-Day Event in May. After a fine dressage score
and faultless crosscountry, he had the last two elements of the last
showjumping fence down, and dropped to fourth place. Mark was
furious with himself for letting the competition slip out of his grasp at
the very last moment. But two weeks later he did exactly the same
again riding Rough and Tough at Kalmthout in Belgium. A clear
showjumping round would have given him the lead but the horse
made a costly error, collected five penalties, and Mark had to be
satisfied with second place. No wonder he says 'whoever invented this
reverse-order lark for showjumping in three-day events is no friend of
mine – or any of the competitors really. It's great for the spectators.
Absolute hell for the competitors.'

Although every rider likes to win a competition, and usually sets out
with that first prize as an ultimate goal, it was a rosette for fourth place
that gave Mark particular satisfaction during the summer. Lincoln
was by no means an easy horse to settle for dressage, and while Mark
has never believed that perfect dressage marks are the key to winning
three-day events, he nevertheless wanted to improve Lincoln's
performance in that sphere. Working with one of the country's leading
dressage instructors, David Hunt, Mark made such headway with
Lincoln that he entered him with Persian Holiday in the premier event
of the year – the Franklin Mint Dressage Championship.

Percy had never turned in a bad dressage test in his life, so no-one was really surprised when he finished second in his class, but Lincoln surpassed himself by coming fourth, and the timing couldn't have been better. Mark had been invited to compete in the final trial for a place in the team that would ride at Fontainebleau, and the sceptics who thought of the horse as unreliable, and weak on dressage would have to think again!

Meanwhile the rest of the team horses were making equally spectacular progress. Going Places collected a fifth, third and second in novice classes at Tythrop Park, Lockerbie and Annick, while Fieldsman came third in the novice class at Eglinton, and then won on his first outing as an intermediate horse at Lockerbie. As for Classic Lines, he continued to prove that he was both brilliant and wayward by winning the regional final of the Midland Bank Novice Championship at Eglinton in Scotland and the following week getting eliminated after a disaster at Lockerbie.

On more than one occasion Toad had demonstrated a rare talent that convinced Mark that here was a horse that had the stamp of greatness about him. Everything he'd ever been asked to do came easy, 'and that was one of his troubles', says Mark. 'Everything comes so easily to him, he thinks he doesn't have to listen to me. Even when he's arguing and playing the damn fool, or tossing his head in the air, he'll

Dauntsey Park – Mark with son Peter and Prince Edward waiting on the ramp of the horsebox (*Srdja Djukanovic*)

suddenly see a fence in front of him – and he's got so much ability he'll just let fly and jump it.' But at Lockerbie he came unstuck. The last fence on the course was a sunken road wide enough for horses to jump in, and either bounce or shuffle one small stride, before jumping out and over a rail on the far side. Mark approached the jump calmly, slowing Toad right down to a trot to give him plenty of time to get through the combination. As Mark got to the edge of the drop, Toad pricked his ears, ignored his rider's aids and tried to jump the whole thing in one. Mark turned him round and tried again, hoping that this time he would have got the message. But no. Toad took another flying leap and slithered down the far bank. It was the last fence, so Mark retired, sent the horses home and headed off to Dauntsey Park on 2 August with Lincoln as one of the twelve short-listed horses to compete in the final trial for the Fontainebleau 'Alternative Olympics'.

The day of the trial was fraught with problems before Mark even sat on the horse. He'd left his riding breeches at home and after a frantic phone call to Gatcombe a groom arrived with them leaving only minutes to spare before his dressage test. Lincoln gave a creditable performance in the arena, and then disgraced himself with a stop in the showjumping. On the crosscountry course Mark had singled out the sunken road as the fence where he was likely to have problems. 'It was a dead cert that if I was going to have problems anywhere, that was where he would try to stop on the way in. But he didn't. He just sailed over, and I was so amazed that I relaxed and as a result we just didn't make it out from the bottom of the 'road' and over the far rail. I turned him, jumped again, and blow me, he did exactly the same thing again. That suddenly concentrated the brain miraculously, and on the third attempt there were no mistakes.' Mark didn't expect the performance to impress anyone, and was very surprised when his name was not dropped by the selectors. The day had dented Mark's confidence a little, but not enough for him to lose all faith in Lincoln, and so although he didn't get a team placing, he was entered as an individual competitor in the hope of picking up an individual medal if everything went right for the horse. In addition it would silence the critics who condemned the horse as a waste of time and money when the Range Rover sponsorship was arranged.

Not that Mark's sponsors were swayed in any way by these opinions. They had complete faith in Mark's judgement and never once questioned his decisions. In return, they were linked with some of the most successful horses in the country, and had the satisfaction of watching three of their team finish in the ribbons at the Midland Bank Championships at Locko Park on 15 August. Persian Holiday was fifth in the open, while in the novice section Town and County came third, with Classic Lines emerging as overall novice champion and winner of the Griffin Trophy. Working on the principle that nothing succeeds like success, Mark set off for Fontainebleau the day after the

Mark chats to Princess Anne – on her thirtieth birthday – while waiting to complete his dressage test on Classic Lines at Locko Park, 15 August 1980 (*John Topham Picture Library*)

championship in an optimistic frame of mind. Lincoln had been given nearly four weeks to get over the disasters of Dauntsey, four weeks in which Mark had regained the horse's confidence and got him jumping boldly and fluently. On the morning of the vet's inspection, Mark rode the horse for a while and then left him with the groom while he went off to take another look at the testing crosscountry course. In the middle of his walk a breathless messenger came running across the course to tell him that 'your horse is lame'. 'I just couldn't believe it. That horse had never taken a lame step in his life.' But sure enough, when Mark got back to the stables, he found that Lincoln was definitely uneven when he trotted. The vet checked him over and couldn't pinpoint the trouble, but by the time Lincoln was called in front of the official veterinary panel – he was passed sound! Everyone was very relieved. On Friday the horse rode a slightly disappointing dressage test without the slightest sign of lameness, but by the end of the day he was on three legs again. The vets re-examined him and still could not pinpoint the lameness to the leg, the foot or the shoulder. Mark couldn't possibly risk riding him across country and had no alternative but to withdraw from the competition. He took Lincoln home and turned him out in a field at Gatcombe and blistered his leg as an insurance policy. All he could do now was wait and see, and hope that the horse would be fit to run again the following year.

One advantage of living with the sort of crowded schedule that Mark has is that it never leaves him time to brood over disappointments. Hard on the heels of Fontainebleau came Burghley, the major three-day event of the autumn season. All through the summer Persian Holiday had been carefully schooled and prepared for an attempt at the Burghley title. The previous year he'd been withdrawn in the trial week with an injury, and had only actually finished the course once – in 1976 when he came eighth.

The Midland Bank Championship in August had been a good pipe-opener and privately Mark was considering retiring his old friend at the end of the year, and wanted to send him out in a blaze of glory. And it almost came off. Dressage day ended with Percy out in front, where he stayed after a faultless crosscountry round. Uncomfortably close behind, in second place, was Richard Walker with John of Gaunt, with a score of 46.4 to Percy's 44.4. Riding in reverse order for the showjumping, Richard had one fence down, and maintained his position. Percy only had to do the same to add the Burghley title to his impressive roll of honour. But it wasn't to be. He had the first fence down and a brick out of the wall and left the arena in second position. For the third time that year Mark had lost the winner's ribbon in the closing seconds of a competition, and it was a bitter pill to swallow. 'In thirteen years I'd never lost a winning place in a three-day event, and within six months of one year I'd managed to lose three – perhaps that will do me for another thirteen years!' Was it bad judgement – or bad luck? Mark's superstitions about numbers are well known in his family, and I suspect he's not altogether joking when he says 'eight has never been my lucky number so perhaps I should just give up in the 80s – I certainly think I'll retire before 1988!'

After Burghley the eventing season tails off a little, but Mark planned at least three more outings that autumn before hanging up his boots for the winter. Classic Lines wasn't left to rest on his laurels as novice champion. Mark took him to Rudding Park in Yorkshire, mainly to see what effect the championship run had had on him, for although the horse had produced characteristic brilliance, a small doubt niggled in Mark's mind. 'In order to win the class he had to go quite quickly in the crosscountry phase, and just galloped at everything. It's the only thing I've ever done with him that I regretted because he thought "this is the way I enjoy jumping". But of course you can't just gallop round, see a fence and accelerate into it, regardless of what's on the other side, or where you go afterwards.'

At the very first fence Mark knew he'd been right to expect trouble. 'I rode at it in what I thought was a perfectly reasonable fashion, he stuck his head in the air and was off – flat out. This little pantomime went on for fence after fence. At every fence we came to he was sticking his head in the air, taking charge and rushing at the fence. After about seven fences I decided that this wasn't doing me or the horse any good, so I slowed him right down, and virtually showjumped him round. Fast enough to give the horse a chance at the fences, but with me in control.' Toad didn't enjoy the experience at all, and neither did the steward who hadn't appreciated the battle of wills that was going on between horse and jockey, and reported Mark for what he saw as bad riding. But Mark was adamant. Toad was incredibly strong, and while his natural ability got him out of trouble over small fences, once he started trying to career off into the massive timbers of an open course, he'd get himself and his jockey into real trouble. At home he was schooled, quietly and calmly, but it took months for his rider to 'get common sense back into his nut and have him jumping in a sensible, relaxed way again'.

For years Mark had managed to avoid any really bad falls or serious injuries. The last time had been in 1973 when he lost the sight of his right eye temporarily after a fall on Columbus at Rushall. But his luck ran out at the end of September when Rough and Tough did a spectacular cartwheel over a fence at Taunton Vale. It was a relatively straightforward obstacle with a palisade in front of a slight slope. 'I

(*left*) Fontainebleau mini Olympics – team effort as Mark watches the water jump and sends information back to the team via the 'runner' – Princess Anne; (*right*) attention for his injured hand after Mark and Rough and Tough performed their spectacular cartwheel at Taunton Vale – nothing broken but extremely painful torn ligaments which kept Mark out of riding for two weeks and required months of treatment (*John Topham Picture Library*)

came absolutely right to jump it, but the horse just didn't take off. He hit it with his chest and I thought, well that's all right – he's stopped. But he didn't, he kept going. His head and shoulders went over the fence and for a moment I thought he was going to come back up. So I was sitting there like a Charlie, hanging on to the buckle with my feet round his ears. Then I saw his tail come in front of my eyes and I thought "God this is going to hurt". There was no way I was going to get clear. The next stop for me was the ground, and he was obviously going to come over on top of me. It was a real slow-motion cartwheel. I went flat onto the ground, and as luck would have it I landed on the slope and slid a bit. As he came over he landed on my legs which wasn't too bad, because if I hadn't dropped down the slope he would have gone over my back – and those are the falls when you can do yourself a real injury.'

While Mark was sitting on the ground with half a ton of horse over his legs congratulating himself that he hadn't been more seriously injured, he was suddenly aware of incredible pain in his left hand. 'It felt as though all the bones in the back of my hand had come out through my palm. I was convinced when I took my glove off that I'd see two bones sticking out. In fact there was no blood, and no bone. But it hurt so much I was beside myself with pain. I couldn't stand up, couldn't sit down, couldn't stand still. I honestly didn't know what to do with myself – it was quite the most painful thing that has ever happened to me. It hurt so much all I could do was laugh.' An X-ray showed no broken bones, but literally a fist full of torn ligaments. In the short term it kept Mark out of riding for almost two weeks, and he received treatment for about six months in all for the hand. That time he had a lucky escape. Riders before him have been crippled, or even killed, when similar situations have gone horribly wrong. But thoughts of having serious accidents have no place in Mark Phillips' philosophy. 'No one wants to have a bad accident, and I have been very lucky. Oh, I have had a few knocks and bumps, and bruises and things, but nothing terrible. Riding, like all sports, is a matter of confidence and if you thought of the injuries you might sustain or worried about hurting yourself over a fence you would never start in the first place. When confidence is high you do things crisply and sharply by instinct and without thinking about it, thereby, on the whole, keeping out of trouble. However, he who hesitates . . . !'

Three weeks and several pain-killing injections later Mark and Rough and Tough were back in partnership. They rode in the team which came second at Wylye, finishing fourteenth as individuals. Wylye also provided another challenge, one that you won't find in the record books but which has £150 riding on the outcome.

In one of those idle moments when riders swop gossip and banter, Mark, Mike Tucker, Ginny Holgate and Judy Bradwell were extolling the virtues of their respective horses and each reckoned they had one of

Mark and Princess Anne being interviewed by Brian Moore in the drawing room at Gatcombe for the LWT television film 'Brian Moore Meets Captain Mark Phillips', shown at Easter 1981 (*John Topham Picture Library*)

the best young horses in the land. It was the usual light-hearted stuff that goes on whenever horsemen get together, and when Mark declared that 'I reckon Classic Lines will get in the first three at Badminton in 1983', it produced a chorus of 'rubbish'. 'After that, I think we all got rather carried away. 1983 sounded a long way off and we all bet each other fifty pounds that one of our horses would be in the ribbons. Whoever comes out on top picks up £150 from the other three' – adding, not too seriously – 'there'll be a lot of pressure on Badminton '83'. But there's a glint in his eye when he says it. Mark doesn't make rash statements about his horses, and he does believe that in time Classic Lines could prove worthy of a place next to Columbus and Chicago as one of the really great horses in his career. He knows that to win Badminton you need a good horse, and good luck. He believes he already has the first – he hopes he'll get the second.

Chapter Twelve

November is usually one of the quieter months in Mark's diary. The eventing season is over, the horses are taking a rest, and the demands of the farm grow less with the shortening days. It's then that he goes shooting, or indulges in his other passion – hunting.

An invitation to the Caledonian Hunt Dinner in Edinburgh took husband and wife north at the start of the season and provided Mark with an opportunity to ride with the Dumfriesshire. A few months earlier Princess Anne's hound, Pleasure, who'd been a gift from the pack, had died after a brain haemorrhage, so needless to say when they visited the kennels she was offered another hound as a replacement. Random, like Pleasure, had no interest whatsoever in hunting. According to Mark 'she got in the van with the other hounds all right, but once they got to the meet and dropped the ramp on the van, all the hounds would run out except Random, who stayed curled up in the far corner. They couldn't get her to come out, so that was that, useless hound number two.'

Random was installed at Gatcombe along with Mark's new dog – Laura the lurcher. Moriarty, the famous black Labrador, had grown old and rheumaticy. The jet black of his muzzle had clouded grey with age, and so he'd been retired to Mark's parents at Great Somerford where he still rules the roost. But Mark missed the companionship of a family dog at his heel and, because he'd always 'hankered after a lurcher', when he was offered a bitch puppy in Kent bred by Brazil's owner Margarite Boucher 'I weakened, and couldn't resist it'. So Laura and Random took up residence at Gatcombe, and on 5 November an announcement from Buckingham Palace confirmed that the house was to have another new arrival. Princess Anne was expecting their second baby. Mark could not have been more delighted. He adores his son and welcomed the thought of another child in the house – demonstrating that blend of pride and pleasure in children that is the stamp of a good family man and father.

Gatcombe is not a home where children are permanently left in the care of a nanny while their parents indulge in their own lifestyles. The Princess takes Peter to and from school every day that she's at home, and nursery teas – especially in the winter – are a family occasion, when Princess Anne brews the tea and father and son grapple on the floor in mock battle, or sit entwined on cushions reading from a story book. It isn't easy to maintain a stable family routine when parents have to spend days, sometimes weeks, away from home on business as

Mark playing with Peter on his slide outside the conservatory at Gatcombe in summer 1981 (*Jim Bennett*)

both Princess Anne and Captain Phillips do, and if anything that has made them more determined to share their lives with their children as much as possible. Though Mark believes that 'I don't spend nearly as much time with Peter as I would like, just occasionally, when I get a free afternoon and probably ought to be doing any one of a dozen other things, I'll spend the time with him. If I'm in the workshop mending something and he wants to hold a spanner, or pass the hammer, it all takes much longer because you have to watch everything and make sure it's safe. But at least he's helping Papa, and as he gets older I hope he'll become even more involved with the farm and things that I'm doing. It's difficult to define what a father's responsibility is – but whatever it is I certainly feel it. It's something I want to do.' As for following in father's and mother's footsteps and taking to riding, there's no doubt in Mark's mind that 'I'm in the fortunate position to give him all the help and encouragement he may need – if that is what he really wants to do. But I'm not going to make him do it. He has a mind and a character of his own. I shall be very happy to teach him, but it's something you have to play by ear.'

So far Master Peter Phillips has certainly shown no fear of horses.

He's as much at home in the Gatcombe stables as he is in the nursery. His first Shetland pony is a prized possession and he's something of a seasoned spectator at horse trials and three-day events. With such a background it's virtually inevitable that he will ride, and if Mark is reticent to commit himself on the subject it's possibly because it is also inevitable that if his talent and interests lie in eventing, he will be constantly compared with his parents, and that is not a spotlight that Mark would wish on anyone. But Peter's riding achievements are very much for the future. In the spring of 1981 Mark's major concern was his preparation for Badminton with Lincoln and Persian Holiday, whose proposed retirement had been postponed until after the competition.

Mark's superstition about the figure eight was tactfully never mentioned when Percy drew that number in the Badminton running order. There's no logical reason to suppose that something as random as a number is going to have a major effect on something as positive as a three-day event. But the jinx – if that's what it is – must have been working at full strength. On a 33-fence course Percy didn't get past the eighth, and was retired at The Quarry. Mark's reaction that 'I'd let the horse down' was typical of his feelings for an animal he regarded as 'an old friend'. These sentiments were not shared by Frank Weldon. In his opinion 'Percy isn't a lucky horse for Mark. When you look at him, he's such a great big slashing sort of a horse you'd think he could eat

Peter riding his diminutive Shetland pony Smokey at Sandringham in January 1981 (*John Topham Picture Library*)

Mark receiving the Butler Bowl as the leading British rider at Badminton 1981 on Lincoln from the Queen, while Prince Philip looks on (*John Topham Picture Library*)

fences. But there's always one leg poking out somewhere. I know Mark loves the horse, but I've said for years, he's the sort of horse that might hurt him.' Mark was hurt, not physically – but inside. Deep down. He believed he'd failed Percy, and that was the worst hurt of all.

But there was elation at that Badminton too. Lincoln demolished all opposition – and won. His triumph gave Mark one of his sweetest victories for years and made Lincoln a virtual certainty for the European Championships. But the jinx hadn't quite finished with Mark. Only weeks after the euphoria of winning, Lincoln was standing on three legs. He'd injured himself while he was supposed to be having a rest in the field and bang went another opportunity to ride for a European title. His record in that area was beginning to sound like a bad joke. Not since the World Championships of '74 had Mark come within sniffing distance of either a World or European title – the one elusive honour that still evades him.

Lincoln's injury was frustrating, but it certainly didn't keep Mark out of the saddle – or out of the ribbons. Classic Lines was upgraded from novice and came fourth on his first outing as an intermediate at

Shelswell and eighth at Clumber Park. The willing gentle-natured
Going Places – nicknamed Simon – tended to be overshadowed by his
boisterous stable companion Classic Lines who demands attention –
and gets it – with his antics. But in April Going Places clocked up a win
at Brougham, then came third at Tidworth, and on both occasions
demonstrated to Mark that he had that perfect combination of ability
and temperament of which champions are made.

The previous summer the first young riders had gone through the
Range Rover Bursary scheme and twenty-year-old Duncan Douglas
was offered a £1500 boost to his career when the British Equestrian
Federation nominated him as the Range Rover Young Rider of the
Year. Alan McLeod's hope that 'a 1984 or '88 Olympic team might
contain three or maybe four people that had been helped by our
Bursary scheme' didn't look such a pipe-dream after all.

On a personal level Mark couldn't ignore the irony of suddenly
finding himself training groups of riders at Gatcombe when that was
the very job he'd assumed he would be doing when he left the army.

The training sessions are held three times a year at the beginning
and end of the summer, each lasting four or five days. Riders are
chosen by the British Horse Society and have their expenses and
training fees paid for by Range Rover. It's a unique and positive
contribution from a company whose major object in becoming a
sports sponsor in the first place was to promote the image, and
therefore indirectly the sales, of its own product. So far no other major
sponsor has followed their lead.

Mark supported the whole scheme, and being a trainer is an experience he clearly enjoys. 'I get quite chuffed when I see a horse and
rider improving as the week goes on and it's really gratifying when
they leave here after five days looking significantly better than when
they arrived.' But above that personal satisfaction there's a genuine
pleasure at being able to make a positive contribution to the future of
the sport. 'I feel I've got so much out of the sport that it's only right to
put something back in. Over the years I've had some marvellous
opportunities to ride great horses and get help and advice from really
first-class horsemen, and perhaps I can now help other riders by
passing on some of that store of knowledge and experience.' Watching
Mark teach, it is obvious that however reticent and tongue-tied he may
be at a cocktail party where the conversation revolves around political
small talk and social gossip, when sitting on a horse with an audience
of eager pupils, he's a master of his craft. After watching a rider for just
a few minutes he can pinpoint precisely their major faults or
difficulties, and his explanations of how to correct them are delivered
with graphic, spontaneous and detailed directions that leave no-one in
any doubt what they should be trying to achieve. 'Teaching someone
to ride a horse is quite difficult really', says Mark, 'because you're not
just trying to get them to assimilate facts and figures. You have to

imagine what they're feeling, and turn that around into instructions they can readily understand. It's quite a complicated process,' but one he manages with stunning professional competence, and when words aren't enough, his practical demonstrations of controlled classic horsemanship usually leave his audience open-mouthed with admiration.

He reserves his own admiration for just a quartet of riders in the world that he finds 'pleasing to watch across country, at dressage and in the showjumping ring'. Britain's Richard Walker and Lucinda Prior-Palmer, the American Tad Coffin, and head and shoulders above the rest another American, Mike Plumb. 'Perhaps he hasn't been as successful a competitor as some others' says Mark, 'but he's had a long and impressive career. Personally I admire him as a complete horseman. When you watch him his horses are always perfectly balanced, and he's as still as a mouse. He's lovely to watch.'

Most aficionados would rank Mark equal in skill and ability beside any of his own top four, but suggest this to him and he'll shake his head saying, 'I know myself too well, my strengths and my weaknesses – so it's not for me to say.' He believes without question that dressage is still his weakest discipline: 'I cannot get that excited about it and treat it slightly as a necessary evil. I enjoy riding the horses so that they're nicely schooled and balanced, but the real pros get every last ounce of bend into the corner, every last bit of movement possible. I

The Range Rover Bursary scheme in action – Mark demonstrates a point to one of his pupils, Frances Hunter on Strike a Light (*Jim Bennett*)

find that difficult because my back isn't as strong and flexible as it should be. Also, although I like my horses to be obedient, I do let them get into little bad habits, like not always standing still, or making sure that they're standing four square, little things I ought to tighten up on really, but I do think that a horse has got a mind of its own, so I am a little bit lax in that respect.'

The class of May 1981 at Gatcombe was made up entirely of girls – Nicola May, Ginny Strawsen, Sue Berbeck, Frances Hunter and Joanna Wrigglesworth – all under eighteen, and each one destined to make an impression on the record books before the end of the year. They arrived on 4 May with quite a few bad habits and problems between them, and left four days later having spent at least three hours of every day in the saddle under the watchful, critical eye of the Captain, getting their problems unravelled and their bad habits gently ironed out. At the end of the course every rider admitted she'd improved some aspect of her riding. They weren't just being polite; in four days you could actually see a difference in the way they rode, sitting deeper in the saddle, having better contact with the horses through jumping fences with even greater confidence. As for Mark, he was satisfied that he'd given them all something to think about: 'That's how I got my riding experience, learning from other people. So next week when they've got a problem perhaps they'll say "Oh, Mark Phillips told me to try this" and if it works, fine. If not, then they'll have to call on what they learned in the pony club, or saw another rider do, and so on. With horses you have to keep thinking and trying things until you come up with the right solution, and if they can draw some experience from what they've heard and seen during these four days, well then we've achieved something.'

What they did achieve was almost a minor take-over of the season's main events, and it gave Mark great satisfaction to monitor the progress of his 'class' as they added even more rosettes to their collections. In particular, Frances Hunter and Strike a Light won their first three-day event at Osberton in September, while Ginny Strawson rode in the gold-winning team at the Junior European Championships in France during August and, but for two fences down in the showjumping, would have taken the individual gold as well. She then accepted the challenge of the Burghley Three-Day Event on Greek Herb, finishing a commendable fifth.

With the exception of one outing to Rufford Park in Nottingham where Going Places maintained his form with another third place, Mark's own competition interest took something of a back seat towards the end of May as he and Princess Anne prepared for the arrival of their second child.

At the beginning of the second week in May, Princess Anne moved to Windsor, while Mark carried on working at Gatcombe. Just after lunch on 15 May he rang the Castle to be told that the Princess had just

Proud father – Mark leaving St Mary's Hospital, Paddington, after visiting Princess
Anne and their new daughter Zara, May 1981 (*John Topham Picture Library*)

left for St Mary's Hospital in Paddington; a phone call to the hospital
confirmed that 'there was no need to rush as nothing much was
happening'. Casting his mind back four years to the scene when Peter
was born, Mark decided that on this occasion he wouldn't mind giving
the birth a miss. 'I know some people feel strongly about it, and that
many women like their husbands with them for moral support, or
whatever. But each to his own. Certainly Princess Anne wasn't fussed
about whether I made it in time or not, which is why she waited at
Windsor while I stayed on the farm. So I must admit that I didn't go
dashing off to London right away. Instead I finished the afternoon's
work, then took a steady drive up the M4 thinking that if I didn't go
too fast, then the baby might be born by the time I got there.' When he
arrived at St Mary's, Princess Anne was still in labour and within
minutes he found himself being robed in gown and mask and

'somehow co-opted into the proceedings', to witness the birth of his daughter at a quarter past eight that evening.

As he left the hospital reporters asked the obvious questions 'Were you at the birth and do you think fathers should be there?' Mark answered honestly that 'Yes' he had been with the Princess throughout the birth and 'No' he didn't think it would be everybody's cup of tea – a remark, as usual made in innocence, that brought another hail of criticism down on his head. 'Oh baby – Mark drops a clanger' was how the *Sunday Mirror* headlined a front-page story in which baby 'experts' who favoured the 'shared miracle of birth' lashed out at him for supposedly saying 'I wouldn't recommend it to other fathers.'

Mark flew to America a few days later and left the row still bubbling behind him, somewhat bemused by the thought that his opinion should be thought so vital to the rest of the fathers in the country, who presumably could make up their own minds on the matter. But then Mark was becoming hardened to reading stories about himself that exaggerated or condemned his actions, and bore little resemblance to the truth – which was just as well, because in June he opened his morning papers to find that a great fuss was being made about a supposed 'Ice-cube Throwing' incident on the ferry back from a competition in Holland. Mark was said to be involved in 'rowdy' scenes in the bar which 'upset' and 'disgusted' fellow-passengers – but the incident simply never happened as reported. Mark received an apology from the ferry company confirming that neither the Captain nor the Chief Purser witnessed any of the incidents that were described in great detail in the press, and subsequent enquiries confirmed that the story had been invented by a reporter who saw an easy way of making money by selling the story to the nationals. It wasn't the first time it had happened – and it certainly wouldn't be the last.

Anyone who doubts the importance of good luck and a benevolent guardian angel as ingredients in a successful eventing career should have walked through Mark Phillips' stables halfway through 1981. He started the year with more than a dozen horses including seven leased to the Range Rover Team, each one holding the promise of at least improvement, at best real achievement. What he was left with by August as far as the team was concerned was effectively a three-horse race. After Badminton Persian Holiday had been retired to hunting, and 'the good horse Lincoln' as Mark called him was given six months off to fully recover from his leg injury. Originally they'd thought six weeks would be enough, but vet Geoffrey Brain advised a double insurance of splitting the tendon and giving him six full months to recover.

The injury itself was still something of a mystery. The only logical explanation seemed to be that, when he was pawing the ground waiting to come in from the field, Lincoln had put his foot through the gate and caught the tendon on one of the bars. But whatever the cause, the effect was conclusive – he was out of competitions until the following year. Mark is used to living with those sort of disappointments, but it doesn't make them any easier. As he says 'anybody who wins at Badminton would fancy their chances in another competition that year because Badminton is generally recognised as the severest, most difficult, three-day event in the world, in terms of those that are held on a regular, annual basis. So the logical process is that if you're good enough to win the most difficult one, then you're in with a chance to go on to the European or World Championships afterwards. But when something like this happens, you just go as normal and try to forget about the disappointments.'

Town and County won Bicton in a blaze of glory during early May, and then went lame on a splint, while Fieldsman's best result for the year had been gained at Kalmthout in June, where he came seventh in what was his first ever three-day event. In every respect it was a daunting introduction to the major competitions. There was a burst of gunfire in the middle of his dressage test, half the crosscountry course was under water, and the fences would have done credit to Burghley in their size and degree of difficulty. Out of more than fifty riders, only eight managed a clear crosscountry run, so Mark was pleasantly surprised when the relatively inexperienced Fieldsman managed to clear all but one of the fences and finished seventh. The performance convinced Mark that Fieldsman was worthy of 'a much higher opinion than I had of him before'.

Completing a three-day event is a major physical test for any horse, so Fieldsman enjoyed a fairly relaxed life for the rest of the season, with only one other outing to Achleschwang in September when he finished fifteenth. As for Highwayman, he didn't compete at all. Mark is a great believer in never pushing a horse beyond its limits and Highwayman had shown that he simply didn't have what Mark looked for in potential or ability to make an international eventer. 'When horses are doing something they enjoy', says Mark, 'they're happy and that's the most important thing. Highwayman isn't right for eventing but he's turning into a good, weight-carrying hunter, so that's what he'll be best at.'

All of which left just Classic Lines and Going Places of the team horses to tackle the rest of the year's competitions. But what they lacked in numbers, they more than made up for with results. Classic Lines won a place in the British team to compete at Hooge Mierde in Holland in June, a team Mark describes as 'containing four of the nicest horses this country has produced in a long time, Three Cups ridden by Richard Meade, Killannan ridden by Richard Walker, Mr Wise Guy with Colin Wares, and Classic Lines. They just looked a picture, each one with the stamp of an ideal three-day event horse.'

The competition was Classic Lines' first three-day event as an open horse and Mark was determined that it wouldn't be an unhappy

Mark and Fieldsman at Kalmthout, 1981; Mark talks us through the fence: (*l to r, top row*) Approach – keeping hold and driving into the last stride; take-off – still keeping hold so that there is no chance of a 'glance off' at the corner; up and over – note how my centre of gravity is still vertical over the horse's withers; over and down – I now start to slip the reins to give the horse freedom and allow my weight to come back behind my leg ready for touch-down; (*l to r, second row*) landing – the horse has all the freedom he wants and I'm safe behind my leg; away – back into the vertical over the horse's withers; second stride – support for the horse through deep ground; re-balance and on to the next fence (*Jim Bennett*)

experience for him. 'I wanted him to finish thinking "oh – that was good" so that he'd enjoy the next outing.' There were a few 'wrinkles' in the dressage test, but nothing that Mark didn't think he could iron out in the future. On the steeplechase course he'd gone 'like a train – I've never had to work so hard to restrain a horse so much' and when he arrived in the crosscountry starting-box he was obviously impatient to get on with the competition. Because Mark was riding as a team member, not an individual, he spent some time discussing how the course was riding, and which fences were proving difficult, with the *chef d'equipe*. While he chatted, the team of grooms went through

their usual routine of unsaddling the horse, washing him down, and quietly walking him round until a few minutes before the start of the next phase. Mark believed that he had plenty of time in hand 'but suddenly I heard somebody say "number 40 – two minutes to go". At this stage the horse was on the other side of the box, the saddle was still on the ground, and he was nowhere near ready. Anyway – frantic panic. We threw the saddle on the horse, tried to get the breast plate done up and were working flat out. At last I trotted him over to the start and was told "you're late – you've missed it". In those circumstances the rules say you're allowed to go straight away because the clock is already running on you. Instead the starter insisted that I wait for his ten-seconds countdown, so I set off not knowing how late I was and how much time had been wasted – it could have been thirty seconds, a minute, I had no idea. I thought to myself, well I could bust a gut and go flat out, and still pick up fifty time faults because of being late in starting. I decided there was no point, I just had all the enthusiasm drained out of me; and then just to make matters worse, as we jumped the second fence, the horse's noseband broke – probably because in the rush we hadn't put it on properly. So all in all, by the time I got to the third fence morale was at zero.'

After the crosscountry at Kalmthout, 1981 – not just a fine weather sport (*Jim Bennett*)

Kalmthout – girthing up during the ten-minute halt between the steeplechase and crosscountry phases (*Jim Bennett*)

The winning British trio at Hooge Mierde, June 1981 (*l to r*) Richard Meade on Three Cups, Mark on Classic Lines and Richard Walker on Killannan (*Findlay Davidson*)

In contrast Classic Lines was firing on all pistons and attacked the course with spirit and determination. It gave his rider particular pleasure to feel him jumping the really difficult fences 'fantastically well' and to finish the course, pulling like a train, 'looking so fit and full of running that he could probably have gone round again'. A clear showjumping round put them in seventh place overall with the combined efforts of the team securing the gold medal. If Mark had been frustrated by the mix-up in the box as it was happening, he was even more dismayed when he saw the final time sheets. If he'd managed to complete the crosscountry course in twenty seconds less, he would have finished third instead of seventh – but then eventing is full of 'if onlys' and Mark's had enough of them to know the difference they make to results.

Towards the end of the year Classic Lines and Going Places competed on the Scottish circuit. Classic Lines won the advanced section at Eglinton, then came fifth at Lockerbie where Going Places finished third in the intermediate.

In many respects the two horses looked almost inseparable in ability and performance but, although at eight years old Going Places was a

Blizzard working through a water jump during the Wylye Three-day Event in October 1981 (*Jim Bennett*)

full year senior to Classic Lines, Mark felt it was the seven-year-old who had the edge on stamina and maturity, especially after his performance at Hooge Mierde. So when the entries closed for the Burghley Three-Day Event in September, Classic Lines got the nomination. Instead Going Places was entered for the Three-Day Event at Wylye, which he won with a faultless performance on 4 October bringing the season to an end in a most happy and satisfactory way.

Trotting in behind Going Places to collect the rosette for second place was an eight-year-old gelding called Blizzard – also ridden by Captain Mark Phillips. The horse was not one of those leased to Range Rover, but his performance at Wylye coupled with a third in the prestigious Midland Bank Novice Championship in August confirmed his potential as a possible future international horse. His owner, Dr Simpson, has kindly agreed to lend him to the Range Rover Team for 1982.

Meanwhile training for Burghley became a family affair as Princess Anne had started riding again within weeks of taking baby daughter Zara home to Gatcombe, and had qualified the Queen's promising young chestnut Stevie B. Mark knew he was taking something of a gamble with Classic Lines, as it was going to be by far the biggest course he had ever jumped, but he reasoned that 'the horse really does have outstanding ability, and is physically very mature. He'll be jumping fences that are bigger and more complicated, and there'll be more people than he's used to. All of that I'm sure he can cope with. What I didn't want was for the horse to have a bad experience by frightening himself and losing confidence. If that happens we'll have to take a deep breath, say "silly boy, I've done too much" then go back to the beginning and start again very slowly.'

Their dressage marks gave neither Princess Anne nor Mark any reason to believe that either of them would go home with the winner's Raleigh Trophy tucked under their arm, but both were convinced that their horses could cope with Bill Thomson's beautifully-built fences and knew that, taken steadily, the experience of riding and hopefully completing the course would be invaluable.

The Princess steered Stevie B around the first two-thirds of the course with steady, sympathetic riding, and the young horse didn't put a foot wrong until he came to the infamous Trout Hatchery, which had stopped dozens of horses in their tracks, and been the real bogey fence of the course. Stevie made a gallant effort over the log, landed badly in the water and gave himself and his jockey a ducking. They were reunited, jumped the next fence well, and at that point Princess Anne retired.

Burghley 1981 – Mark performing his dressage test with Classic Lines before their contretemps at the Lower Trout Hatchery in the crosscountry phase (*Jim Bennett*)

They returned to the stables, wet and bedraggled, to be joined less than an hour later by the Captain and Classic Lines – also wet, also bedraggled and definitely disappointed. At the start of the crosscountry, Mark had believed that Classic Lines could beat one of the major contenders for the 1981 title, Lucinda's horse Beagle Bay, and in a rare burst of pre-competition optimism he declared 'he's all systems go. I really think he could win this one.'

So, what went wrong? What the spectators saw was horse and rider taking an early bath at Fence 6, the Lower Trout Hatchery, and for once Mark isn't able to give a stride-by-stride analysis of why. 'It's a complete mystery,' he says. 'We've even watched the action in a slow-motion replay and we still can't work out what happened. Up until that fence he'd been really going well, listening to me and concentrating on the job. When we got to the water he came back to a trot and went into the stream, took two strides and was all set to jump the rails coming out, when suddenly we both went under. It was unbelievable. It's possible, I suppose, that he crossed his legs or caught a toe and got in a tangle, but I really don't know what happened.'

Mark has always said that he didn't want Classic Lines to come away from a major three-day event feeling that the whole thing had been a frightening and unpleasant experience, so he too retired, and the Phillips family prepared to pack up, and drive home. It had been an unhappy day all round, but the following morning held an even nastier shock for them. The press was full of rumours that their marriage was breaking up and that they were heading for a divorce. The story had originated with an Australian newspaper report headlined 'Anne and Mark to Split' which went on to claim that the 'marriage is on the rocks' and that 'Mark is being sent to Australia to think things over'. They even suggested that 'the Queen is unhappy about a close relationship her son-in-law has with a television personality' – and as far as at least three British newspapers were concerned, that meant me!

The fact that Mark's trip to Australia had been planned months before so that he could ride in the Melbourne Three-Day Event, and that his marriage to Princess Anne was both happy and sound, were the sort of truths that just got in the way of a 'good story'. Once again, investigation proved it to be nothing more than a collection of half-truths, lies and innuendo invented by a 'hack' who was handsomely paid for his 'exclusive' by the Australian press.

Mark and Princess Anne have learned to weather that sort of attack on their lives together. It's one of the things that makes their relationship so strong. They work as a team, always supporting each other whether they're training horses, fulfilling their varied and various public roles, or creating a loving family home in which to bring up their children. And perhaps as much as anything else, it is that mellow, comfortable eighteenth-century house – Gatcombe – which is the key factor in their lives. It's a heritage they plan to leave to their children, and the one oasis in a goldfish-bowl existence that guarantees them privacy and the pleasure of a normal family life, where they can argue over breakfast, play football with Peter, share bathtime with Zara, have a cuddle watching television, and know that it won't appear in tomorrow's papers. After years of being a very public Princess, Mrs Mark Phillips puts a high value on her private life, believing that 'you have to have something to call your own. Once your public life becomes interesting to a wide audience I'm inclined to think your private life becomes much more important to your mental stability, never mind anything else.'

Princess Anne accepts that being a 'Royal' means that much of her life will be regarded as public property, but she also feels that 'sometimes people forget just how public our lives are, and because we've done television programmes like *The Royal Family*, in a way it almost makes it more important to preserve what's left, and in my case, I suppose, I am just prepared to argue for it a bit more.'

Mark Phillips doesn't pretend that he finds the role of public man an easy one to live with. He sees himself as an 'ordinary' person 'who just goes about my own business', and he would quite clearly have been perfectly happy to live a fairly anonymous life in the country with his only claim to fame being his equestrian achievements. But such is the irony of life that this very private man has been catapulted into a permanent spotlight by marrying into the most public family in the land, and however much he may want to be 'ordinary', it isn't easy when your mother-in-law is the Queen, your brother-in-law the Heir to the Throne, and protocol demands that you refer to your wife in public not as 'darling', 'my wife', or even 'Anne', but the formally correct Princess Anne.

The fact that he has managed to achieve such an easy balance between 'Royal' husband and 'common' man is, in the circumstances, to his eternal credit. No-one could pretend that his life is hard, or that marriage hasn't brought him advantages he could never have dreamed of as plain Mark Phillips – army officer. He lives comfortably in a beautiful house, with a fairly privileged lifestyle that allows him to indulge his passion for hunting, shooting and eventing. But he's never surrendered his independence, or lost his own identity – doing his duty as a 'Royal' when necessary, but remaining very much his own man and being prepared to work hard for what he gets out of life.

As a father he is loving and over-indulgent. His children are two of the great strengths in his life, and while he's 'old-fashioned enough to be glad I had a son first', daughter Zara is the darling of the household. But even though their mother is a Royal Princess the children remain plain Master Peter and Miss Zara Phillips as Mark has no title of his own. When Tony Armstrong-Jones married Princess Margaret he became Lord Snowdon, but Mark stays Captain Phillips – not because he has refused a title, but because he has never been offered one and it isn't something that bothers him. His attitude is that 'if the powers that be thought it would be a good thing then I would have accepted it, if that's the order of the day. But if no-one thinks it's necessary, then I'm perfectly happy. What are titles anyway? It's what you are, and who you are that matters – not what you're called.'

There is, of course, one exception. A title that Mark wants more than anything else in his career. But it's a title that will be earned by his own skill and endeavours as an eventer, not one handed on a velvet cushion or delivered at the end of a regal sword.

The man who has won Badminton four times, represented his country as an Olympic horseman and earned himself the universal acclaim of his peers as 'one of the most brilliant horsemen in the world' still hungers after an individual Olympic, World or European title. He's still only thirty-three. In a sport where age is no barrier he has plenty of time, and his own view of the future is quite clear. 'When I was twenty I always said I would give up at thirty because I thought that by then I would be feeling too old. In fact when I got to thirty, I found I got a new lease of life. I think what made the difference was showjumping. I really got into the whole thing and for the first time started to understand in far greater depth the mechanics of how the horse works. His balance and rhythm. I started to get a deeper understanding of how I could make the whole thing work more efficiently, which was rather exciting. I am sure I'll know when I want to give up. Whether it will be my back that will stop me, or a bad fall so that I start to lose confidence and no longer enjoy the sport or whatever, but right now I still love competing and I still love winning. So while I'm still enjoying it, while I think I am still riding well and still think I'm as good as the next man, I don't see why I shouldn't go on competing – and hopefully winning.'

PART TWO   BADMINTON 1981

Prologue

When the Duke of Beaufort opens the gates to the public of the 550-acre park around Badminton House in Gloucestershire every April to play host to the famous Badminton Horse Trials, something like a quarter of a million spectators flood onto the course. That is more than fill Wembley Stadium for the Cup Final, or pack the terraces on the 18th green for the British Open. The Badminton Three-Day Event is one of the equestrian highlights on the British sporting calendar. Those who watch in their thousands on site and the millions who watch on television vary from the dedicated aficionados and hopeful contenders to the mildly interested who enjoy a day out in the country. Most understand the purpose of the competition, some the skill and courage required, but very few can appreciate the preparation, both mental and physical, for rider and horse that makes any major three-day event possible at all. It isn't something that happens quickly. It builds over years of training and competition, success and failure. No-one can ever hope to know what goes on inside the mind of a horse or the soul of a rider. But watching the concentrated preparation of Capt Mark Phillips, as I did before Badminton 1981, gives a rare glimpse of the work, frustrations and skill that take a rider to the top – and the tension and emotions that keep him there.

Badminton Preparations

28 DECEMBER 1980

The weather in Gloucestershire was as hung-over as most of its inhabitants.

The big black horse stood by the gate in the corner of his field, head down, hooves impatiently pawing at the ground. It was cold and damp. His thick woolly winter coat kept out the worst of the east wind that clipped across that exposed hillside on the edge of the Cotswolds. Just a few feet away on the other side of the farmyard there was a warm straw-filled loosebox. No draughts would wrap around his legs in there, no rain settle between his shoulders or blanket his back. Admittedly there was freedom in his field, he could gallop and buck and roll with no walls to hem him in, and doze stoically under the low branches of the huge sycamore in the middle of the field. But he'd had enough of this spartan life. So while his human keepers sat down to a lunch of yet another variation of left-over Christmas turkey, he kept his station by the gate and demanded attention. The splosh of wellingtons through mud told him that the wait was almost over.

'Come on Lincoln.' Shelley Whitbourne's shrill voice cut through the afternoon gloom. At the sound of his name he pricked his ears in anticipation. Shelley unhooked the gate and walked up to him. There was no point in suddenly darting away and playing 'catch me if you can' as he had when he was a youngster; it had been fun then, but now all he wanted was to get back inside his warm stable. So he stood quietly while she clipped the leading rope onto his head-collar and then followed her through the gate, up the slope to the yard, onto the concrete, through the huge double-doors of the stable-block and inside to the warmth and smell of home. As he passed the other looseboxes a few horses bobbed their heads over the half-doors to see who was clattering through and disturbing their afternoon. The fourth door on the right, his door, was open. Inside the straw was deep and inviting – just asking to be rolled in. The hay-net swung on its hook, bursting at the seams with sweet stalks. Later there would be a warm bran mash, and then he'd sleep indoors for the first time in four months.

Tomorrow he'd wake to the clatter of buckets, the chatter of stable grooms and the rigid routine of a well-run yard. But more than that – he would have stretching before him four months of planned, rigorous training to make him one of the finest equine athletes in the country. For Lincoln, the big, black, bold eleven-year-old gelding, was the

The Range Rover Team grooms (*l to r*) Sandra, Shelley, Zena and Jane (*Jim Bennett*)

horse that Captain Mark Phillips had decided to ride at the Badminton Three-Day Event in April 1981, when his strength, ability and courage would be put to the supreme test. The events of the next fourteen weeks could be the most important in his life.

29 DECEMBER 1980

When Shelley threw a saddlecloth over his back at eight o'clock that morning and began the pattern of placing the saddle, buckling the girth and fitting the bridle, it was the first time he'd worn the old familiar clothes since last summer. That was at Fontainebleau where he'd gone as an individual to compete in the alternative games. His dressage had gone reasonably well; 63·8 points had left him in fourteenth position, but on the evening before the crosscountry he'd been declared lame and that was the end of that, except that the cause of the lameness had remained something of a mystery. Neither the British Team vet, Peter Scott-Dunn, nor Capt Phillips' own vet, Geoffrey Brain, could pinpoint anything. As Mark Phillips recalls somewhat ruefully, 'We never did get to the bottom of it; we went through the whole list – foot, leg, tendons, shoulder – there wasn't really a lot left. All the time we'd had him he'd never been taken lame – it was sickening really.' So Lincoln was sent home to Gatcombe Park where Geoffrey Brain took another look at the offending leg, the off fore, and suggested 'give everything a blister for good luck, and turn him out'. Which is what they'd done. Four months later, everything *looked* fine, but the question mark would be there, niggling in the background, every day until the end of the competition on 12 April.

That first day was a leisurely introduction to the rigours that were to follow. He still wore his shaggy coat and only had shoes on his front feet. His stomach was slack and his muscles flabby, so for half-an-hour he ambled through the woods on the west slopes of the farm, then after lunch Bernie Tidmarsh the blacksmith arrived to trim his feet and fit a new set of shoes all round. Tomorrow the real work would begin.

30 DECEMBER 1980

The countryside around Gatcombe is like a big dipper. It is impossible to travel anywhere within a five-mile radius without going up or down something at least one in ten. Mark reckons 'it's a bit like living on the side of a mountain; rotten for weather – but ideal for training horses'. After threequarters of an hour of steady walking with Shelley in the saddle along the tarmac lanes, up and down a few gentle hills, Lincoln was back in the stable. While he munched away on a bulging hay-net, Shelley took out her other two charges, Town and County and Going Places who, like Lincoln, are both part of the Range Rover-sponsored Team. There are never less than twelve horses in the Phillips' yard – usually more – all in the care of four girl grooms. They feed them, groom them, clean their tack, exercise them, travel with them to every show, and become protectively attached to their own special charges. Lincoln's groom had left before the winter, so in those first few days Shelley was trying to build up a relationship with her temperamental newcomer. She admits that she didn't really like him much to start with. He's a naturally arrogant, aloof horse who has never enjoyed the sort of sloppy fussing that so many of the others look for. 'He's a funny horse,' says Shelley, 'very sensitive and at times very annoying. You just have to take each day as it comes.'

That day was going to be something of a test. Lincoln had to be clipped out of his shaggy winter curls into a neat, cooler, hunter clip. He's quite calm about the process until you get to his head. 'Everyone said you'll never get his head clipped without a twitch,' recalls Shelley, 'but I thought, no, I'm going to try it. I just worked at it bit by bit. There was nobody else about so I couldn't get angry – if I had that would have been the end of it – I wouldn't have got anywhere.' The whole exercise took almost two hours. At the end of it Lincoln looked as though he was ready for work and Shelley thought she'd scored a minor triumph. As a concession she'd left his ears – they really were impossible to clip – but there hadn't been any tantrums or fights and they'd parted on reasonably good terms. From now on things could only get better.

31 DECEMBER 1980

Lincoln saw the old year out wearing new shoes, a newly-clipped coat and doing a walking circuit around Gatcombe that had increased to an hour. Over the next few days that would gradually build up until by 4 January he'd be walking for two hours a day, a steady rhythmic pace that strengthened his legs, loosened the joints, tightened his muscles – the sort of gentle physical build-up any athlete needs to get his body back in tune after months of inactivity. The big black horse became a familiar sight on his morning outings around the villages and hamlets surrounding Gatcombe, Nailsworth, Avening, Amberley and Box. At first the long haul up the testing one in seven chicane to Box village left him heaving and gasping like a chain smoker but by the end of the month he was taking it in his stride.

Throughout January and for the first week of February Shelley was the only person who rode Lincoln. The man who would pilot him around Badminton had only peered at him over the stable-door and monitored his progress as an observer. With so many horses to school, a farm to run and a diary full of official engagements, it's clearly convenient for Mark Phillips not to have to while away two valuable hours of every morning just swanning around the lanes of Gloucestershire. But there's sound psychological reasoning behind it too. Mark freely admits: 'If I'm riding a horse I tend to nag at them a little bit. I always want them to be bending a little bit one way then the other. I'm always working with them, getting at them, and I think they have enough of that when they start to work with me in the school on the basic dressage movements. But when they're out with the girls, although they might work quite hard physically, they're not under any mental strain at all. They can get on with trotting up the hills, shying at paper bags and bricks – just enjoying themselves.'

And even when he does start to work with them in the school, he still hands them over to the grooms afterwards for their daily hack round the lanes. Again it's convenient – while one horse is doing basic roadwork with a groom, another can be put through his paces in the school. If it sounds a bit like a conveyor belt, that is exactly what it is – but the strategy is still sound. 'It's a real advantage when I've been working with a horse and find I'm going down a blind alley – getting to the point where he is getting a mental block and I'm not getting any further. Then I won't ride him at all for two or three days. I'll sleep on it and think about what I'm doing wrong, and he can hack out and forget about it. Then we might start again and suddenly find the problem isn't as difficult as we thought it was. We were both just getting up-tight with each other.'

That's the sort of luxury that only a few riders can afford but it demonstrates the importance they place on keeping their horses happy. So while Mark Phillips rode other horses and got on with running the farm, Shelley did all the groundwork, and Lincoln was out having fun.

4 FEBRUARY 1981

At 7.30 am Mark Phillips downed his usual weight-watching breakfast of black coffee and half a grapefruit, read through the main stories in the morning papers, then went out into the vast stone-flagged hall to put on his riding 'gear'. The butler/valet had made a neat pile of leather chaps, riding boots and tweed cap on a chair in the hall. The chaps were pulled on over cord jeans, feet slipped easily into old boots that gaped at the sides where uppers no longer met bottoms and had splits in the leather that exposed his toes – but Mark is notorious in his family for never throwing anything away until it virtually falls to pieces – and these were his most comfortable boots! Finally the cap, so familiar a part of him that he'd feel – and look – undressed without it. Then out onto the gravel drive, into the blue Range Rover and off up the winding drive behind the house to the farm buildings and the stableyard. The routine was a carbon copy of the days before, and the days that would follow. What made *this* morning different was that he planned to ride Lincoln for the first time since Fontainebleau.

The indoor school at Gatcombe is a massive echoing hanger that serves as garage for the the horseboxes, cover for the tractors and trailers and dry store for fertilizer and small machinery as well as housing cavaletti and showjumps for the horses. In here they do their 'circuits and bumps' – his slang for the dressage exercises that take them round and round at the walk, trot and canter. Each day the rider asks for a little more bend, a little more flow, a little more perfection. It's a ritual that Lincoln knows well, and after six weeks of walking at a steady pace for two hours a day, he is ready to move on to stage two of the build-up. From this morning onwards the circuits and bumps would be a regular part of his daily routine.

As he walked into the school for the first time he had a good look round – ears pricked, nostrils flared, and a spring in his step that anticipated something a bit more energetic than boring walking.

He moved around quietly at first, getting the feel of the deep fibre under his feet; then as he was nudged gently into a trot he shot forward – all legs and exploding energy. After twenty minutes or so he was moving with more purpose, but still only listening with half an ear to what was being asked of him. He rode down the centre of the school – came to an almost square halt and the reins were dropped loose. 'That'll do for today' declared Mark. The big horse stretched his long neck, and blew hard down his nose showering everyone close by with a slobbery mist. It had been a hard twenty minutes' work – but the morning wasn't over. Shelley swapped places in the saddle with the Captain and rode him out to make up the rest of his daily two hours on the lanes and hills.

Mark's verdict on the morning was: 'He wasn't doing what you'd call "dressage" but I didn't expect that. What I was really pleased about was that he was feeling so well and strong. He really was bursting out of his skin with exuberance and good health. He was very strong when I started trotting; I thought he was going to buck for a minute and that I was going to be decanted before I'd even started. He was so full of himself that I couldn't really ride him forward at all – I was busy trying to restrain him all the time rather than being able to get any good paces out of him. But I'll be working him every day from now on so he should get more and more sensible – I hope!'

At this stage Lincoln was on three feeds a day of steamed rolled barley, nuts and about 8lb of oats, with as much hay as he wanted. The food and exercise were turning the grass fat into muscle, and the hours of walking hadn't shown up any weakness in the suspect leg. But that evening vet Geoffrey Brain came to check him over and what he found was, in Mark's words, 'disappointing. He found some hardening in his tendon which he couldn't really remember being there before. We'd just have to be careful – not do too much too soon. He thinks he'll be all right – but that's a worry we'll have to live with between now and Badminton.' It was a bad end to the day – and the start of the next morning wasn't much better. Lincoln had had an erratic session in the school: 'He's just being so stupid I can't do a thing with him' was Mark's frustrated reaction. 'He's just so tense we're not getting anywhere.'

An hour-and-a-half out in the country, a night to sleep on it, and on

Friday they were making progress. From the rider a more hopeful report: 'He's starting to relax. I'm beginning to get a better contact in my hands keeping him between my hand and leg. At last he's listening, now we can think about working on a few movements. Nothing too complicated – just shoulder-ins, ten- and twenty-metre circles, but all the while managing rhythm and balance.'

7 FEBRUARY 1981

A change of gear for Lincoln from second to third, with a bit of canter work in the school. It was all a bit phrenetic to start with as you might expect, but by now Lincoln had obviously acquired enough mental discipline to know that after the initial burst of enthusiasm he was expected to knuckle down and produce some concentrated effort. At the end of the session his rider was clearly pleased: 'He's still a bit excited about the cantering job – but gradually he's beginning to relax. I think by next week we'll be able to start doing a few counter canters with him, maybe even a little bit of lengthening, but the whole time keeping him steady and calm, keeping him balanced.'

11 FEBRUARY 1981

I was sitting in the middle of the covered school at Gatcombe on Classic Lines – affectionately known as Toad, because he is one! Beside me Hamish Cameron, the young New Zealand sheep-farmer who's spending a year with Mark Phillips to improve his riding and hopefully follow in the footsteps of Australian Andrew Hoy who beat a path to Gatcombe before him, and walked off with the Burghley trophy in 1979 riding Davey. 'Sickening, isn't it' said Hamish, in a tone that cloaked envy with admiration. What he was referring to was the combined action of man and horse that circled round and round us. Mark and Lincoln were working together in that unique state of concentrated harmony that comes when rider and horse are speaking the same language. Mark made the rider's job look effortless, and Lincoln responded with a swinging trot and a rhythmic canter that were a joy to watch. It was a short session – just ten minutes or so – but one of the most successful to date. And the rider couldn't have been more pleased. 'He's going better and better every day. I cantered him round the school in counter canter several times on each rein. He was getting more and more relaxed and coming safer and safer in my hand. I've kept the session short this morning because I'm a great believer in "little and often". I think that if they work hard for a short period of time, then in a funny sort of way they enjoy it. Like this morning – he had his ears pricked all the time and wasn't worried, he was really happy about his work. If I'd gone on and on at him eventually he would have become bored or fed-up or cross. We have ended up at cross-purposes, and then we'd have started to go backwards. So I stopped before we got to that stage and sent him out for a hack.'

FRIDAY, 13 FEBRUARY 1981

Unlucky for some – but not for Lincoln. Geoffrey Brain called to check his legs and pronounced them clean.

16 FEBRUARY 1981

A horse with Lincoln's scope and ability will think nothing of popping over a show jump at four foot six. So the casual observer may have found the elementary trotting poles and six-inch high fence that confronted Lincoln that morning something of an insult. Not a bit of it. As Mark explains, 'They were an exercise in psychology, not equitation. Lincoln is eleven now, so I'm not trying to teach him to jump because he's done it all before. All I'm working with is his attitude of mind.' Lincoln has always been a bold, enthusiastic jumper so no-one, least of all his rider, expected the morning's jumping to be a leisurely affair. He wiggled and screwed into the fence, and bucked out of it. After each landing Mark cantered him quietly round at one end of the school before turning for another approach. Each time he saw the fence Lincoln threw his head back, pranced on the spot, then launched himself at the poles. It was hardly a demonstration of world-class showjumping, but it didn't bother the Captain. 'He's bulging with excitement and anticipation, and I think there was probably a bit of worry there as well. It's almost as though he can't control himself. But he obviously enjoys it by the way he bucks and fools around afterwards.'

Each day for the rest of that week the jumps got higher and were arranged in a way that needed great concentration. First a small bounce of cross-poles, six inches high and nine feet apart, just enough to make him drop his head, take a good look and react instead of dashing off on landing. Then an avenue of five jumps built like a staircase. Each pole slightly higher than the one before, with a bounce between the first four, and a stride to the last, which stood at three foot six. By the end of the week the small course included a parallel and upright at three foot. He'd got all the initial 'fizz' out of his system, and was concentrating on each obstacle. There was nothing too complicated or too big, and the Phillips' philosophy was simple: 'I've spent the last two-and-a-quarter years riding him. He knows me, and I know him. If I can consolidate that, and improve what I've got by working on his attitude of mind, keeping him calm and relaxed all the time, then he'll take a lot of stopping. Because he's got all the ability in the world.'

21 FEBRUARY 1981

Stable duties started early that morning. By 6am all the horses had been fed, groomed and watered. Lincoln and some of his stable companions had their manes plaited and an extra bit of sheen worked onto their coats. By seven o'clock they were loaded into the lorry and

A corner of the tack room at the Gatcombe stables with Jane, Sandra and Shelley at work (*Jim Bennett*)

bumping their way down the farm track. Their destination – a small indoor jumping show at Urchinwood, some thirty-five miles away near Weston-super-Mare.

The programme for the day was to enter each of the horses in two combined training competitions – dressage and showjumping at novice standard. If anyone recognised the black horse as a possible Badminton contender they might well have wondered, after watching his first attempt, if he would ever make the competition. The dressage test was the novice horse trials test Number 12 – a combination of walk, trot and canter at its most elementary. When Lincoln entered the ring he clearly wasn't concentrating; every time he went from trot to canter he threw in an almighty buck, then in the showjumping that followed his performance was, in Mark's words, 'diabolical. I couldn't get him to settle to a rhythm. Every time he saw a fence he just stuck his head in the air and was off. He wasn't jumping too badly when he actually got to the fence, so we managed to negotiate a clear round – but it wasn't a very stylish operation! Nevertheless, he managed to finish in third place, and by the evening he'd settled down considerably. His second attempt at the dressage test was a much more collected affair. Again he chalked up a clear round showjumping, and this time won the class. It had been a most satisfactory day. In the Captain's words 'he thought that was the greatest thing since sliced bread. Nothing too difficult – just a nice outing for him. It's helped him get a lot of the stupidness out of his system.'

On the drive home, up the M5, it started to snow. The lights of the big lorry finally swung into the yard at Gatcombe just before ten o'clock. It had been a long session so tomorrow the horses would have a day off.

23 FEBRUARY 1981

By Monday the fall of snow that had looked so attractive on Sunday lay in grey ugly heaps on the side of the roads. The sting of the cold wind that blew through the Cotswolds had humans buried in warm layers with collars turned up, but it was a welcome relief to Lincoln as he trotted relentlessly up the twisting mile-long hill to Box village. When he reached the top, Shelley turned his head, led him back down the hill at a walk, then trotted back up a second time. While the air and ground froze, he sweated, and his stamina went up another ten points.

24 FEBRUARY 1981

Anyone who works closely with horses and looks for some measure of success in the eventing world has to develop the patience and philosophical calm of a saint. One outburst of anger at the wrong time during a training session could destroy a whole morning's work, and it's no use expecting horses to always comply with your carefully laid plans for a steady progress of work because they won't. Mark sums it up this way: 'Horses are like people – they're not machines. Whether they go well for you or badly, there's always a number of contributing factors. Not the least of which is which side of the bed *you* got out of.' Clearly both horse and rider got out on the right side of the bed that Tuesday morning. They worked in the school for twenty minutes and achieved the sort of harmony that made the grind of the past eight weeks worthwhile. Lincoln's concentration was keen, his paces fluent and accurate. His rider couldn't have been more pleased. 'This morning he rode better than he's done in all the time I've owned him. I don't think I could have got him any better – he was absolutely right on the spot. He's concentrating, thinking and listening, and the whole thing is starting to slot into place.'

With six weeks to go before Badminton everything was on schedule. Neither horse nor rider had any hang-ups. The only black cloud on the horizon was the weather. The ground had frozen solid. By mid-week there was no sign of a thaw and on 26 February, when Lincoln should have had his first gallop, he was restricted to the covered school, and the familiar hour-and-a-half hack through the lanes. It was disappointing – but not disastrous, providing the thaw came soon.

David Hunt is regarded by many event riders in Britain as one of the
best dressage trainers in the country. His technique is admired, his
opinion valued, so when he arranged a training session at the indoor
school at Badminton twelve of the riders hoping to compete in the
three-day event turned up to be put through their paces – including
Mark and Lincoln.

Each combination rode the full FEI test as they would in the
competition itself under the critical eyes of the judge, David Hunt, and
the unforgiving eye of the television cameras. As with so many other
sports, the electronic gadgetry of the video recorder has proved an
invaluable aid to training. However the riders may *think* they rode,
they can *see* the good, the bad and the indifferent when the tapes are
replayed later in the day.

The session began well for Mark. In the practice arena the horse was
relaxed and willing, and looked as though he would give a good
account of himself before the cameras. But then there was a delay –
and as Mark recalls things went from bad to worse: 'I had a longer gap
than I thought between warming-up and going in to do the test, and I
think he must have got a bit cold in his back, because when I finally
went into the ring and started the test, I couldn't sit on him. Every time
I went to sit in the saddle, his back just dipped away from me as if he
was saying "oh – don't sit in the saddle". I couldn't ride at all. I just
had to sit there and suffer and just trot through the test without asking
for anything. It was a disaster.' And not one that he could just walk
away from. That evening, over dinner, the tapes were replayed while
all twelve riders sat in judgment on each other and David Hunt pulled
them to pieces. 'It was awful. I said he's got cold in his back and went
stiff on me. David Hunt said it was because he wasn't going forward
into my hands correctly balanced. In the end it was probably six of one
and half-a-dozen of the other.' Whatever the reason it hadn't been a
very constructive day. The only positive thought that Mark could
salvage from the day was 'better make a mistake here now than in five
weeks time'.

Sunday morning brought the first signs of a thaw and found Lincoln
back in the lorry on his way to Wylye in Wiltshire, for an indoor
jumping competition.

On the first round he spooked at every other fence, but still managed
to go clear. By the second circuit he'd calmed down, and went clear
again. When he entered the ring for the final competition of the day he
looked like a horse that was ready to do a workmanlike job, and set off
with style and purpose. Over the first half of the course he established
a steady rhythm, met each fence well, and landed clear. Then suddenly
he put in a stop. Mark turned him, made another approach, and

Lincoln cleared it effortlessly. He went on to finish the round without further incident. It had only taken a split second, but it showed up a major flaw in his concentration and his rider was understandably furious. 'He obviously had it in his mind he wasn't going to jump the fence and was off back home. *I* was looking at the jump but *he* wasn't, and when I said "Oi – there's a fence there", he said "not on your life Dad" and that was that.'

On the drive back to Gatcombe the weather outside the lorry was as depressing as the atmosphere inside. It had been a disappointing two days and as the week drew to a close the morale in the Phillips' camp dropped to a new low.

2 MARCH 1981

When an event horse is in training, every stage of its progression from a grass-fat plodder to a racing-fit competitor is carefully plotted and calculated. Weeks of walking to tighten and strengthen muscle and sinew; the steady introduction of trotting to build muscle and expand the lungs. Each day as the horse gets fitter and stronger the work load is increased, mental attitude and physical stamina building together on a steady upward curve of athletic performance. No two people train their horses the same, and Mark's system has been geared to suit not just his own theories about fitness and training, but also the facilities and landscape around him. His horses don't gallop every day, and when they do it's a steady, strong pull up one of the Gatcombe hills to exercise their lungs without putting too much strain on their limbs.

By the first week in March, Lincoln should have had at least two gallops worked into his schedule, but the snow and ice of late February had left the ground rock-hard so gallops were impossible. And when the thaw finally came it brought endless rain which turned the ground into a bog. The morning of Monday, 2 March, was overcast – but dry; although the ground still wasn't ideal, Lincoln's training programme couldn't be held up any longer, so after a fifteen-minute work-out in the school he was walked quietly down through the woods to the start of the Gatcombe Gallops.

The park in front of Gatcombe House drops steadily away between two folds of hills, past a small lake and finally disappears at the bottom of the valley where it is swallowed up by the dense undergrowth and spindly trees of a young plantation. From the boundary of the wood to the front of the house it's a good half-mile of steady uphill work. As Lincoln set off from the bottom of the hill he took a hold on the bit and thundered over the exposed shale on the path. When his hooves hit the grass of the parkland he changed gear and steadily accelerated up the hill splattering mud and rain-soaked turf behind him. At the top he was blowing with the effort, but the slow walk back down the slope brought his breathing back to normal, and then he was off for a second uphill run. The exercise was repeated three days later on Thursday, and again on Sunday. Each time his huge lungs coped more easily with the effort like a huge powerhouse being stoked up with reserves – the only thing to suffer was the park. It rained steadily all week, and as Lincoln galloped relentlessly through mud and water he turned the path across the grass into a quagmire. Mark stood at his front door and viewed the scene philosophically. Lincoln may have done untold damage to the ground but he had to have his canter work. When something as important as the Badminton Three-Day Event was at stake, nothing was sacrosanct – not even the view from Gatcombe Park!

9 MARCH 1981

With four weeks to go before the start of Badminton week, the tension in competitive yards all over Britain was building up as trainers and riders began the final countdown to 9 April. For most horses fitness was no longer a problem. At this stage it was a silly injury during training, a sudden lameness or infection that could bring the whole machine grinding to a halt.

At Badminton itself the course-builders were on target with the construction of their formidable solid-timber obstacles. Foreign competitors started to arrive to settle their horses to the English climate and at Gatcombe Lincoln maintained a steady, daily two-hour schedule of dressage, jumping and hacking, with a hard canter in front of the house twice a week. The competitions he'd done to date were all potboilers geared mainly to give him a day out, get the frustrations out of his system and put confidence back into his stride. None of them were done in the intense atmosphere of major competition. But from now on the pressure would start to build, and each day's performance would be judged as an indication of his potential to tackle the main goal in April. The shift in attitude was subtle – but it was enough to make a day's competition of dressage at Wylye on 9 March something of a yardstick.

Looking around the lorry park you might almost think you'd stumbled on an important international competition tucked away in the quiet of the English countryside. There were competitors from France and Italy, as well as most of the top British competitors, and the World Champion, American Bruce Davidson, who'd flown into Britain just four days before with his brilliant grey horse Might Tango.

Mark planned to ride two tests. One in the morning as a warm-up, with the major FEI test – the one he would ride at Badminton – in the afternoon. Although the test was to be ridden under cover in an indoor arena, the horses had to warm-up outside and, like the rest of the country, Wylye had been rained on for almost a week. Everything was waterlogged, and within an hour the only practice field available to the riders had been churned into a mudflat. Lincoln has quite a loose, extravagant movement, and was demonstrably unhappy at having to splash through the sticky conditions for twenty minutes. When he went into the arena to be judged the horse was still unhappy, and the result pleased no-one – least of all Mark. 'I think it can only be described as a disaster' was his verdict. 'I can't tell you how many noughts I scored – but basically, we barely performed the test.' In these circumstances it would be so easy to lose your temper, blame the horse for not concentrating, for letting you down. Most people would understand the need to lash out and loose off some of your frustrations. But riders know that's the last thing they can do. It's no good upsetting a horse further by a show of temper, and you can't take them to one side and give them a pep-talk! Instead Lincoln was left to stand quietly in his box while his rider watched the rest of the competition, and looked for somewhere dry to ride-in for the afternoon session.

Three hours later they were warming up again – this time on an all-weather surface outdoor arena. The going was one hundred per cent better, and Lincoln settled to the job. He rode the test well, a complete turnabout from the morning, and clocked up a score of 156·5 which put him in the lead. It looked as though that was how the day would end, but then Bruce Davidson entered the arena. If either horse or rider were suffering from jet lag after their marathon journey from Pennsylvania, it didn't show. They swung into a near-perfect demonstration of how the test should be ridden, and the score of 167·5 pipped Lincoln into second place. Mark was still well pleased with the way Lincoln had performed, but Bruce Davidson had clearly hoisted his flag as the man they were all going to have to beat, and the Phillips' camp knew Lincoln wouldn't have two chances at getting it right at Badminton.

15 MARCH 1981

Shelswell Park sits snugly in the gentle hills of Oxfordshire tucked away down single-track lanes just north of Bicester. Every March, two weeks before the estate cattle are turned loose to graze on its lush grass, the Park plays host to the Midland Bank sponsored horse trials with classes at intermediate and open intermediate standard. It's a good course for those young horses making their debut after qualifying out of novice classes. But more than that, like so many of the one-day events held towards the end of March, it provides a perfect testing ground for some of the potential runners at Badminton.

Lincoln had been plaited and groomed at 6.30am, fed by 7.00am and three hours later was bucking and kicking like a two-year-old on the end of a lunge rein at Shelswell.

The weather at Gatcombe had maintained its sorry wet state and there'd been no opportunity to get the horse out of the indoor school and into the flat practice field to work on his dressage. 'They need to get used to having the wind up their tails and the rain on their backs,' explains Mark. 'All the things that are likely to distract them. But it's been so wet we've had to keep on working indoors. Hardly what you'd call an ideal preparation for his first one-day event of the season.'

Fortunately there was neither wind nor rain to distract any of the competitors. It was cloudy but dry, and the occasional break in the clouds let the horses feel the sun on their backs. Lincoln was due to ride his dressage test just before noon. As Mark quietly worked him on the practice ground, it was obvious that Shelswell was being used as a pipe-opener for most of the top competition horses. Clarissa Strachan was there with her two horses Delphy Kingfisher and Merry Sovereign, Rachel Bayliss and Mystic Minstrel, Lucinda Prior-Palmer with Mairangi Bay, Mark Todd, Richard Meade and Jane Holderness-Roddam. It was like a roll-call for the British team selectors. And moving quietly among them all, Bruce Davidson and his unmistakable grey. 'Why is he here so early,' I asked. 'Quite simple,' I was told, 'he wants to win Badminton!' Mark worked Lincoln steadily for threequarters of an hour. Glancing down at his watch he nodded to the groom Shelley as if to say 'that'll do' and, letting Lincoln relax on a long rein, made his way between the string barriers to the field where the four dressage arenas had been marked out.

Jane with the Range Rover team horsebox and the tack needed for a one-day event (*Jim Bennett*)

On the way into the field he passed Clarissa Strachan who was beaming from ear to ear. 'Good test?' he enquired. 'Not bad' was the response, which somewhat underplayed the fact that she'd just ridden what was to be the best test of the day and place her in the lead with a score of 32.

At major three-day events everything runs quite literally like clockwork, with riders starting each section of the competition exactly on time. Not so at some of the one-day trials. At Shelswell they were running almost fifteen minutes late and riders were left with the dilemma of not wanting to overwork their horses and take them off the boil, but equally not wanting to let them stand around and get cold or bored. So for a quarter of an hour Lincoln walked round and round the edge of the field with a blanket over his quarters while his rider talked with other competitors who were in the same boat – each trying to stay calm and pretend that the delay didn't really matter.

At last the steward called out Number 311 and Lincoln was ridden into the arena. For eight minutes every movement was scrutinised by the judge, and recorded by the rider. When they left the arena they'd achieved second place with a score of 34 and Mark admitted to being 'quite pleased with him. He was much more safe and secure in my hands and didn't go fragile on me at all.' There had been just three small hiccups. 'After he halted at the start he put in a little canter, and his first canter strike-off proper was a bit of an explosion. Then towards the end after the medium trot he came back to me too much to a walk when he should have gone into a working trot. But they were only little things, on the whole he's very settled and I'm very pleased. If I can get him going regularly like that over the next few weeks, I can build on it and ask for some real brilliance.'

As the day wore on the crowds thinned out and the temperature dropped. Lincoln stood in the massive blue Range Rover Team horsebox and shivered – but not with the cold. 'It's just his nerves,' said Shelley. 'He'll be all right once he knows he's going to start showjumping.'

It was another two hours before he entered that second stage of the competition, and before he started Mark knew he was going to be difficult. 'The ground is a bit sticky,' he said. 'That means he'll just stick his nut in the air and fight me all the way round. We'll just have to keep going – and hope.'

His prediction of a difficult ride was not far off the mark. He landed awkwardly over the first, stuck his head in the air on the approach to the fifth, took a long look at the double and pecked slightly on landing and made a rush at number eight, the brick wall. He finished the round clear, still in second position, with a four-word report from the rider 'that was *hard* work'.

Maybe, but as in any one-day event the hardest work was still to come – flying over twenty-three solid fences round a three-thousand metre course in an optimum time of five-and-threequarter minutes. Mark had walked the course early that morning and already ridden round once on another Range Rover Team horse, Town and Country, so the route was fixed firmly in his mind, as were all the likely pitfalls.

Before either could set off there was yet another change of 'clothes'. For the dressage test Lincoln had been ridden in a flat-sided dressage saddle, with an eggbut snaffle and crossed noseband. When they entered the showjumping arena Lincoln's saddle had been changed to a well-padded jumping saddle and a running martingale had been attached to the reins – while his rider was resplendent in the red jacket of a British team member.

But for the crosscountry phase everything was geared for speed and comfort so, in addition to the saddle and bridle, Lincoln had each leg dressed in specially-coated crepe bandages wrapped over padding – they would protect his legs and give his tendons support. Shelley took her time binding each leg. The blue bandages were made of a stretchy waterproof fabric. Tie them too loose and they'd drop off and hinder the horse, too tight and they could do untold damage. Shelley told me that one day they'd tied some of the fabric around one of the other groom's arms and pulled it tight, just to see what happened. 'Within minutes her arm was going blue – the blood just wasn't circulating.' Getting it just right came from skilful practice. She slipped an index finger between skin and padding to judge the tension; when it was right she began stitching the ends in place – much safer than relying on tapes or velcro which could fly loose in the heat of the moment and cause trouble.

The needle and cotton then transferred to the bridle. On the second plait back from the poll I could just make out a small loop of black cotton. Shelley proceeded to stitch the top of the bridle to the loop 'just in case the Captain comes off' she explained. 'If the Captain holds on to the reins and the bridle comes loose it won't pull off the horse's head and leave him free to dash off.' Simple, but effective – and hopefully a precaution that wouldn't be put to the test!

Mark emerged from the changing-room at the front of the lorry wearing his familiar black silk over the crash helmet, and an ancient white polo-necked sweater that had so many holes along the right hand shoulder that it looked as though the moths had been feasting on it for months. 'Another one of your lucky talismans?' I asked. 'Not really' he grinned, 'I just can't bear to throw anything away until it absolutely falls to pieces.' I knew what he meant, but from the way Princess Anne eyed it I felt that its days were numbered.

Her Royal Highness had arrived midway through the morning accompanied as usual by her detective and the two family dogs, Laura the lurcher and Random the Dumfrieshire hound. As Mark was legged into the saddle the public-address system boomed out the tally on Bruce Davidson's round. He'd had a run-out halfway round the course, so 20 penalties to add to his dressage score of 39 – a disappointing result.

As Princess Anne drove along the edge of the course to a vantage point from where she could see most of the fences on the undulating figure-of-eight course, her husband and Lincoln jogged steadily down to the start. Clissy Strachan had gone fast and clear on Delphy Kingfisher so he knew he had everything to ride for.

As the starter dropped his arm, Lincoln pulled strongly off the line and flashed effortlessly over for the first three fences. If he was going to have any problems at all it would be in this first half of the course over fences four and five – a set of angled rails at the top of a small rise. As the fences loomed up he rode Lincoln steadily – almost showjumping in – to make sure that he never took his eyes off the first part of the fence and wasn't surprised by the second obstacle, which came up quickly after a sharp left-hand bend. They were over safely, and Lincoln's bold jumping made nothing of the rest of the course. He finished the round still full of running with his rider full of compliments 'he really went well for me, he got into a good rhythm, and was pulling strongly into the fences as if he really meant business – he didn't look or feel like stopping once'.

Making their way back to the lorry with Lincoln gently steaming through his anti-sweat rug, the tannoy boomed out the best news of the day. Lincoln had gone round the course just fractionally faster than Delphy Kingfisher, enough to put him in the lead. While Lincoln was being washed down and rugged up for his journey home, Mark sat down to his 'lunch' at 4.30. As usual he hadn't eaten anything all day, but now that the tension of the day was over he was ravenous. He tucked into Coca Cola, two hard-boiled eggs, salad sandwiches and cold grilled sausages. At five o'clock the weather finally broke. Leaden grey clouds rolled in from Oxford, it started to pour with rain again, but nothing could wipe the satisfied smile off Mark's face. As Lincoln was led up the ramp into the box, his rider slapped him on the rump and declared 'I just can't believe that the old donkey has actually won.'

16 MARCH 1981

On Monday, Lincoln had a day off. The girls in the yard made a fuss of him and called him 'The Champ'. In the afternoon the vet came to inspect his legs and passed them A1. Whatever had made him lame at Fontainebleau the previous year hadn't been resurrected by the gallop around Shelswell. Everyone heaved a sigh of relief – and for the rest of that week the training programme slipped quietly back into gear.

For the first half of the week Mark and Princess Anne drove like 'yo-yos' up and down the M4 between their home and the studios of London Weekend Television. LWT had spent a year making a film about the Captain, and now that they'd reached the final stages he was needed to record the commentary and approve the final cuts. So it was

Thursday before Mark sat on Lincoln again. It was a day of good news and bad news. The good news was that it stopped raining long enough for Lincoln to be schooled outside in the field for the first time that year. The bad news was that foot-and-mouth disease was confirmed on a farm in Jersey and restrictions placed on the movement of all animals from Ringwood Market in Hampshire. While Lincoln worked on turns and transitions, farmers throughout the country held their breath and prayed that the outbreak wouldn't hit the mainland.

21 MARCH 1981

The rain came down in stair-rods. The horses hated it – so did their riders – but the morning routine went on without interruption. By 2 o'clock everyone had dried out and settled down to a 'wet afternoon in'. The horses munched hay and ignored the rattle of rain on the roof, while Mark watched the Rugby International on television. But the peace didn't last long. A fire broke out in one of the barns and for two hours it was literally all hands to the pump to save the building. Fortunately there were no straw bales in the barn, just loose straw on the floor – and little doubt about how it started. 'I think it was just kids sheltering from the rain,' he says. 'I suspect they had a smoke – and just accidentally set fire to the straw. It didn't do too much damage but instead of having a nice peaceful evening, I got in after ten, and the poor old Fire Brigade didn't finish damping down till about 2 am.' So much for a quiet evening in!

The following morning he took two horses to a novice one-day event near Yeovil, and a further outbreak of foot-and-mouth was confirmed near Yarmouth on the Isle of Wight. In the horse world they took the precaution of cancelling a number of competitions in southern England, though at Badminton the course-builders worked on. If the disease spread to the mainland everything would be cancelled but while a strip of water held the virus at bay the preparations went on uninterrupted.

25 MARCH 1981

If Lincoln had started to become bored with his strict training routine, he concealed it well, but this morning there was no pretence, just a total breakdown in concentration and effort. 'It's what I call a real "don't touch me" day,' said Mark with resignation. 'Every time I touch his mouth he went "oh", and every time I put my leg to him he went "oh". There was no way I could get him to do a thing. So instead of a ten-minute job, I suppose it must have taken me an hour to get any sense out of him.'

A steady canter through the length of the Park took some of the tension out of him, but when horse and rider met again next morning, Mark knew it would have to be a case of 'softly, softly'. Anyone who feels that getting a horse to compete is just a matter of building up muscle, then aiming them at the fences, should have watched the careful psychological coaxing that went on over the next two days. 'I had to repair some of the damage and get him really settled again' said Mark. 'I just couldn't afford to have another argument with him on either Thursday or Friday. I wanted him calm, and confident, ready for his next one-day event on Sunday.'

29 MARCH 1981

With just nine days to go before the start of Badminton Week, the horse trials at Brigstock in Northampton provided a last opportunity for many of the entrants to give their horses a serious work-out under competitive conditions. The twenty-eight fences on the crosscountry course aren't as daunting as those at Badminton, but they're sufficiently challenging to make this outing something of a curtain-raiser to the main event.

When Mark let down the ramp at the side of the Range Rover Team lorry, two horses emerged from it – Lincoln, as expected, and Persian Holiday. 'Percy' had spent the winter with Mark's parents, being hunted with the Duke of Beaufort's hounds. While Lincoln had been the centre of attention at Gatcombe, Mark's sister Sarah and his mother Mrs Anne Phillips had taken on the job of getting Percy fit around the lanes of Great Somerford. Did this mean that Percy was to make another appearance at Badminton? 'I don't know,' was the cautious reply. 'Let's just see how he goes today.'

Percy of course had seen it all before. Over a career that spanned almost ten years he'd been one of the most consistently successful horses in the Phillips' stable with a whole string of trophies and ribbons to his credit. As he faced the prospect of yet another dressage test followed by showjumping and then a dash across country, his attitude was decidedly phlegmatic. Lincoln, in contrast, was full of beans. While Persian Holiday waited calmly to perform what turned out to be an immaculate dressage test, Lincoln thrashed about on the end of a lunge rein, bucking and rearing like a rodeo act. 'That's quite normal for him' was Mark's reaction. 'Put him on the end of a piece of string and he loops the loop, but it gets all the tensions out of his system. If he had to do that with me on his back it would just make him neurotic. But this way he takes it out of himself, not the rider, and when I eventually sit on him he's ready to accept the bit and do some work – hopefully.'

Lincoln's dressage had been timed to start at 12.30pm. Three-quarters of an hour before, horse and rider began their 'warm-up'. At five minutes to go Lincoln was 'like velvet' – but a hitch in the proceedings meant a delay of almost fifteen minutes and by the time they finally entered the arena he'd gone 'off the boil' and was clearly bored by the whole procedure. His mark was 42 – no disgrace by any means but, for his rider, disappointing. 'When he started this morning

I really thought he was going the best he's ever gone. But once he got bored he started to lean on my hands; that made him lose balance, and then he got tense – it was just a vicious circle. After Shelswell I expected something good, but now he's taken a step backwards and that's just a bit disheartening.'

The next stage of the afternoon didn't do much to lift spirits. Persian Holiday had ten faults showjumping after a disaster at the last fence and dropped down the placings. But no rider can allow disappointment with one horse to affect the chances of another. If he took any emotions at all with him into the ring for Lincoln's round, it was only the determination not to make the same mistake twice. He didn't and finished with a clear round.

Two heavy rain showers had altered the going dramatically on the crosscountry course from the conditions that existed the evening before when most riders had walked round. Early competitors found the ground deep and soft, but towards the end of the day many of the take-off points had been churned into a boggy, clinging morass. The bullfinch took a particularly bad hammering and had a number of

Mark riding Persian Holiday through the water at Brigstock in March 1981 – the last competition before the Badminton event (*Jim Bennett*)

horses sprawling into it on their chests after a greasy take-off. Persian Holiday made heavy weather of the course and was 'a bit argumentative' over the early fences. He went clear and finished in seventh place, but as he was led back into the stable after the run, still sweating and heaving, Mark was clearly unhappy. He sat on a pile of straw bales and talked the course through, stride for stride, fence by fence, with Princess Anne and anxiously watched as the big chestnut horse came all too slowly back to a normal rate of breathing.

The general air of gloom was relieved by the appearance of Hamish Cameron claiming that Mark owed him £5. 'How do you work that out?' he asked. 'Simple,' said Hamish. 'When you're teaching you're always saying that every time you see my hands come up when I'm jumping you'll fine me £5.00 – well I just saw you hail a cab [fling the whole arm in the air] going over the ski jump – so you owe me a fiver.' The debt was mentally chalked up on the slate, while Mark considered the next vital question of the day – whether or not to run Lincoln in the rapidly deteriorating conditions. 'He's not a horse that likes deep going,' he explained. 'His balance is very important to him. After Shelswell he's so full of confidence that if he just slipped and frightened himself here – we'd look really stupid. And besides, it's just not worth risking something important like Badminton for the sake of a bad mistake at a one-day event – not now we're so close.' But there were no real disasters on the course, and as no rider ever expects perfect conditions, just before five o'clock Lincoln was saddled-up and prepared for the last phase of the day.

After his performance in the dressage arena it was clear that he wasn't going to repeat the success of Shelswell and win, but that wasn't what his rider wanted. 'I'd like him to finish third,' he said, 'and I'll tell you why later.' Princess Anne cast her eyes heavenwards and said 'It's just him being superstitious about numbers! He thinks sevens are lucky, and eights unlucky. Let's just hope they don't give him an eight at Badminton, or we'll probably never get him out of the stable.' The remark was made in good humour, but proved to be uncannily prophetic.

Lincoln made his way to the starting-box just after ten past five. He was being ridden in a running martingale, grackle and thick german snaffle – and the combination evidently suited him. He set off like a rocket and pulled strongly into each fence from start to finish. A slight slip in front of the bar before the pheasant feeder provided the only anxious moment – but it didn't break his rhythm or his nerve and when the pair galloped over the finishing line Mark was beaming. 'He just went from strength to strength,' was his verdict. 'In fact I think that's the best he's ever gone – I really do.'

When the trophies were handed out at the end of the day Lincoln collected a rosette for third place – exactly as the Captain had hoped. Why third? 'Quite simple,' he said. 'When I won Badminton on Great

Ovation in '71 and '72, I was first and then third at the two warm-up competitions on both occasions. It was the same with Columbus in 1974. He was first at Downlands, third at Windsor, then won Badminton.' Mark's superstitions about numbers are viewed sceptically by the rest of the family, but when they doubt his reasoning he points to what happened with Persian Holiday in 1977. He was first at Rushall, then second at Brigstock, and in the Badminton Championships when Mark was well fancied to win the competition for the fourth time, his reins broke in Huntsman's Close and he was eliminated. But Lincoln had now notched up two results which followed the winning streak and even if no-one else noted the significance, as far as Mark was concerned it was a good omen.

30 MARCH 1981

Ever since 1968 when Mark took part in his first Badminton on Rock On, he's followed the same ritual pattern in the week before the competition. He takes his Badminton horse (or horses) down the M5 to Devon to put the finishing touches to their combined performance at Great Rapscott, the South Molton home of his friend and trainer, Bertie Hill. The change of pace and scenery make it something of a

Lincoln in his last pre-Badminton work-out at Brigstock, 1981, where he finished third (*Jim Bennett*)

working holiday, and there's no doubt that the soft Devon air and relaxed hospitality dilute many of the 'pre-match' tensions that might otherwise creep into those last vital days.

He'd planned to leave Gatcombe together with Lincoln, Persian Holiday and the groom Shelley, at 1.30pm on Monday afternoon. In the morning there had been that anxious moment when both horses were walked out of their boxes and 'trotted up' on level ground to make sure there were no lumps, bumps or signs of lameness from the previous day's exertions at Brigstock. But both were one hundred per cent, so the grooms began loading the lorry with enough equipment and food to last them a week.

While the girls looked after the horses, Capt Phillips spent the morning working on the farm, moving cattle, buying in hay and attending to all the administrative minutia that was essential to keep the farm running in his absence.

1.30pm came – and went – and the jobs just kept piling up. It was 10.30 at night before the lorry rolled down the drive and headed west, and the small hours of the morning before they arrived at South Molton.

Everyone, the horses included, had something of a lie-in the next day and a leisurely start to the week. A quiet walk around the hills and lanes for two hours was topped by twenty minutes just standing in the cool water of the river that runs along the boundary of the Hill's farm. The horses were relaxed, the foot-and-mouth outbreak had been contained by the Ministry and all threats of cancellation at Badminton lifted. With just seven days to go everything was set for a week of concentrated effort and the daily routine of training went on much the same as before.

The flat meadow below Rapscott provided the perfect schooling arena, and the one-in-six Devon hills surrounding them an ideal 'mountaineering course' for topping up the strength already built into legs and lungs.

After lunch the horses relaxed – and so did their rider. With neither the farm nor official business to make demands on his time, Mark and Bertie indulged in yet another pre-Badminton ritual, and went fishing. North Devon is famous for the salmon and trout that course through its rivers, with the Torridge almost within casting distance of Rapscott. It's the one and only time in the year that Mark goes fishing and, as well as being a ritual, it's become something of a standing joke. 'In all the years I've been coming here,' he explained, 'I've never caught a thing. I'm determined to sooner or later, but in the meantime it's a good way of switching off.'

On Friday morning the horses were driven for half-an-hour north of Rapscott to Bratton Down – a string of fields perched high on the edge of Exmoor where Bertie maintains a complete steeplechase and hunter trial course. It's about as exposed as you can get up there. The wind rattles in off the Atlantic coast and chills everything on those exposed, north-facing slopes. If either horse needed an excuse to play up during their dressage work, the weather gave them plenty. The wind niggled around them, and the air was cold and damp with a fine veil of moorland drizzle. But Percy performed with the calm and willingness that's made him a dressage champion, and Lincoln did his best to please at what he obviously finds the least enjoyable of the three disciplines. To round off the morning they were given a gallop around the field and then popped over a few small jumps for fun. Later in the day Mark confirmed that he still hadn't made a decision one way or the other about taking Percy to Badminton. For many riders, just having one horse qualified for Badminton would be enough; to have two would be something of a luxury. But as he explained, Percy was by way of a safety net. 'If anything happened to Lincoln then I'd certainly run him – but apart from that it will depend very much on the going. If it's like a bog patch then there's no way I'd enter him. But if we have a run of dry days, and I thought he'd enjoy the outing, then I'd run him as a last fling because after this season I intend to retire him.' So in many ways, although Percy's training was as demanding as Lincoln's, there wasn't as much pressure on him to emerge as the number one contender from the Phillips' yard when the entries were finally confirmed on Wednesday, 8 April. It was Lincoln that carried their expectations – and with only four days to go, how did he rate?

Mark was cautious but objective. 'In his dressage he's very nearly going well. I haven't tried to teach him anything new, just consolidate what he can do already, but I know I haven't got it truly established yet. His canter strike-offs aren't as relaxed as they could be, his rein-back's aren't too good, nor are his halts. He tends to get tense in his back, go hollow and stick his nut in the air. I'll keep working at it – but not under too much pressure. The last thing I want is for him to get worried about anything. At this stage he's got to feel relaxed, because if he's not relaxed now outside the arena I've got no hope when we get inside the ring with the stands flapping, the boards, the crowds and the judges.'

And what about his jumping – surely after Shelswell and Brigstock he *had* to be confident about that? Again, there was caution in his answer. 'He's just starting to get himself warmed-up but he's a difficult horse to school in cold blood, so over the first two or three practice fences he'll back himself off and just hop over them, or even stop, so when we're schooling it's very difficult to get him enthusiastic about the job. But at a three-day event it's easy because you've got the steeplechase course to get him going before the crosscountry fences. In some ways one of the most difficult fences for him at Badminton is the

Persian Holiday's dressage test, Badminton 1981. With empty stands he failed to rise to the occasion

first fence on the steeplechase course, but by the time he's jumped two or three he'll be flying. He's certainly fit enough to run for his life, and the thing I'm really pleased about is that he's not at all worried about life this year.'

To hear a rider talking about the psychological state of his horse would probably sound a bit neurotic to someone not involved with the sport. But when the partnership of rider and horse have to face the Badminton test of physical endurance and courage together, it's important that each half of the team respects and understands the other half. No horse can tell a rider how it feels, it can only hope to have a jockey who's sufficiently sensitive to read its moods and react to them. Watching Mark at work with Lincoln, there was no doubt that such a mutual understanding exists. But would it be enough to make them winners. 'In my heart of hearts I don't think so,' was the candid reply. 'I understand that the course is going to be less complicated this year with fences that are big but straightforward, and more galloping in between so if the going is half-decent they might get ten or twelve rounds inside the optimum time. Which means, and I could be very wrong, but I think the dressage marks could be very important this year. Obviously we've got to jump a clear round, but assuming he can do that, I still think he's going to need a lot of luck at Badminton this time.' His reaction was pessimistic – but realistic.

Eighty competitors would arrive at Badminton, including some of the greatest horse/rider combinations in Britain and a strong contingent of overseas competitors headed by world champion, Bruce Davidson, with just one goal in view – to win at Badminton. In the circumstances not one of them, Mark included, would be foolish enough to rate their chances publicly – whatever they might wish for privately.

On Friday evening Princess Anne drove herself down to Devon bringing her ever-present detective, and the Captain's running shoes.

4 APRIL 1981

The weather was warm and sunny, an atmosphere reflected in the mood at Rapscott. After a week of concentrated effort Mark took stock of the situation and decided that 'perhaps I was over-doing it a bit – asking too much of them, particularly Lincoln'. So Saturday was a 'quiet and happy day'. With the sun on his back Lincoln relaxed into a morning's work that made no demands on him, mentally or physically. 'We did a few transitions, nice simple stuff, without asking for any extensions, and then I lobbed him over a few poles before going off on a steady ride around the hills.'

Tucked into the side of one of those hills is a local beauty spot,

No – not a late night. Nerves before the start of Phase A at Badminton, 1981

Charles Bottom, with a restaurant bordered by an inviting grassbank. In keeping with the switched-off feeling to the morning, the riders and horses stopped for a coffee break. While Lincoln and Percy nibbled at the lawns, Mark and his groom savoured the early spring sunshine. They rounded off the morning with a gentle stroll back to the farm, and a paddle in the cool refreshing water of the river.

In spite of the sunshine Saturday afternoon found everyone indoors watching television. The Grand National was the first attraction and the Boat Race next, followed by one of Mary Hill's farmhouse teas. 'But I think I must have eaten too much' admits Mark, 'and what with being stuck in all afternoon, I just felt grotty – so I went for a run, something I haven't done for ages.' His route took him down across the valley from the farm, through the meadow and up the steep hill on the opposite side. He admits to being 'a bit puffed at one stage', but the sudden burst of energy marked an end to the day off, and on Sunday the horses went back to their regime of schooling, jumping and trotting up and down the hills. At the end of the morning the two animals were sweating and blowing with the effort but like athletes they had reached a peak of physical fitness and each day's work pushed back the limits to their stamina.

The fish in the Torridge still weren't running, or obliging, so on Sunday afternoon Bertie Hill and his pupil went horse-hunting, and a visit to a local farm produced two more youngsters for the Phillips' yard. They hadn't intended to buy, but as Mark says, 'You can drive thousands of miles and not see what you want. Then suddenly, something turns up.' What 'turned up' in that Devon farmyard were a two- and three-year-old described by Mark as 'two of the nicest horses I have seen for a long time. They're lovely, big, scopey horses with bags of quality.' If they live up to that confident description perhaps in a few years time they'll make the return trip back to Devon to be trained at Bertie Hill's for one of the major events. But as Monday dawned and Badminton Week slipped steadily into focus, Lincoln and Percy were the centre of attention. After fourteen weeks of concentrated effort to blend obedience with style, build muscle power and confidence, their training had come to an end. 'I can't get them any fitter than they are,' said Mark. 'From now on the important thing is to keep them in good health right through till Sunday.'

7 APRIL 1981

A keen wind clipped across the top of Bratton Down as Lincoln and Percy were led out of the lorry for their last gallop across the Devon turf before they made the four-hour journey to the stables at Badminton.

Percy was the first to go – eating up the ground in long easy strides around the perimeter of the huge field. When he finished the circuit he was walked quietly on a long rein to get his breath back – and his rider looked worried. 'He hasn't done anything wrong,' he said, 'but it's taken him nearly five minutes to come back to normal breathing. I've known all along that he's not as fit as Lincoln but I'd rather he hadn't blown quite as much.' Clearly the doubt about running him was still large in his mind; 'and I still, honestly, haven't decided' he admitted. 'Percy is an old friend, I don't want him to make a fool of himself – so we'll just have to see.' Lincoln on the other hand 'surpassed himself'. During the brief schooling session he 'floated across the ground with tremendous elevation in his trot' and when he set off on his canter, according to Mark, 'he literally took off. He wanted to go about ten miles an hour faster than me. It's marvellous to know he's catching hold and wanting to go, but I'm not sure if I'm going to be able to last four-and-a-half miles with him going like an express train.' And so as the horses, complete with their entourage of groom, supporters and rider, set off for Gloucestershire, the only doubt about Lincoln in Mark's mind was 'what do I ride him in – bit-wise – on crosscountry day to make sure that he feels comfortable in his mouth, and I don't get my arms pulled out!' Considering that the Badminton fences would need a surfeit of strength and stamina – it wasn't a bad problem to have!

Badminton

The lorry drove into the old stableyard behind Badminton House just after three o'clock. The ageing stonework was mellowed by the afternoon sun and the courtyard echoed with boots on gravel, horseshoes on slate. Lincoln and Percy rolled in an eiderdown of fresh shavings in their stables, and came up looking like abominable snowmen. Shelley and Sandra Kee, the groom who would cosset Percy, set to unloading the lorry and stacking the equipment they'd need in the empty third stable next to Lincoln. The Captain had been given a set of three boxes in a block built onto the side of Badminton House, a few yards from the stable accommodation. It gave him the privilege of space and privacy that the other competitors could not enjoy. But although the competitors regard each other as equal, the press and public do not. Throughout the week Princess Anne would be following her husband's progress, and while they would take their share of attention out on the course and in the competitive rings just like everyone else, the discreet block of three stables closed off to the public would give them a chance to get out of the spotlight and, even more important, make the ever-necessary job of Royal security slightly less of a headache for the men of the Avon police force.

As the afternoon wore on a procession of lorries and trailers arrived at the yard, each one unloading a cargo of horseflesh that rippled with strength and energy.

Lincoln and Percy were saddled-up and taken on a gentle stroll through the parkland, past the tented city that had sprung up to house the banks and shops, the beer-tents and hamburger stalls, along the edge of the lake past the dressage arena and the starting-box. At the height of the competition they'd all be crammed with spectators, but on Tuesday evening only the flags waved and the ducks watched as the horses ambled and their riders gossiped in groups of twos and threes. It was more like a Sunday morning in Rotten Row than the eve of a world-class competition, but this was the last chance the riders and their horses would have to relax, and they were making the most of it.

As the horses were settled down for the night, Persian Holiday's week was still in the balance but there were no doubts from Mark over Lincoln. 'I have never had a horse better than he is now, he's never been going better in his dressage, he's never been fitter, and he's never jumped better than he did at Brigstock. You just can't ask for more than that. If I can produce that form here at Badminton, and we get beaten, then it would not be by the conditions or his performance, but by a better horse and rider.' Whether or not that 'better horse' was at this moment standing somewhere in a stable at Badminton only the next five days would tell.

WEDNESDAY, 8 APRIL 1981

Badminton Park looked like a half-finished watercolour. As we drove through the gates at eight o'clock in the morning a light curtain of grey mist was draped across the skyline. Horses soundlessly walked and trotted, rhythmically cantered in and out of the veil. There was no distinction between green grass and blue sky – just a colour chart of greys with dark figures, soft-edged and blurred. The place was alive with horses being schooled, but the mist kept them anonymous.

Over a breakfast of grapefruit and black coffee the conversation at Gatcombe had been all about the weather. The forecast had been for rain; just a little would keep the going springy, too much and traditionally soggy patches on the course would become bogs. But as the Range Rover crunched across the gravel into the stableyard at Badminton, the sun was making a brave effort to break through the cloud and take the dampness out of the chill morning air.

For Lincoln and Percy their morning routine was unbroken. Mark rode each horse for about twenty minutes following the strict patterns of the main dressage exercises and then sent them off with their grooms for the obligatory hour-and-a-half ride. In the echoing servants' hall at Badminton House the copper pans glinted in the light of a huge open fire, and row upon row of stags' heads looked down with glassy eyes on a gaggle of riders and grooms snatching a quick coffee or late breakfast. The American, Bruce Davidson, demolished a quick breakfast of eggs, bacon and sausages, while he and Mark made solicitous enquiries about the other's horses and guarded comments on their own.

It's a feature of any major competition that all competitors bring a groom with them. Whether it's a paid employee or a willing member of the family, it provides a reliable pair of hands that can clean the tack, groom and feed the horse, and accept the role of dogsbody for four days leaving the rider to concentrate on the competition itself. So while grooms busied themselves with morning exercises and lunchtime feeds, the eighty competitors made their way to the Badminton Village Hall for the traditional 10 o'clock briefing from the competition's director, Col Frank Weldon.

Although Badminton is always referred to as a three-day competition, it actually takes four days to complete – two for the dressage section, and one each for crosscountry and showjumping. Crosscountry day itself is divided into four sections; Phase A is a 2¾-mile hack around the roads and tracks of the estate, Phase B is the steeplechase course, Phase C is a further 6¼ miles of roads and tracks,

Col Frank Weldon, director of the Badminton Three-Day Event, briefing competitors after the drive round the roads and tracks section (*Jim Bennett*)

and then Phase D – the section that pulls in the crowds and provides the real spectacle of the competition – is the 4½-mile ride over 33 crosscountry fences. Every year the 16-mile course is altered slightly; as they entered the hall before the briefing, each competitor was handed a 15 × 20in ordnance map of Badminton showing the exact route to follow and the location of every fence so none of them could get lost.

The purpose of the meeting was to familiarise the competitors with the competition judges, remind them of the rules and penalties and give them the sort of administrative pep-talk that encompasses everything from the location of the secretary's tent to a reminder about keeping dogs on leads. It's followed by a procession of vehicles through the park to trace the exact route of the roads and tracks. Although the route is carefully flagged and signposted, no-one wants to risk taking the wrong direction on such a relatively easy section of the course and so, with Frank Weldon at the head, a snake of Land-Rovers and the occasional intrepid saloon car headed off to inspect the first part of the course.

Competitors Polly Lochore, Angela Tucker and the American, Sandy Pflueger, all piled into the Range Rover with Mark who tagged onto the end of the conga as it made its way bumper to bumper under the arched entrance of the stableyard and through to the start of Phase

A. A quick glance into the Phillips' stable block told him that neither horse was in its box – and they should have been. There was no sign of them in the yard, nor on the lawns outside the house, and a mild sense of alarm had Mark tugging at the wheel, breaking away from one column of cars and bouncing off across the parkland in search of the two horses. They weren't in the dressage practice arenas, nor on the long gentle sweep of tree-lined grass where the horses got their best gallop of the day. There was no reason to suppose a disaster but every excuse for indulging in the possibility of it, with a major competition less than twenty-four hours away. Everyone looked for the familiar black and chestnut outlines of the two animals while Mark made another sweep around the exercise areas. As we drove back towards the house there they were, heads down, quarters swathed in light-blue towelling rugs, nibbling on a feast of grass with Shelley and Sandra in tow on the end of halter ropes. The atmosphere lightened and the Range Rover re-joined the guided tour.

The roads and tracks section of the competition is the unglamorous bit, the part that few spectators, if any, ever bother to watch, and many don't even know exists. The route followed newly cleared paths through a young beech plantation; wood anemones, primroses, and violets splashed cheerful colour along the verges, but it was the depth of mud and the way they might best avoid its strength-sapping pull that concerned the riders. A lone magpie flapped up through the trees, and was ignored. Seconds later when its mate appeared, a cheer went up inside the cab. One magpie is unlucky, but two – a good omen. For nearly three miles the convoy bumped and slurped through rut and mud before turning across the grass landing-strip of the local flying club and onto the steeplechase course. The eight fences were set out in a figure-of-eight that would demand a steady gallop at around twenty-six miles an hour to finish the phase in the four minutes allowed. On paper it looked simple enough. There was no way a rider could get lost, and no trappy fences to catch them out, just bold brush fences built in the style of steeplechase courses throughout Britain. And yet each competitor and follower religiously walked every inch of the course just as they would ride it. Judging the lie of the land and condition of the turf in front of each take-off, gauging the camber to left or right as they swung off the rails at the end of each circuit, noting the rough poached circle that straddled the quickest route from fence three to the first left-hand curve. The fences were solid and straightforward – but no one took them for granted. Chris Collins had a crashing fall on the circuit at Burghley, and no-one would forget the horse at Fontainebleau the year before who misread the open ditch, tried to bank the brush, and broke its neck. So every pace was measured, every fence judged, and then like the customers on a Cook's tour the figures climbed back into their vehicles and set off to drive the six remaining miles of roads and tracks.

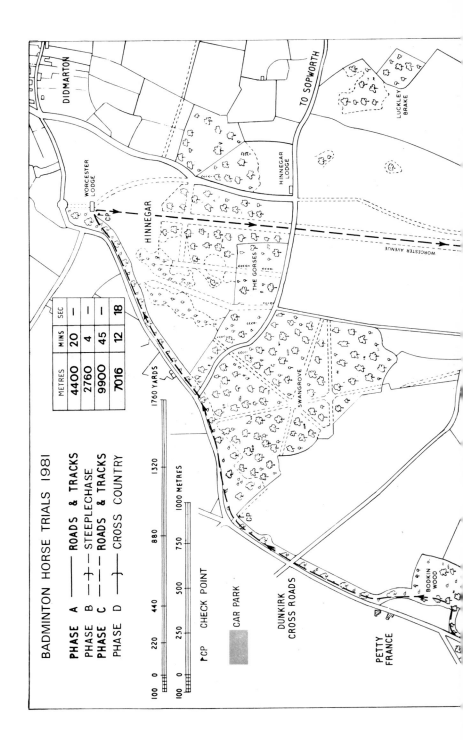

BADMINTON HORSE TRIALS 1981

PHASE A ———— ROADS & TRACKS
PHASE B —†— STEEPLECHASE
PHASE C —†— ROADS & TRACKS
PHASE D ——→ CROSS COUNTRY

METRES	MINS	SEC
4400	20	1
2760	4	1
9900	45	1
7016	12	18

▶CP   CHECK POINT

CAR PARK

DIDMARTON

WORCESTER LODGE
CP

HINNEGAR

HINNEGAR LODGE

THE GORSES

TO SOPWORTH

LUCKLEY BRAKE

WORCESTER AVENUE

SWANGROVE

CP

1760 YARDS
1320
880   750
500
440   250
220
100 0   0

1000 METRES

DUNKIRK CROSS ROADS

PETTY FRANCE

BODKIN WOOD

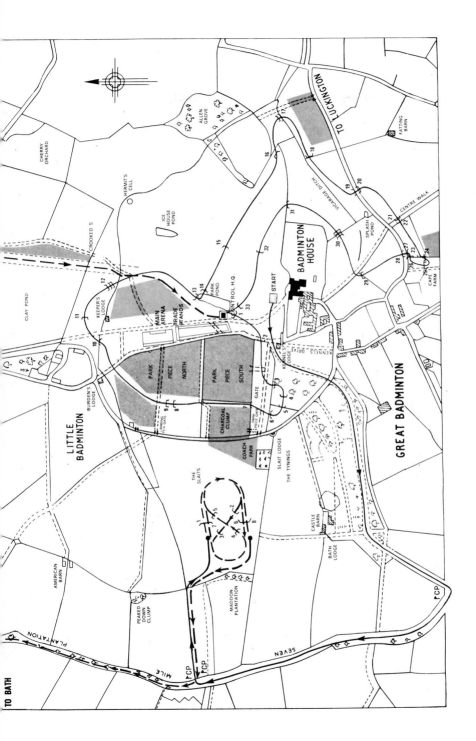

Lucinda Prior-Palmer walking the steeplechase course; she was lying third on Mairangi Bay at the end of the dressage section (*Jim Bennett*)

Lunchtime was a leisurely affair that Wednesday before Badminton. There was no panic, no outward show of nerves among riders and grooms. Just a quiet, efficient bustle as horses were fed, groomed and shampooed ready for the vet's inspection at five o'clock.

The brass catches and hinges on the doors to Lincoln's and Percy's boxes glinted in the cool, semi-gloom of the small stable-block, and the bars in front of each box were decorated with the telegrams and cards wishing Percy 'Good Luck'; Lincoln 'A Good Ride' and the grooms 'Lots of Success'. But while Percy munched away at his lunch at a steady contented pace, Lincoln stood stare-eyed and rigid. 'It's his nerves,' said Shelley casually. 'He's highly strung and he knows something's up.' His rider displayed none of Lincoln's nerves and tucked into a picnic of sausages and eggs, cheese and biscuits. Then, donning the familiar tweed cap and a pair of well-worn plimsolls, he tied Laura, his lurcher bitch, to a piece of binder twine and we set off to walk the thirty-three fences on the crosscountry course.

No-one expected the course to be as imposing or difficult as the previous year (1980) when the British team selectors were looking for a likely Olympic squad. But at the same time, no-one would ever expect the wily Frank Weldon to build a course that didn't pose problems or make demands on the fitness and ability of the competitors.

During the next few days Mark would walk the course at least three times and on each occasion, like every other competitor, he would follow the exact route that he planned to ride. No haphazard trotting from one fence to another, just looking at the take-off and landing. He wanted to know the condition of the going between the obstacles, where there were lumps and bumps in the ground, how it rose and fell on each approach, plotting in his mind exactly how he would swing into every bend, cut every time-saving corner. By the time he rode round in the heat of competition on Saturday, the route would be finely etched in his mind as clearly and exactly as if there were white arrows painted on the ground, and although he'd ridden the course many times before, he approaches each Badminton as though it were his first.

Fence 1, Whitbread Barrels, lay in a direct line straight off the starting-box, a double row of silver beer barrels at 3ft 10in high – a nice inviting fence to get the horses started. 'But you can bet your life,' said Mark ruefully, 'that if a horse is going to play you up they'll suddenly decide they don't like the look of the shine on the metal, and then you're in trouble before you've even started.'

No. 1 WHITBREAD BARRELS   No. 2 LAMB CREEP

The thatched roof of the Lamb Creep, Fence 2 on the course, stood at 3ft 11in. The approach was clear and the landing offered the prospect of a long steady gallop with a left-hand bend into a combination of four fences tucked in between the trees which kept the riders alert and the crowds enthralled. Fences 3 and 4 – Arrowhead and Huntsman's Leap – made up Huntsman's Close, with Post and Rails as Fence 5 and Elephant Trap as Fence 6.

The first fence in the quartet was a set of 3ft 11in rails set in a ditch with an angled approach, and a mighty sycamore splitting the fence and growing right where any sane rider would want to land. A quick 'right hand down a bit' and then, less than ten strides on, a 3ft 9in spruce hedge with a big drop on the other side. Just time to land and gather your reins, then a dodge either left or right around the trees to another set of post-and-rails into a clearing, with the formidable-looking Elephant Trap fence off to the right. Although each fence was marked separately and judged as an individual obstacle, they came upon horse and rider so quickly, with the landing from one relating to the take-off for the next, that each competitor needed to look at the four as a whole.

Nos. 3 & 4 HUNTSMAN'S CLOSE

No. 5 POST AND RAILS   No. 6 ELEPHANT TRAP

Mark walked backwards and forwards through the trees, lining up each approach and take-off, weighing the advantages of one approach over another before making the decision to go on the route that was shortest and fastest – but would need the most accurate riding. He paced out his approach to the first ditch-and-rails keeping the large sycamore on his left and landing so that the horse would be lined-up to meet the spruce hedge near the centre. 'The problem here,' he observed, 'is that as the horses jump they have a huge tree in their eyeline, and the tendency is for them to think that they're going to jump into it. So as I land I have to be ready with pressure on the right rein to take the horse down under the tunnel of overhanging branches and squeeze through the Christmas trees and over the next fence; then, still steering to the right, gallop boldly at the Elephant Trap.' Sounds simple doesn't it? But those four fences straddle a path that weaves and dodges for less than 200 yards. It needs courage and precision to pack so much riding into so little space.

From the Elephant Trap the ground dips away towards one of the many tarmac roads criss-crossing the estate, and then rises a little to the site of Fence 7, the Watertrough, a block of timber 3ft 11in high with a drinking trough 5ft 6in wide set inside. 'A big bold fence' said Mark. 'I shall be happy if Lincoln's really taking a hold by here. Pulling, and showing that he's keen to get on with it. What I don't want is to have him going along with his nut in the air gazing at the crowds.' The crowds are such a natural consequence of any large sporting event that it's perhaps difficult for a non-competitor to think of them as one of the 'natural' hazards. For most of the year horses are

No. 7 WATERTROUGH

worked and trained in relative isolation and compete at events where only a few hundred people are scattered around the course. 'But Badminton is unlike anywhere else,' said Mark. 'You get the biggest crowds of all here. For four-and-a-half miles all you can see is a little green carpet rolling out in front of you – the rest is a dense sea of faces.' So plotting the route from start to finish includes not only getting the take-off and landing right, and hopefully choosing the right route through the fences, but also taking into account what effect the crowds are likely to have on the approach, and making sure that the horse has the clearest possible view of the obstacle without his attention being distracted by the press of people.

As we strode along the 'green carpet' clearly marked with a continuous barrier of tape on either side, it was obvious that Mark was riding every stride of his two great horses in his mind, anticipating the strength of pull, the eagerness in their stride. 'By here,' he said, indicating another road crossing, 'Lincoln should be taking a strong pull paying attention and if he's going as well as I hope, this is the point at which I'll have to start steadying him down ready to take the next fence.' We were still several yards away from the wide sweep of clear ground in front of Fences 8 and 9 – The Quarry – but Lincoln's 'braking distance' in relation to his speed and strength was considerable, while for Persian Holiday the 'steadying' point was much nearer the obstacle.

The Quarry is one of the crowd-pullers at Badminton. The fences are set in a small amphitheatre giving the crowds a superb view of horsemanship at its best or worst. The way into The Quarry was over a stone wall; the way out on the opposite side, up a set of steps or a ramp leading to a small 'platform' with a rail out over a drop. Had either fence been in the middle of a flat field they would have done credit to the pony club, but built into the sides of the Badminton Quarry, Frank Weldon had set his competitors a demanding obstacle. The jump into The Quarry offered a choice of a sloping, slightly lower end to the wall on the right or a wider, square-topped section to the left. On landing the ground ran steeply away from the lower side of the wall but gave a slightly better gradient after the higher element. In both cases there was hardly time to gather the reins before scurrying into the first of the three big steps, or swinging round to take the ramp on the left-hand side of Fence 9. At the top of the climb the riders found a square of turf barely four yards wide edged by a set of rails three feet high, with a drop on the landing side. The bold rider on a bold horse would go right through the middle – over the highest part of the wall, up the steps and straight out over the rails at the top.

Nos. 8 & 9 THE QUARRY

But there were at least four other obvious routes to take, and the more riders looked at the problem, the more alternatives they found. Mark had a double problem to solve here as he would be riding two entirely different horses – one explosive and eager to chew up the fences, the other older, more careful and less inclined to heroics. 'Percy has never found steps very easy,' admitted Mark, 'and because he's going early in the day I wouldn't have the benefit of watching anyone else go through – so I *think* my best bet is to go up the ramp. But I think Lincoln might jump the steps. He's going towards the end of the day and by that time there should be some sort of pattern emerging as to which is the easiest way of jumping it. If everybody has gone up the ramp and made it look like a pony club fence then it's pointless going up the steps – and vice versa.'

For almost half-an-hour he walked backwards and forwards from take-off to landing, up the steps, then up the ramp, trying to imagine the speed and strength each horse would give him, and which combination of stride and jump would suit them both. At last he collected Laura from the post where she's been tied and had waited patiently watching her master weave to and fro over the same piece of ground. 'I'll sleep on it' he said and we set off down the hill towards Number 10, the Keeper's Rails – two massive tree-trunks at 3ft 11in set at an angle across a ditch. There was no agonising over this fence; as we approached it off a gentle downhill gradient he made for the left where a small smooth-topped hillock made the take-off slightly uneven. The obvious point to jump was right in the centre where the ground was even, but he explained 'by the time Lincoln rides round, about seventy other horses will have gone through there, and it's bound to be cut up. By keeping to the left we should get good dry ground and a better footing.'

No. 10 KEEPER'S RAILS   No. 11 HOGSBACK

Fence 11 was the semi-circular Hogsback of spruce perched on top of rising ground and approached through a series of hillocks and troughs that would have done justice as a hazard on a golf course. The verdict – the fence was pretty straightforward, it was the approach that would need safe riding.

Next on the agenda was one of Frank Weldon's new fences that had already attracted a lot of comment from the riders – the Crooked S. It was exactly what the name suggested. A set of rails ranging from 3ft 6in to 3ft 11in built in the shape of an uneven S, and placed on a downhill slope on uneven ground. By the time we arrived a group of riders and trainers was already weaving in and out of the fence lines, striding purposefully across them to work out the distance between each element, shaking their heads and trying another approach, every expression, every movement, indicating that the fence lived up to all the horrors they'd been led to expect.

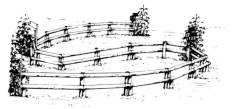

Nos. 12A, B. & C. CROOKED S

The Quarry, Badminton 1981 – a worrying moment as Lincoln catches the top of the wall and brings the pole down (*Hugo Czerny*). However, he recovers well (*opposite*) and sails up the steps and over the final element

The Crooked S – nobody looks happy at the prospect; with Mark are Angela Rippon and Martin Whiteley (*Jim Bennett*)

Mark leaned on the first rail and looked at the straightest, quickest and most difficult route right across the centre. He leaped over the fence and ran on down to the second element, carried forward by the momentum of the slope. He shook his head; 'No – I don't think so,' he said, and then began pacing out the easier but longer route, at each edge of the S. A group of riders sat on the rails, just taking it in and swapping ideas on the merits of alternatives. None of them came to any decision – except that it was a fence that would need a lot of thought and the knowledge that whichever route they chose would demonstrate not only the horse's ability but, more importantly, the rider's own courage and confidence. 'Another one to sleep on' said Mark, and we made our way across the park and up the hill behind the trade stands and dressage arena to Fences 13 and 14, the famous Badminton Lake.

There were three ways into the water; the easiest route over a 2ft 6in fence was the slowest and wouldn't appeal to those riders looking for a fast round. That left a jump over the boathouse at 3ft 6in and a long pull through The Lake to the jump-out, or the shortest route over rails at 3ft 2in with a big drop into the water, then a short scamper to the opposite bank and the upturned punt that together made up Fence 14. Mark was in little doubt about the route he intended to take on

(*above*) Victory lap past the Royal Box; (*below*) The Saddle of Honour presented to Mark as the winning rider to the obvious pleasure of the Queen, the Duke of Beaufort and Prince Philip

Lincoln: 'I'll go the shortest,' he said emphatically, 'the rails offer a "pop" over and then a drop down into the water, and I think it's easier for a horse to do that than ask him to land in water with a splash after a big spread, which is what you'd have to do if you went over the boathouse. It is, of course, the big "splash" that attracts the crowds to The Lake. They come in their thousands, blotting out the grass with a tangle of bodies, clapping and cheering every rider that tackles the combination successfully, gasping, oohing and aahing and sometimes laughing at those who get a ducking.'

Nos. 13 & 14 THE LAKE

Mark has his own horror of the Badminton Lake from 1976 when he took an early bath on Brazil. He had the crowd roaring its delight, and provided the popular press with some unusual photographs as he lay on his back on the grass bank with his legs in the air letting the water run out of his boots. 'There wasn't much else I could do,' he recalls, 'I was so wet, even if I'd got the boots off I would never have got them back on again and I couldn't go on riding with all that water sloshing about inside.' It wasn't an experience he wanted to repeat, so the rule for The Lake is steadily in and safely out and, if your luck holds, the chance to ride the big fences on the second half of the course on a dry saddle in dry breeches!

The next two fences have been a familiar part of the Badminton course for a number of years – the Whitbread Drays of Fence 15 and the Park Wall at 16. Both big fences, but neither of them posing any problems for a bold horse galloping on.

No. 15 WHITBREAD DRAYS   **No. 16 PARK WALL**

Mark walked the route he'd taken in previous years and, apart from taking note of the going and checking on the height of the branches on an overhanging tree, he spent little time at either obstacle, moving on instead to another of the new fences, the Cirencester Rails.

Nos. 17A. & B CIRENCESTER RAILS

Frank Weldon had designed Fence 17 like a huge X straddling the banks of a small stream. On the left the rails were angled sharply giving a cautious rider the chance to jump in onto flat ground, line themselves up to leap the ditch, and then get in a short stride before jumping the rails on the far side. On the right of the cross, the alternative was much the same, except that the rails were set at a much shallower angle producing in effect a small 'coffin' fence with rails in, a bounce across the ditch and then out. The quickest and again most difficult route was through the centre of the angled rails which stood at 3ft 9in with a big spread, but there was a clean approach and good landing for the rider who aimed just left of centre providing the horse jumped well out – which is where Mark decided he would go.

The Cricketers Arms, Fence 18 on the course, was an attractive construction of giant cricket bats topped by a pole to mark the Duke of Beaufort's association as President of the Gloucestershire County Cricket Club. 'Aim for the middle and ride on' was the uncomplicated decision at an equally uncomplicated fence.

Then on to Fences 19 and 20, the First Luckington Lane Crossing – a ditch in front of a bank with a drop down onto the lane, one stride up onto another bank, and off over a set of rails. The Luckington Lane is not a fence for the faint-hearted. It needs to be ridden with rhythm and balance, with the horse going forward taking each element without checking its stride; a lack of heart, especially at the top of the second

No. 18 CRICKETERS ARMS

Nos. 19 & 20 FIRST LUCKINGTON
LANE CROSSING

bank, will bring the combination to a grinding halt and make any recovery a messy business with little room to manoeuvre and no chance of regaining any impulsion. As with a number of fences on the course, Mark had jumped the banks many times before. He's come to the decision that, provided you kept the horse balanced and kept going forward, you'd be out cleanly and on your way to the two big hedges at Fences 21 and 22 known as the Centre Walk.

Nos. 21 & 22 CENTRE WALK

Called the Aintree Chair and Becher's Brook, neither fence stood as high as their namesakes on the Grand National course, but at 4ft 2in and 4ft respectively they were quite big enough to meet threequarters of the way round the course. The ground after the two hedges was soft and boggy. 'This is where you could have problems with a tired horse,' Mark reflected. 'Once they get into boggy ground and find the going a bit heavy, they're likely to think "oh no, I can't go on any more" and once they drop like that they lose their impulsion and, to a certain extent, their heart as well. And even though the ground dries out immediately afterwards, you've lost your rhythm, and you've lost the spark.' If the fences that followed were not too difficult that wouldn't be much of a problem, and the rider would have chance to re-kindle any 'lost spark' over a few easy fences, but immediately after the Centre Walk is the combination of Cotswold stone fences known as Tom Smith's Walls.

Nos. 23, 24 & 25 TOM SMITH'S WALLS

Fences 23, 24 and 25 stood respectively at 3ft 11in, 3ft 10in and 3ft 9in. When the competition is over and the estate returns to its main function as a commercial farm, these walls form part of the square enclosure to one of the many farmyards, but for the Three-Day Event they provided an imposing, solid trio of obstacles. There was no 'easy way' over them – the degree of difficulty was only lessened by the speed and angle at which a rider decided to approach them. Mark walked a path that took him to the right of the first wall, giving himself room to land, sweep round on the left rein and meet the second wall dead-centre, with horse and rider ready to immediately swing right-handed to the third element, which itself offered four options. They could either trot carefully through a partially opened gate and then swing right to jump the last wall, or jump the gate and the wall. The third option was to jump the wall beside the gate and then bounce across the angle to the last wall; finally – a route for the really bold – they could jump the corner, and save the precious seconds that would be eaten up by the other three routes. 'If I get this far I don't think I'll want to take any chance,' said Mark, so he decided to take what for him would be the safest and quickest route – jumping the gate, and then out over the final obstacles.

Nos. 26, 27 & 28 SECOND
LUCKINGTON LANE CROSSING

The Second Luckington Lane Crossing was another combination of three fences that offered a choice of routes. In essence, Fences 26, 27 and 28 were nothing more than a set of rails in a field, with a hedge on either side of the lane. The easy way round was to jump the 3ft 9in rails, then turn left-handed and over the hedges across the lane, but the corner made an inviting fence and offered the shortest route across the lane. Mark walked both alternatives and confirmed that the choice he made on the day would depend on the ground and how the horses felt on this last stretch of the course.

The Zig-Zag at 29 was a familiar fence. Previous experience had told him to jump on the right where the take-off was even and the landing would line him up well for the next fence on the course,

No. 29 ZIG-ZAG

the Brandy Glass. There were five possible routes through Fence 30, but Mark considered only two of them – jumping the bowl of the Brandy Glass with bounce between the two elements, or straight across the 'stem' in one. At that point the poles were 3ft 11in high and the spread almost 6ft. 'A bold horse will make nothing of that,' he said, 'but again, we'll see how they're going on the day.'

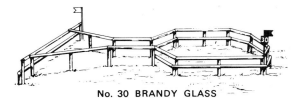

No. 30 BRANDY GLASS

Three from home and the Pardubice Taxis loomed large under the trees. At 4ft 6in Fence 31 is a big obstacle in its own right, but on the landing side the ground falls away into a ditch. 'I've never had a good landing at this fence,' said Mark ruefully; 'the horse always seems to go down on his nose a bit' and he shrugged – almost acknowledging that only the luck of the day would decide whether he came out of that mighty leap well or not.

As we walked down the home stretch with Badminton House on our left and only two fences to the finish, Mark admitted that when he gets to this stage on the course he needs to keep a grip on his concentration. 'It's very easy to think "well that's it" and just coast home,' he said. 'The second time I won here on Great Ovation the

No. 31 PARDUBICE TAXIS   **No. 32 FALLEN TREE**

penultimate fence was a log pile. I think I must have eased-off a bit then because the horse stood off. For a moment I thought he was going to put a foot down and bank it. We'd have gone a purler if he had; that shows you can't stop concentrating for a minute – especially when you're in sight of home' . . . as we were now, with just a single log and the famous Whitbread Bar between us and the finishing line.

No. 33 WHITBREAD BAR

Anyone who'd got that far wouldn't find Fence 32, the Fallen Tree, a great problem and the Whitbread Bar, Fence 33, was there as an attractive advertisement for the competition's main sponsors rather than a trap for the horses. But each fence was walked, and the line of approach carefully plotted. Mark's professional attitude was simple and uncompromising: 'Never take anything for granted. No matter how many times you've jumped a course, or how well you think you know it, you walk it and judge it as if you're doing it for the first time; when you don't – that's when you get caught out.'

As we walked back to the stables, I wondered what conclusions he'd come to about the course. 'Fast and fair,' was his immediate reaction. 'There's plenty of scope for mistakes, and The Quarry, Crooked S and Lake are going to be problem fences. If it stays dry and people go flying round, then the dressage marks will become very important. But if it rains before Saturday, and the going gets sticky, then there'll be a lot of skill needed and it will be up to every rider to judge how much petrol they've got left in the tank to tackle the big fences on the second half of the course rather than just going flat out.'

That first walk had taken us well over two hours. It had established an overall impression of the course, but there were clearly fences that would need to be looked at again, and again.

'The Quarry, The Lake, the Second Luckington Lane, Tom Smith's Walls, they're all places where Lincoln could make a fool of himself,' admitted Mark, and they were among the fences that would get special attention the next day when we walked the course again.

But with the time rapidly approaching five o'clock, the state of the fences had to take second place to the condition of the horses. Before anyone could declare themselves a competitor their horse had to be passed fit by the Veterinary Committee. The inspection was timed to begin at five o'clock precisely and, as we walked back into the stables, the courtyard was already filling up with some of the fittest, most athletic equine talent in the country.

Each horse had been turned out to perfection. Their manes and tails were plaited, their legs cased in colourful protective bandages, their coats gleaming from the effort of shampooing and grooming. Most of the humans looked pretty good too. The comfortable well-worn stable gear of jeans and wellies gave way to tweed and cavalry twill, to cashmere and Hermes scarves. The yard had the look of the President's enclosure at a County Show, and all the atmosphere of a bloodstock sale. Sandra petted and fussed over Percy, who clearly enjoyed all the attention. I got the feeling that if he'd been a dog he would have willingly rolled over on his back with his legs in the air demanding even more of her attention.

In the box next door, Lincoln was his usual aloof self, shaking off any affection like a tetchy old bachelor. Each horse had its competition number printed on a small disc that was attached to the side of the bridle. Percy was number 8. Princess Anne had already singled that out as the one number her husband thought really unlucky – but no-one acknowledged the fact as Percy was led out into the afternoon sunshine just before five o'clock to join the thirty or so already gathered.

The archway at the far end of the courtyard led onto the gravelled drive in front of Badminton House. It was here, with that beautiful old building as a backdrop and the lake in front of them, that the panel of vets took their seats to view and examine the hopeful contenders. A steward by the arch called each horse by number to be trotted up in front of the vets minus bandages or blankets. The pattern was the same for each competitor. When the horse arrived level with the judges it stood foursquare and still to have heart, lungs and legs examined. Then the groom or rider walked the horse away from the panel, and trotted it back. If all were agreed that the animal was sound it was given the nod, and the name and number, followed by the word 'Passed', boomed out over the loudspeakers. Number 8 sauntered up to the judges, satisfied them that he was fit and sound, and then dragged a grinning Sandra back to the stable. There was well over an hour between his appearance and Lincoln's, so Mark saddled him up and took him for a quiet stroll around the park while the steady roll-call of numbers worked their way down to Number 87 – Lincoln. At the call of his name and number Shelley walked Lincoln into the arena, and had a tussle with him to get him to stand still. When at last he stopped fidgeting, he put his head in the air and took an arrogant sweep of the spectators who were leaning on the barriers. His walk and trot were sound, and the announcer boomed out 'Passed'.

As we drove out of the park that evening, a fresh breeze was tugging at the canvas walls and the flags of the trade stands. It was a drying wind that held the promise of good going for the crosscountry on Saturday, so when the official entry list of competitors closed that night, both Range Rover Team horses were on it – Lincoln *and* Persian Holiday.

THURSDAY, 9 APRIL 1981

For two days the atmosphere at Badminton had been one of busy anticipation. The change of location from home to competition hadn't interrupted the daily round of stable chores, nor the programme of exercise and schooling for the horses. There'd been meal tickets to buy for the grooms, forms to fill in, tack to clean, courses to walk, reunions with old friends and a dozen other things to do, so if anyone had been suffering from an attack of pre-competition nerves, most of them had done well to disguise it under a camouflage of 'carrying on as normal'. But on Thursday morning there was a distinct change of gear. The scrape and clatter of grooming and feeding, the hollow ring of steel-clad hooves on flagstones, bounced around the four walls of the stableyard and accentuated the near-silence. The chatter and banter between grooms was reduced to a murmur, and the riders seemed to seal themselves and their nerves behind a wall of concentration.

Persian Holiday's dressage test had been timed to start at ten o'clock. Sandra, his groom, was up at five o'clock and feeding him breakfast a quarter-of-an-hour later. He was groomed and plaited,

Relaxation after the first vets' inspection; Mark on Percy and Shelley on Lincoln, with Mrs Anne Phillips and Mark's sister Sarah looking on (*Jim Bennett*)

rugged and cosseted and ready to be ridden when Mark arrived just before eight o'clock. Lincoln wouldn't be riding his test until late the following afternoon, so while Shelley led him off for a session on the lunge line, it was Percy who was the centre of attention in the stable. Everything was very calm and businesslike. The grooms were sensitive to the tensions building up in their employer and didn't want to do anything that would upset him or break his concentration. As Percy was led out of the box, Mark noticed that the small disc displaying his competition number was missing from the bridle. It should have been stitched to the end of the browband so that it would sit, without flapping, on the side of the horse's face, just below his ear. For a second the air snapped: 'I'll lynch that girl' he exploded. And in the silence that followed he located a needle and cotton, and began sewing the disc on himself. He fumbled with the last knot, snipped the cotton free, then grinned and said 'This is really a job for the female members of the team' and handed the sewing kit back to Sandra.

As Percy was led off to the practice area Sandra let out a sigh of relief and said '*that* was treading on dangerous ground'. But it was a minor niggle and within minutes had been forgotten, leaving horse and rider to concentrate on preparing for the dressage test. A dozen or so riders were working on the flat turf of the practice area behind the main dressage-ring. Lucinda Prior-Palmer, the first competitor of the day, already resplendent in top-hat and tails, was putting the finishing touches to her work on Killaire, while others walked and trotted, circled and bent under the discerning eyes of trainers, owners, grooms and a growing number of press photographers.

As Sandra and I watched Percy slip with apparent ease into a controlled and measured pace, she admitted that all week she'd been trying to con the old horse into believing that he wasn't going to a competition at all, but on a holiday. I wasn't quite sure how you could convince a seasoned campaigner like Percy that the familiar sights and sounds of Badminton were there for his entertainment and not to be taken seriously, but Sandra was sure that it had worked. 'He's a cunning old horse,' she said. 'If he thought for one moment that he was going to have to compete, he'd have gone lame on us – he's very good at faking lameness when he thinks he's going to have to do some hard work. So we all keep very calm, and try to keep the tension and excitement of the competition away from him.' There was no way of knowing whether or not their confidence trick had worked – except that Percy was very definitely *not* lame, and was in fact applying himself to his morning's work with all the appearance of a horse that was having fun!

Just before nine o'clock Mark walked Percy into the collecting-ring to watch Lucinda ride the test. A few feet away Clissy Strachan waited patiently on her lovely bay Merry Sovereign, while Richard Meade evoked impressions of an aristocracy long gone as he sat astride

Speculator III in an elegant topper and buff-revered tail-coat, having his horse rubbed to a shine by one groom and his boots polished by another.

Lucinda left the ring to a light ripple of applause from the handful of dressage devotees who were already positioned in the covered stands and Percy was walked quietly back to the stable. Mark changed from jeans and checked shirt into the formal dress of white breeches, top-hat and tails and, at a quarter to ten, Percy was led out for him to mount. The old horse shone, his saddlery was spotless – and the numbered disc on his bridle was hanging loose. So with fifteen minutes to go Mark was involved in another attempt at makeshift needlework. 'It's a good job it's you, Percy, and not a few other horses I could mention' he joked as the big horse stood motionless while the needle wove backwards and forwards around the leatherwork. The job done, Sandra rubbed over the bridle for the twentieth time eking out every last bit of shine, and Mark polished up his topper with a handkerchief. He dropped a glove by Percy's front feet and, as he bent to retrieve it, the horse crashed his foot down in an impatient stamp – missing his fingers by a hair's breadth. There were a few gasps from the onlookers, then a nervous giggle; 'I think we're more nervous than he is' said Shelley, as horse and rider walked casually out of the yard.

In the collecting-ring, friends and relatives of the competitors were piled onto a flat-topped trailer watching each test. Princess Anne leaned on one corner and their young son, Peter, was given a grandstand view by sitting at the front. Number 8 was called and, as Mark rode into the arena, the concentrated silence was broken by a high-pitched 'Hello Papa'. The reply 'Hello Peter' carried back on the wind, but then there was an unbroken silence for the next ten minutes while Mark performed the test.

As the points for each movement in the test were flashed up on the three electronic scoreboards there were murmurs of disapproval from the onlookers. Most thought he was being poorly marked, though when the figures were totted up at the end of the first day Percy was lying in 4th position on a total of 58·2. Nevertheless, his rider was disappointed. 'I know he can do so much better,' he said. 'We went into the ring and he just didn't light up at all. His trot work was accurate, but flat. His canter work was all right, but laboured. He just didn't have that spark.'

Percy had the rest of the day off, to be cooed at and mothered over by Sandra. Now all attention turned to Lincoln.

His dressage was less fluid and needed more concentrated effort than Percy's, and so for an hour horse and rider worked under the scrutiny of dressage trainer David Hunt. When Lincoln was returned to his stable, Mark looked pleased and admitted 'He's going nicely.' The session had put a note of optimism back in his voice and the smile on his face, and by the time he set out to walk the crosscountry course after lunch, the disappointment of the morning had been overtaken by the anticipation of what was still to come.

That second walk around the course was done in the company of a growing number of spectators, those who'd come for the four days of the competition and wanted to get a good look at the fences before the mass of crowds that would arrive on Friday and Saturday. They clustered around each obstacle, looking in awe at the size of timber, the depth of drops and the wide expanse of ditches. Every so often one figure would break out of the group and identify himself or herself as a competitor by striding purposefully in a straight line, counting the number of steps, and glancing back at a take-off or landing point. It wasn't easy for them to see exactly where they wanted to jump as small knots of spectators wandered in and out of their line of sight, so the occasional friend or helper would have to ask politely 'Would you mind – just a second – while we have a look at the fence?' and on more than one occasion I heard the surprised and unlikely remark 'I had no idea the competitors walked round the course before they rode it'. But walk they do, as we were now, to commit every inch of the four-and-a-half-mile course to memory and plot with precision the way each fence would be ridden.

Fences 1 and 2 were walked up to, and passed by without comment. It wasn't until we reached Huntsman's Close that Mark traced his steps backwards and forwards, walking each of the alternatives he'd considered, and then settling on the line he'd thought of originally.

The Elephant Trap and Watertrough were galloped at mentally, and left to the comments of the spectators. Ahead lay The Quarry, and that still needed a lot of thought.

A precocious pony clubber announced to doting parents 'Oh that's easy, you just go over there, down there, up the steps and out.' Mark and the competitors already considering the obstacle clearly didn't share her dismissive views. They were all aware of the subtle traps concealed in the sloping banks, the pitch of the steps, the closeness of the penalty zone to the base of the ramp, and they judged each option carefully before coming to individual decisions.

Mark's jaw had been set as he stormed first the steps, then the ramp. It relaxed when he finally decided: 'I shall take them both up the ramp. I can see it in my mind. A nice steady curve into the first wall, a gentle pull to the left on landing, then up the hill, over the top, and out – both of them – flowing over nicely.' He smiled, and inclined his head, as if adding 'with a bit of luck that is' and we set off once again past the next two obstacles to the real headache on the course – the Crooked S.

There was already quite a crowd around the fence, as there would be on each of the following days. Its notoriety as a hazard was already established and people came in their hundreds just to gaze at the complexity of it, and wonder at how any horse would ever ride through it. For a quarter of an hour Mark paced out a series of possible routes, and finally confirmed 'I'll take the longest route.' It meant approaching the fence to the right, jumping through the first curve of the 'S', then turning to jump the second curve, and then swinging uphill to go through the third element. Once again, had the fence been on flat ground it would have been a fairly straightforward bounce through the centre, but the land dipped and curved away down the left-hand side of a steep slope, and it was that which made the obstacle more of a puzzle.

At The Lake, Martin Bewick was considering the way to ride his horse Schweppes. 'I suppose it's not too bad if you take the easy route,' he suggested. Mark laughed. 'Which *is* the easiest – I'm still trying to find it,' and then indicated that, easy or not, he was still going the quick way over the post and rails.

At the Cirencester Rails, two of the competitors were manfully trying to pace out their route over the angled rails to the left, in spite of the mass of people who were crowding over the fence and walking through the stream in the ditch. Mark walked his approach, swinging wide to the left, then popped across the ditch and looked back at the fence from the landing side. 'Yes' he said emphatically, 'that's absolutely the right place to jump. I didn't notice yesterday but the landing here is flatter than the one offered on the other side.' As we walked away, another surprised spectator asked enquiringly of his companion 'Did *you* know they walked round the course first?'. We didn't wait to hear the reply!

An Irish competitor was perched on top of the second of Tom Smith's Walls. 'How the hell did I jump this the last time?' he asked no-one in particular. 'All I remember is that it was very un-comfortable' and one of the French contingent commiserated with him as together they considered the advantages of one route over another.

Mark considered two possibilities, and pulled a face as a Nelly Knowall declared loudly 'That's nothing more than we'd tackle when we're out hunting.' 'She's not a competitor' said the Irishman dryly, and the group who were competing turned their attention to the Second Luckington Lane Crossing.

Throughout the walk whenever Mark approached a fence he went through the same series of almost unconscious actions. He would stride up to the fence, clicking his tongue in encouragement to his phantom horse, plant his feet firmly together at the point he intended to take off, and then sling his arm out, as if to indicate a clean straight leap over the obstacle. He did this now as we walked towards the corner of the Luckington Lane, and then again at a point further along the first of the three fences. 'No decision here' he said, 'I'll see how they're going by this one. If they're pulling and going really strong then I shall certainly go by the quick route over the corner. But if I feel they need a bit of nursing it would be silly to make a mistake having got this far round, so I'll take them across on the right-hand side of the tree and give them a straight run into the two fences each side of the lane.' The rest of the fences on the course needed no second opinion. He'd decided how he was going to jump them and so the rest of the walk merely formalised the route he would take on the gallop between each obstacle.

On the way back to the stable, we met up with Bertie Hill. 'Come and look at a couple of fences with me' Mark asked – so off we went again.

Bertie stood at the top of the bank at The Quarry, screwed his nose up as Mark described the route he intended to take and finally said 'If I was you I'd go up those steps – no messing,' and then explained his reasoning. He was worried that Percy would trail a hindleg over the rail at the top of the bank. 'The chap is getting a bit leggy in his old age,' he said, 'and I think you'd be safer going that way.' For twenty minutes they walked the alternatives, each trying to persuade the other that his route was the best. Bertie even worked out a devious route along the top of the quarry that avoided both the steps and the bank, but they threw that out as being too complicated and too time-consuming. At last Mark conceded; 'I think, Bertie, I'm going to lose this one,' he said. 'I think you've convinced me that the steps are right.' 'Look buster,' was Bertie's reaction, 'you come into this fence absolutely right, really going on. Take a good jump over the wall, with a good landing, then providing you pick up your reins and pick up your horse and keep going, you can do anything you like.' Mark didn't look totally convinced. 'The trouble with you, Bertie,' he said fondly, 'is that you're getting old.' 'I don't know about that,' replied Bertie, 'but I'll tell you what – you're a damn sight more difficult to convince now than you used to be.'

So with an entirely different course plotted in his mind for The Quarry, we now made our way to the other unsettled question on the course – how to jump the Crooked S. 'I've already worked out how I'd do this one,' said Bertie and then proceeded to walk one of the most difficult routes taking the left-hand side of the first element, two strides to the centre rail, and another two out over the far side. 'Well there's no argument about *that* one,' answered Mark emphatically. 'I'm simply not going to do it.' They then argued about the relative merits of those horses that *would* jump Bertie's route. 'Now if you were riding a Columbus or a Chicago that's the way to go,' declared Bertie. 'But I'm not, so I won't,' was his pupil's stubborn reply – so together they paced the easier options. For a quarter of an hour they considered every angle until Bertie was drawn to comment 'Old Frank Weldon knew what he was doing when he put this one up here.' Suddenly Mark's face lit up. 'I've got it,' he said, and walked a route that followed his original plan for the first element, but went slightly uphill at the second. This put him on a land that would give a short sweep downhill to the left offering a straight line through the centre of the last element. It was just a subtle shift of direction, but enough to gain a few vital seconds on what looked like being a fast course.

Mark now had the pattern of his ride locked away inside his memory. 'But I shall walk the course again tomorrow,' he said, 'just to make sure.'

FRIDAY, 10 APRIL 1981

'Tomorrow' dawned, sunny and warm. As we drove through the park towards the lovely façade of Badminton House, we could make out the shape of a big black horse circling round and round on the end of a lunge line. 'There's the good horse Lincoln' said Mark, and we watched a while as Shelley lunged him obediently round and round, first on one rein, then the other. He rippled with strength and exuberance, rearing occasionally, impatient to break out of the circular prison into a full-blooded gallop. We left her restraining him and drove on to the stables where Percy was waiting for an early-morning gallop.

Horse and rider made their way out of the park, across the main road that led to Badminton village and into the huge field where the steeplechase course was laid out. The Hon Robin Cayzer was already walking his horse Rough and Tough around the perimeter of the field and the two riders fell in beside each other; they steadily pushed the horses from a walk into a gentle trot, and then a steady canter before turning the corner at the top of the field and stretching both animals to the full speed of a gallop. They completed a single circuit around the edge of the course and then eased back until both horses were walking on long reins, their heads nodding and stretching as they caught their breath. 'He enjoyed that,' said Mark, 'and he wasn't even blowing as much as Rough and Tough.' It was a good note on which to start and it meant that the day began without any of the tensions that had jangled on the previous morning.

Lincoln's dressage test was timed for 5.10pm, He was one of the last competitors to go, which gave Mark the rest of the day to school him, calm him, and put him in the right frame of mind to produce one of his 'purple patches' of brilliance. Within minutes of starting to work in the practice area it was evident that Lincoln was not prepared to give either a willing or relaxed session. He resisted the bit, and argued over transitions from trot to canter and back again. The loudspeakers announced that Lucinda had gone into the lead with a mark of 47·4 on her second horse Mairangi Bay. That was the standard the rest would be aiming for, and Lincoln still seemed determined not to co-operate. Mark's concentrated silence was contrasted strongly with the only other rider working in the practice-ring, Jane Starkey. Her impressive grey, The Baptist, was giving an almost perfect demonstration of some of the more elegant movements in the test, while she chatted away enthusiastically to her trainer. You got the feeling that her hands and seat almost worked independently and would have produced exactly the same result on the horse if she'd been giving you a recipe for coq au vin at the same time.

Gradually Lincoln's huge Roman nose dropped lower as he began to flex and stop arguing. I was joined by Hamish Lochore, one of the Captain's closest friends. His look and tone conveyed admiration as well as friendship. 'He'd make a donkey look good,' he said, and after a pause, 'you know there were people who said he was a fool to buy that horse because it was a nothing but look at him now – he's every inch a champion.' Lincoln certainly did look impressive at that moment. He was going through one of his more co-operative patches, covering the ground with grace and balance. Hamish continued 'I'm sure there are people who don't appreciate what a very good horseman he is. Many of the riders have their horses made for them, then just come along and continue to make them look good, whereas Mark is always finding youngsters or horses that other people have no confidence in and turning them out on the line. Making them world-class, world beaters.' They were the sentiments you'd expect from a friend – but few in the horse world would disagree with their accuracy.

In front of us Lincoln came to a halt; Mark dropped the reins and patted the horse's thick muscular neck. There was a look of resignation on his face, and disappointment in his voice. 'He's in one of his sensitive moods this morning, keeps wanting to stick his head in the air. The one thing you don't want to do the morning of a dressage test is to have a fight or an argument with the horse. I think I've taken him on a bit too much this morning and had too much of a head-on clash.' Perhaps Lincoln *was* just having one of his 'off days', or perhaps the build-up of nerves and tension was starting to work on them both. Either way, the result was volatile and Mark knew he wouldn't be able to ride the test with any of the fluency he'd been working for all these months. 'He'll still be uptight when he comes to do the test,' he said. 'All I can do is work him for a few minutes before we go in just to keep him happy and quiet. But I think it's too late.'

Lincoln was returned to the cool of the stable, and Mark set off with Laura to walk the course for the third and final time. When he got back he sat in the front of the Range Rover, put his feet up and pulled his cap down over his eyes – to grab a half-hour snooze. If its purpose was to calm him down – it hadn't really worked. 'I feel sick,' he admitted. 'There's no reason why I should. It's not as though I'm going to do anything dangerous. I'm just going to go round and round in circles, doing walk, trot and canter – but I feel sick. It's just like having examination nerves.'

The least I could do for the good horse Lincoln while waiting for the prizegiving in the ring

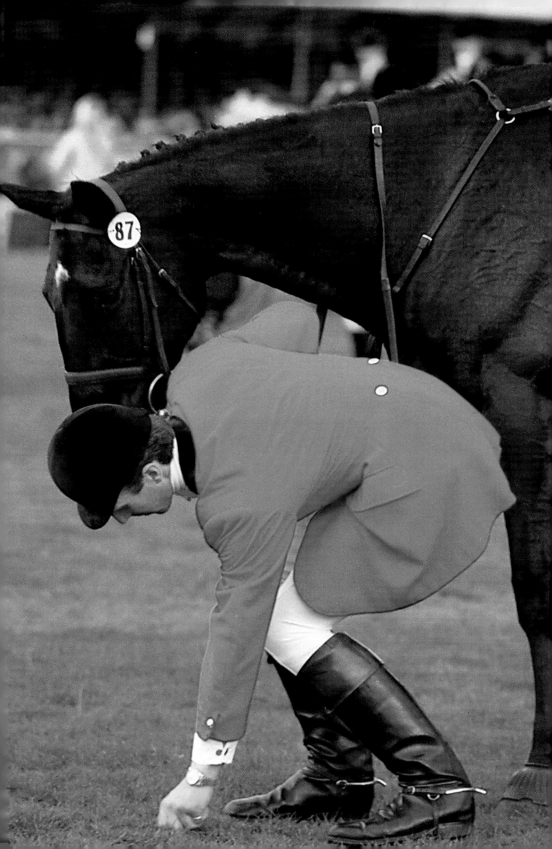

At the far end of the stable Princess Anne perched on a bale of straw and watched as horse and husband prepared for the test. Shelley was rubbing baby oil around Lincoln's nose and on his tail to add an extra shine to the already impeccable glow of his coat, and vaseline around his mouth because 'the Judges like to see a nice wet mouth'.

Mark slipped his arm into the sleeve of his tail-coat. 'It's shrunk,' he said. 'No darling,' said Princess Anne calmly, 'that's my jacket – your's is out in the car.' And then, as he pulled on a pair of highly polished though battered top-boots 'I don't know why you must wear those old things. You've had new ones for seven years, and another pair you've just ordered.' It was the gentle bantering of a wife who's only too well aware of her husband's superstitions about his riding kit and so the reply that 'I'll try the new ones out next time – but not now' came as no surprise.

In the collecting-ring the press cameras clicked endlessly like a plague of tsetse flies at young Peter Phillips. 'Why are all those men taking pictures of me, Mummy?' he asked. Before Princess Anne had a chance to reply, Malcolm Wallace, team *chef d'equipe*, answered 'They're not – they're taking pictures of *me*' so Peter lost interest and went back to his game.

As the afternoon progressed the lead in the dressage section had changed hands yet again. Bruce Davidson had ridden a superb test on Might Tango, and his score of 41·4 was now the standard to beat.

Mark walked Lincoln around the enclosure on a long rein, keeping himself and the horse calm. Immediately before him in the running order at five o'clock was Rachel Bayliss on Mystic Minstrel. With minutes to go before her test she should have been sitting astride her horse waiting by the steward to be sent into the ring; instead she was lying flat out on the grass clutching her stomach and being sick. Her trainer was agitatedly blowing smoke into her face to make her retch, while her skin turned the colour of parchment. The ring steward had already confirmed that it was impossible to either delay the competition, or allow her to ride the test later, so at five o'clock she hauled herself into the saddle, and trotted into the arena prepared to ride a ten-minute test while suffering the appalling effects of food poisoning. Only the competitors and a handful of supporters in the collecting-ring knew that she was ill, and as it turned out it would have taken quite a lot to persuade the rest of the audience of that fact. In an astonishing display of mind over matter Rachel rode a near-perfect test and collected a mark of 36·2 that gave her an unbeatable lead. 'Follow that' was the unspoken challenge as she left the ring – and Mark rode into the arena prepared to do just that.

Lincoln and Shelley after the prizegiving at Badminton 1981. Horse and groom – the picture tells all

Mark and Lincoln performing their dressage test; a poor test left them in sixteenth position at the end of the dressage (*Jim Bennett*)

Unfortunately, Lincoln was not. He resisted the bit, broke into a canter when he should have trotted and the stream of low marks that flashed on the scoreboard told the rest of the story. His final score was 57·8 and he finished the day in 16th position out of 80 runners.

In the stable, disappointment hung in the air like a wet blanket. Mark stood at one end leaning on the windowledge just gazing out blankly. Princess Anne had taken Peter off to see his Grandma and the grooms moved around the stalls unsaddling the horse and rugging him up for the night with silent mechanical precision. Past experience had told them it was best to keep quiet when their 'boss' had suffered a disappointment. Bruce Davidson popped his head around the door and asked 'How did he go, Captain?' 'Terrible.' The word, and the tone it was delivered in, spoke volumes, but Bruce was enough of a friend not to dwell on the disappointment too long, and turned the conversation instead to the following day's crosscountry. The two discussed the various routes they'd decided to take through some of the more complex obstacles. 'What about The Quarry?' asked Mark, and listened as Bruce Davidson described the sweep he would take away to the left before riding up the ramp. 'But if you go that far out,' suggested Mark, 'won't you be riding way outside the penalty zone?' It was a prospect that hadn't occurred to Bruce Davidson so, with the possibility of picking up 20 penalties for riding outside the limit of the jump when he was securely placed in second position after the dressage, he dashed off to take another look at The Quarry, and replan his route.

Captain Phillips put on his Public Face and went to attend a Press Conference arranged by his sponsors, Range Rover. Was it true, asked one of the reporters, that the start of the following day's crosscountry competition had been brought forward an hour because he was one of the last to go and Princess Anne had insisted that he had to be home in time for a dinner engagement? 'No – it wasn't true, the time had been advanced because there were so many competitors that the last riders would be going round in the gloom of early evening – and not only would it be unfair to the riders, but the television cameras wouldn't get any decent pictures. The decision had been taken by Lt-Col Frank Weldon out of commonsense, but the press still couldn't resist the temptation to turn it into a possible gossip story.

On the drive back to Gatcombe, Mark's mood matched the weather – dark and overcast. Then the first heavy rain drops burst onto the windscreen, and with them his temper. 'I just got it wrong from the beginning. It wasn't as good as it should have been,' and displaying the mark of a good horseman, he continued to put the blame for Lincoln's performance not on the horse but squarely at his own feet. 'When he set his mouth against me this morning, I should have kept on trying to work it out of him, and not get all uptight about it. But I didn't. I said "hey – come on – listen" and the worse he got, the more determined I got and it just wasn't on. I really wasn't very clever today – I just made a right mess of it.' He allowed himself a little consolation in the fact that there were sixty-four horses worse than Lincoln – and tried not to think too much about the fifteen that were better!

SATURDAY, 11 APRIL 1981
How can you describe the tension that exists when people are wracked with nerves before an important event? It isn't something tangible that you can grasp, or push to one side. Yet when it exists it's as real as an unwelcome stranger sitting solidly in your midst and at Badminton, that crosscountry morning, the air was full of it. There was no rush or panic. People walked calmly from A to B as though they were treading on eggshells, and conversation was low and muted, as if raised voices might charge the atmosphere and send sparks flying. Overnight rain had changed the going from good to soft, so many riders had to rethink their strategy. Friends and wellwishers came to pat the horses and offer words of encouragement to the riders, but on the whole

agreed they felt 'pretty useless' so went off to rewalk the course, and pick vantage points from which to watch the crosscountry.

Mark sat at the wheel of his Range Rover – not wanting to talk to anyone. He kept his nerves to himself, and left the horses in the capable hands of the two grooms. Sandra and Shelley had been up since 5.30am to work together at getting Percy fed, groomed and saddled in time for the twelve o'clock start. They had a routine to follow that didn't leave room for nerves and anyway both felt a responsibility to keep themselves and their horses calm, while acknowledging that their employer was anything but. The casual visitor like myself couldn't fail to notice the tension in the atmosphere. The one person who remained oblivious was Shelley. She'd joined the yard the previous summer and had lived through four highly-charged days at Burghley in September. She admits that the experience left her wondering what she'd let herself in for: 'The Captain was so nervy, I never thought I'd be able to stand it, but Princess Anne told me not to worry, that he'd be all right after the competition, which he was, so now I don't take any notice. If anything I feel rather sorry for him' – that delivered not in a patronising tone but with a genuine understanding of the emotional demands of the sport which can effect a private, inner hell on even the coolest customers on the circuit.

Don Deakins, a retired policeman who helps repair all Mark's saddlery, arrived to check every stitch and buckle on the saddle and bridle. No-one wanted to repeat the tragedy in 1977 when Percy's rein broke coming out of Huntsman's Close, so everything was checked and double-checked, with nothing left to chance.

With Her Majesty the Queen and at least five members of the Royal Family inside Badminton House, the stableyard and starting-point for the roads and tracks was soon jammed with a mass of people wanting to catch a glimpse of the 'Royals', and detectives trying to pretend that they weren't policemen at all.

Just before noon Mark went off to the starting-box to be weighed, and to check his starting time. Sandra led Percy through the crowds, and then walked him round and round the enclosure with the other waiting horses, while the minutes ticked by. His number was called, Sandra gave Mark a leg-up into the saddle and, without any rush or panic, he crossed over the starting-line at a steady trot on the first stage of the roads and tracks.

As soon as he'd gone Princess Anne loaded the grooms into the Range Rover and drove them off to the steeplechase course. In practical terms they had to be there in case horse or rider needed anything before setting off round the eight-fence track, but it also gave them the only chance they'd have of watching the horse tackle some of the fences.

Phase A was nothing more than a gentle hack through the woods, so Percy arrived at the chase course looking ready for a good run. He set off at a steady gallop, but by the half-way marker it was clear that the horse wasn't jumping with any spark and as he raced over the finishing-line he was eight seconds over the time limit of four minutes.

His canter away from the course took him towards the start of the next section of roads and tracks, and as he dropped out of sight behind a dry-stone wall, the Range Rover nudged its way back through the crowds to the starting-box for the crosscountry section.

When Percy arrived in the box the girls would have just the ten minutes of the compulsory stop between phases to wash and cool him down, check his saddlery and get him ready for the most demanding, spectacular and important section of the contest, his round across country.

From the back of the Range Rover came the buckets and boxes that held all the equipment they'd need. Like the groups of stablehands who'd arrived before them, they laid a groundsheet on the grass and set out each item with a surgeon's precision – and then waited. Percy came into the box with time to spare, not looking particularly sweaty or tired. Within seconds his saddle was off, he'd been sponged down and was walking around at a leisurely pace draped in a sweat-rug. His rider stood with hands on hips, watching for a moment, and then disappeared inside the tent in the middle of the box where closed-circuit television screens monitored the progress of the horses already out on the course. When he emerged the vets had passed Persian Holiday fit to run, so the saddle was replaced, girth tightened and rider tossed up into the saddle.

The starter began his countdown 'five, four, three' – Sandra looked anxiously at her charge – 'two, one – go', and as Percy raced towards the first, we all raced towards the television screens and arrived in time to see him safely over the second fence, heading at full gallop towards Huntsman's Close.

He came out of the Close strongly, powered over the Elephant Trap and Watertrough and headed for The Quarry. What happened next was shown again and again in slow motion on television all that weekend. Percy jumped well out over the wall, shuffled towards the steps, made a half-hearted attempt at the first and crashed, chest first, into the second. His legs crumpled under him as he rolled to the left, and his rider was catapulted out of the saddle to land in an ungainly heap in the corner. Sandra's hand flew to her mouth – 'Oh no' she said, obviously fearing the worst. But the old horse pulled himself up on four sound legs, and started to nibble the grass on top of The Quarry, while his rider nursed an injured hand. Captain Phillips remounted and touched the brim of his cap with his whip – a signal to the officials that he was retiring. The grooms collected their tarpaulin, threw it in the back of the Range Rover, and Princess Anne drove them silently back to the stable.

As she led Percy quietly back into his box, Sandra hid her tears by rubbing her face into the chestnut's soft nose. With Shelley's help he was unsaddled, had his legs cleaned and checked for damage, and was taken off for a quiet walk. His rider stood with his hands on his hips – head bowed. His disappointment was profound, and tinged with the regret that he'd 'let an old friend down'. The object had never been to win with Percy – just to get him round safely and bring him back sound, and while the horse happily wasn't damaged, he'd failed miserably in the other objective. 'I'm so annoyed with myself' he said bitterly – and began to recount the events that had led up to the crash. 'He didn't jump well on the steeplechase course – he didn't like the going – and I knew in my heart of hearts that I shouldn't be taking him across country. And yet while half of me was saying 'don't go' the other half was saying that I was just looking for excuses. Throughout all the ten kilometres of the second bit of roads and tracks, after the steeplechase, I kept tossing it about in my mind. You get loyalties on both sides tearing at you, so I suppose when I came into the starting-box I took the chicken option and just kept going with events instead of being strong-minded.' Mark felt he'd gone well over the early fences 'especially Huntsman's Close which wasn't an easy fence for him' but what happened at The Quarry was something of a blurr. 'I knew I had to go into The Quarry strongly and he jumped it properly, but he landed further down the slope than I'd expected. Then in the next stride he felt as though he pecked, and went down on his nose. I thought I've got to get him and myself back together but, as I picked him up, nothing happened. He just seemed to run straight into the bottom of the step. I stood up and thought, well he's an old horse, and I knew in my heart of hearts that I shouldn't have taken him, so I quietly retired him, and that was that.'

The finality was in fact complete. Not just for Badminton, but for Percy's whole eventing career. This was his last appearance as a competitive horse and Mark was clearly regretting not being able to send him into retirement on a high note. 'My parents bought the horse for me as a four-year-old – so that was ten years ago. In between he's won competitions for me all over the continent and at home, so I've always had a soft spot for him. He's been a great friend and I'm just a bit sick that I didn't stick to my guns, and do what I knew was right and pull him out. If you like, it was a gamble that didn't come off. If it had, and he'd jumped round well, he would have looked a hero – as it was we didn't.'

At that point in the afternoon, morale could not have been lower. Percy was out of the competition and Lincoln was standing well down the placings with a poor dressage score. Mark kept silent company with his own anxieties and the steady trickle of friends and supporters came and went with the quiet understanding of people who find themselves in a house where the master has a mighty hangover. There was a steady through-traffic of gleaming horses and riders walking out to the start, and sweaty heaving animals coming back. Out on the crosscountry course, the source of that transformation, a quarter of a million people cheered, oohed and aahed as one horse and rider after another thundered over the turf and leaped with varying degrees of agility and horsemanship over Col Frank Weldon's testing course. But the noise and the crush and the heady atmosphere of competition hardly touched the quiet of the stableyard.

While Mark tried to snooze, Lincoln was all pricked ears and alertness. With just under an hour to go to his starting time at 17.11, Lincoln was led out of his box into the passageway of the stable – and the countdown began. Shelley had allowed herself threequarters of an hour to bind his legs in the protective vetwrap, neither so tight that he would break down, nor so loose that it would work free. Don checked the saddlery yet again, and Sandra diluted some of her earlier disappointment by pitching in and checking off the equipment needed for the 'pit stop' after the roads and tracks. Mark went through his own process of preparation, dressing in the white breeches and sweater that have been his crosscountry 'uniform' since his days in the pony club, pulling on his comfortable old top-boots and arming himself with his 'talismans' – the battered black 'silk' to cover the crash helmet, and the silver-topped whip. He put the paper that gave the timings for each section of the roads and tracks into his pocket and checked his stopwatch. Those first three sections of the competition needed to be ridden with split-second precision. Twenty minutes for Phase A, four minutes round the steeplechase course, forty-five on Phase C. If he took longer than that he'd incur penalty points, so the list and the stopwatch would keep him on time.

The start for Phase A was less crowded than it had been earlier in the day. Most of the spectators obviously found the leisurely beginning to roads and tracks tame in comparison to the spectacle offered by the crosscountry jumps, and even when Lincoln rocketed round the steeplechase fences and crossed the finishing-line in exactly four minutes, there were few people to witness the event.

In the crosscountry box Shelley and Sandra ticked off their equipment. Spare saddle, bridle, reins, sweat-rug and studs, the bucket, sponge, scraper, dishcloths and lard. The measured tone of the starter counting down each competitor to the 'off' was punctuated every few minutes by the cheers of the crowd as yet another horse and rider galloped over the finish in a lather of sweat and mud.

The anxious faces of those who waited mingled with the relief of those who'd finished, and from the television tent a commentary of cheers and groans monitored the progress of those still out on the course. Lincoln's appearance in this arena threw his team into a frenzy of activity. The saddle came off, and a dishcloth was wrapped around each leg to keep the cooling water being sponged over his body away from the temperamental crepe bandages which could tighten if they got wet. He was scraped dry, had the studs in his shoes tightened and then had lard smeared over his legs to help them slip over the fences without chaffing. While Shelley walked Lincoln quietly around the perimeter of the box, Mark was deep in conversation with Princess Anne. She'd been watching the progress of the earlier riders and was able to tell him that every one of the overnight leaders after the dressage test who'd already ridden had incurred massive time penalties on the crosscountry. Her husband's face brightened. They both knew that Lincoln was an exceptionally fast horse across country – he only had to go clear to be with a chance to get back up among the leaders.

As Lincoln powered away from the start, his 'team' of supporters made a dash for the television screens. Everyone held their breath as he approached The Quarry, and as he rode in over the first wall there was a clatter and crash as one of Lincoln's hindlegs caught the top of the brickwork and brought down a shower of stones and a broken pole. But it didn't impede his stride, and he launched himself deftly up the steps and pinged out over the top bar leaving the cheers and relief of the crowds behind him.

Riding ahead of Lincoln was Rachel Bayliss, now fully recovered from her food poisoning and setting a cracking pace on Mystic Minstrel. The television cameras had swung their attention to her as she approached the Crooked S, and a mighty cheer went up in the tent and out on the course when she aimed for the centre of the combination and made the fast, downhill, difficult route look as easy and uncomplicated as Frank Weldon always said it was. The television pictures and the public tannoy kept a tally of the riders' progress and before they were half-way round the course it became clear that Rachel Bayliss was having the ride of her life, and Mark and Lincoln were chasing her stride for stride every inch of the way.

Through The Lake, over the Cirencester Rails, past Luckington Lane – these two riders were setting the course on fire.

Mark admits that 'After the dressage I thought I was out of it. It wasn't a difficult course so I guessed Rachel, Bruce, Lucinda, Richard – one of them *had* to come up trumps. But by the time Lincoln went across country the leading scores were in the 80s and as Lincoln's dressage was 57 I thought we were in with a chance. Because some of the leaders had gone so slowly, they'd left the door half-open – so we went on the chase.'

As a spectator you can appreciate the visual impact of what happens when horse and rider meet fence after fence, but only the rider counts every heartbeat and Mark's memory of that ride is a record no camera could ever capture. 'I was as nervous as hell before I set off,' he remembers, 'but I knew we were in with a chance. He jumped the first fence quite well, not brilliantly, but OK, and then took the second fence super. The going into Huntsman's Close was soft and he was labouring a bit, so I just kept telling myself to bide my time. Then on the tannoy I heard that Mystic Minstrel had been through the Crooked S on the fast route and I thought, bloody hell, if he's going as well as that there seems no way I'm going to catch him – so I'm now riding for second place. Then Huntsman's Close came up and I went over the Arrowhead, had a good turn to get right for the hedge, which he jumped well, and then had a good turn again into the last rail. Then stupidly I moved him on a lengthening stride to the Elephant Trap and he only just went. He thought about it, went high, and landed almost stationary. Silly boy, I thought, remember what this is all about. Keep a hold of him, keep him on his feet and not lengthen too much. So I hooked him back a bit for the Watertrough and made a better job of it. Riding up to The Quarry he was going well, and so I steadied him down, and perhaps overdid it a little bit because three strides out his head suddenly came up and he started to drop me. Then all the red lights and the warning signals started flashing in my head, so I gave him two down the shoulder, which had the desired effect. But instead of jumping, he just launched himself at the wall, and I thought "Oh Christ we're going to land a long way down!" I didn't want him to do what Percy had done and land too steep and fall on his head. So I let the reins go a bit, so he'd land with his head up and balanced, and then just caught him in the teeth a bit, which is why he dropped his hindlegs slightly and caught the top of the wall. It looked spectacular on television, but in fact it wasn't that dramatic to ride, and it meant that he landed four-square and balanced so I was able to go up the steps

Crosscountry day – a competitor negotiates the Crooked S, the fence feared by many of the riders (*Jim Bennett*)

and out, and his jump was super. I turned him away from The Quarry, he caught hold of the bit and said "Right dad – I'm off". And really I had nothing more to do, my problems were over, because although Lincoln always takes a long time to warm up, once he says "right – that's it", providing I give him half a chance, he's off. At the Keeper's Rail and the Hogsback he stood off, and for the Crooked S he was real. I came the long way round and he jumped the first and second parts super, then he just looked coming into the third so I firmly pushed him on – three strides – and we were over and off towards The Lake. He came in steady and never even thought about it – just popped through, landed a bit flat-footed but I put my leg to him and he just took off, coming out in three strides instead of four and then pinged over the upturned boat as though there was no tomorrow. He jumped the Drays well, then he fired into the Park Wall, and about five strides out from the Cirencester Rails, I felt him catch hold of the bit as if to say "right dad – I'm going", so I was able to just hold on and go with him.'

Like many top-class riders, Mark has a natural stopwatch that ticks away inside his head telling him just how fast or slow he's going without having to keep on glancing at the real thing on his wrist. To make any impression on the contest at all he knew he was going to have to aim for a fast round, but how fast – that was the thought that nagged at him through the first half of the course. 'I knew I wasn't far off the maximum bonus time,' he says, 'but I kept on worrying about whether or not he could keep it up. I had time to think from The Quarry to the Keeper's Rails, and from the S to The Lake. I was tossing over in my mind whether I should slow down a bit or keep going, and then from The Lake to the Drays and the Park Wall I kept thinking, should we be going slower. But then I decided he's going so easily within himself, probably better to leave him and let him cruise at his own speed and I think, with hindsight, that was the right thing to do.' Perhaps it's because he was still thinking about the speed of his run that he stopped concentrating for a split second on the way into the Cricketers Arms as it was there that he made another mistake.

'At the Cricketers Arms I lengthened him a bit too much – he jumped well, but a bit flat because I'd asked for too much. Again I thought "silly boy – careful, don't get over-confident", so as he came to the First Luckington Lane Crossing I held him to it and he popped through just as clever as a cat, and then at the Centre Walk he was brilliant. He took a bit of spruce with him – but it was good.'

Any rider will tell you that once they start on a major course like Badminton, their concentration is so intense on the job in hand that they're rarely, if ever, aware of the crowds, the cheering, or the tannoy that follows their progress. But as he cleared the Centre Walk and lined up to approach Tom Smith's Walls, Mark remembers hearing a snatch of commentary saying that Rachel Bayliss had just cleared the

Pardubice only four fences away. 'I thought "Damn me, I should be four minutes behind her, because we start at four-minute intervals, but it isn't going to take me that long to get from here to the Pardubice so I must have caught up on her".'

What Mark didn't know was that riding away from Tom Smith's Walls Mystic Minstrel had stumbled, throwing his rider off. It had taken precious seconds to get Rachel back in the saddle and discover the cause of the accident. Mystic Minstrel had lost a shoe – and with it all chance of the championship as 31 time and 60 jumping penalties were added to his impeccable dressage score. All Mark would be aware of was that he was now chasing Rachel's tail and the the horse under him was still powering on like an express train.

'Coming into Tom Smith's Walls he took a long look but I kept him to it, and he was brilliant. Then we were on a right mover to the Second Luckington Lane Crossing. We gave the corner a miss, took the short route over the rails, then deep into the first hedge and deep into the second and he made it look just like a little pony club fence. I'd got my line all worked out for the Zig-Zag to keep on the good going, which worked well. He'd left me a bit flat at the Cricketer and a bit flat at the Elephant Trap, and I thought I'm not going to make the same mistake here, so I kept hold of him, rode to the bottom of it, and he pinged out over as though there was no tomorrow. Then we jumped the Brandy Glass over the parallel bars – easy except that he was being

Mark and Lincoln taking a line over the stem of Fence 30, the Brandy Glass (*Findlay Davidson*)

just a bit stupid I think, and then, about a hundred yards from the Pardubice, he suddenly started to tire on me a bit. So I sat still and moved him quietly at the fence, which he didn't jump as high as he should, but he landed well so there was no real problem. But there was some very deep going right afterwards and he was tired. We'd been going at a fair clip all the way, but suddenly he was tired, so I thought, this is the time to sit still and not do anything stupid. Just bring him home quietly and safely. Coming into the log, I just sat still, let him get into the bottom of it then pop over. He didn't hit it, but he slithered over it a bit, so I just let him cruise down in front of the house. I didn't ask him for anything, I just thought "quietly does it", then as we came into the dip just before the Whitbread Bar I asked him for some work, and said "click, click, come on" and made a positive effort to push him up together and held him so that he showjumped the last. In fact he gave it feet to spare, so much so that it made me duck my head because I thought I was going to get clobbered on the roof. But he jumped it real. I wasn't able to accelerate into the finish – he didn't have a lot there. I just let him cross the line in his own time.' That 'time' was just three seconds over the twelve minutes eighteen seconds allowed. It meant he had 1·2 penalty points against him, but Lincoln's was by far the fastest time of the day and catapulted him straight into the lead.

The air was euphoric. The emotions of the past few days exploded in a fit of backslapping and grins. Shelly draped Lincoln in a sweat-rug and led him off to the quiet of his stable where she could wash him down and pile compliments on his head, while Mark was grabbed by Raymond Brookes-Ward to be interviewed for the BBC. 'Congratulations, it looks as if you've won,' he was told. 'Not yet,' was the cautious reply. 'There's still that fellow to contend with' and he indicated Richard Meade who was just about to set off on Kilcashel. For thirteen minutes Mark watched every stride Richard Meade took on the closed-circuit television monitor in the BBC commentary position. Richard went clear – but slow; when the scoreboard was made up at the end of the day, the main focus of attention was the name six up from the bottom of the list. The legend read 'Number 87, Lincoln. Dressage score 57·8. Crosscountry time penalties 1·2. Position at the end of the second day – First.'

It is part of the tradition at Badminton that the end of the crosscountry day is celebrated with a dance in the elegant halls of Westonbirt Girls School, just a few miles up the road from Badminton village. The dancing began at 10.00pm, with breakfast of bacon rolls and coffee in the small hours, but for a group of fifty or so specially invited guests including Princess Anne and Captain Phillips, the evening was ushered in with a posh version of the school dinner at 8.30pm. Not unnaturally the talk over the roast beef and two veg was of the day's competition: those who'd been retired or eliminated, the changing fortunes of those who'd figured in the first fifteen after the dressage, and the new contenders like American Sandy Pflueger and Gerry Sinnott from Ireland who'd taken second and fourth places, with Richard Meade moving up from fifth to third.

At ten o'clock, just as the dancers started to arrive and the band struck up the first notes of the evening, Mark excused himself from the diners and drove down to the stables at Badminton. It was rather eerie driving through the acres of deserted parkland that only hours before had been jammed with noisy spectators. Eerier still to swing into the stableyard and watch the headlights of the Rover trap long, skinny shadows against the grey walls, then to switch off the engine and hear the silence. A door creaked, then scraped across flagstones and Shelly walked out of the darkness.

After Lincoln's incredible run, she'd taken him back to the stable, taken the vetwrap off, released the studs from his shoes, and given him a shampoo in the bath-house to get the sweat off his back and the lard off his legs. For the next half hour she just walked him patiently up and down the drive, round and round in circles, while he dried off and got his breath back. Then he'd gone back into his stable to eat supper and have his legs wrapped in kaolin poultices. Shelley explained 'we always do that as a precaution, just in case he's given himself a bash. That way you start treating any problems before they even show.' She confirmed that when the vetwrap had come off it had been badly ripped on the left hindleg where he'd hit the wall going into The Quarry 'so that was one bit of damage saved' she said. 'And in fact his legs are in good shape.' But no rider leaves his horse's soundness to luck. Which is why, five hours after his legs had been treated, we were standing in the deserted stableyard and Lincoln was being led out into the spotlight of the car's headlamps. If he had done any damage, now was when it would show. Shelley walked the horse away from the car in a straight line and then trotted him back. Mark pulled a face. 'I'm not sure,' he said, 'try again.' Shelley wasn't sure either. 'He feels a bit stiff, not lame, but not sound either. It's funny – he's sort of pokey on his front legs, but it's obviously one of the back legs that isn't quite right.'

It was easy for the shadows to play tricks on the eyes with only a thin corridor of light to pierce the gloom of the night – but there was something wrong; not a lameness, as Shelley had said, but a subtle unevenness in the way he trotted. 'Get the kaolins off,' said Mark, and the back legs were stripped clean so that he could feel for any sign of swelling, or heat. A cut perhaps, or a splinter. But there was nothing. 'Whatever it is, it's not much,' said his rider, and decided that the best thing would be to put more kaolin on the legs, look at them again first thing in the morning – 'and if you have any doubts at all,' he said, 'however slight – ring me before seven.'

We left the silence of the stable and drove back to the noise of Westonbirt School where the dance was in full swing. That any of the riders had enough energy left for the gyrations of the disco and the reggae band that thumped through the night is a credit to human endurance. But while most stayed for the cabaret and until cockscrow, Captain Phillips left with Princess Anne at one o'clock; although his success on the crosscountry was worth celebrating, nothing was finally won until he'd jumped the last fence in the showjumping phase, and it wasn't worth risking the lead on a thick head and bleary eye!

SUNDAY, 12 APRIL 1981

The Sunday morning peace of Gatcombe Park was shattered just after seven by the harsh jangling of the telephone. Forty minutes later Mark was bowling along the Gloucestershire country lanes in reply to Shelly's anxious call. She'd been up at 6am to feed Lincoln his breakfast and wash off the kaolin poultices. Just after 6.30pm she'd trotted him on the flat ground of the stableyard and decided that something still wasn't quite right. That's when she'd rung Mark, who told her to take him for a gentle ride to work out any overnight stiffness, and that he'd be at the stables before 8.00am.

On the drive through the park we passed Jane Starkey making slow progress on her powerful grey. 'Everything all right?' shouted Mark. She screwed up her nose, and gave a thumbs-down in reply. 'This is one of the worst parts of a three-day competition,' said Mark grimly. 'You can spend months getting your horse fit, do a good dressage test, and go round the crosscountry course clear, but if the animal isn't sound on the Sunday morning – then it's all been for nothing.' That might well have been a summary of his own position if he arrived in the yard and found Lincoln on three legs!

He was standing in his box waiting for rider and vet to inspect the damage. Shelley trotted him out for Mark and he looked level; the ride had removed any trace of stiffness. When the vet arrived he went through the same procedure and after a closer inspection the vet passed him sound, and the relief in the Phillips' camp was like a breath of fresh air. The official vet's inspection was due to take place at 10am in front of Badminton House but riders had a horror of being 'failed' at these public demonstrations, so it wasn't unusual to see the vets moving with professional judgement from one stall to another in the hour before the main event.

Just before ten o'clock the yard was full of grooms, riders and horses decked out in Sunday best for the final vets' inspection. At one time only the competitors and a few staunch supporters turned up for the ritual, but over the past few years it's become one of the showpieces of the event and people turn up in their thousands for a glimpse of the gladiators. It was just as it had been on the first day. Numbers were called, horses paraded, and the judgement delivered. Only now there were gaps in the list. The first was Number 8, Persian Holiday. The word 'retired' beside his name told only part of the

Shelley leading Lincoln before the vets for inspection on the final day; Prince Philip, the Queen, the Duke of Beaufort and Prince and Princess Michael look on (*Jim Bennett*)

sadness of his round. Altogether nine of the original list failed to make the inspection including Jane Starkey's grey, and a further two who did were declared unsound and withdrawn from the final jump-off.

Lincoln passed A1, and Bruce Davidson was one of the first to congratulate Mark on the horse's performance and fitness. 'But you weren't too happy?' queried Mark. 'Nope,' said Bruce and then admitted 'I made a tactical error on the steeplechase course by simply going too fast; I overcooked him. It meant that when I went round the crosscountry he just didn't have as much fire in him as I would have liked. He gave me a super ride, but I didn't want to push him too much – so we got a slow time.' Mark had already commented on how odd it was that someone like Bruce should fly thousands of miles across the Atlantic to win a major competition, and then just cruise around the course; now he knew why.

Mark went off to attend morning service in Badminton Church with the rest of the Royal Family. The hymn 'Ride on, Ride on in Majesty' was an appropriate choice in view of the competition still to come and, as the final strains of the service were carried by loudspeaker over the parkland, riders were already walking the route of the showjumping course. For the first two stages of the competition the horses are ridden in numerical order, but on the final day every last ounce of drama and tension is squeezed out of the event by having the riders jump in the reverse order of their competition placing at the end of the second day – which meant that as Lincoln was in the lead on 59·0, he'd be the last to go. Sitting right on his tail in second place was Sandy Pflueger riding Free Scot with a score of 63·2 and Richard Meade who was third on Kilcashel with 66·4.

In eventing, every fence knocked down in the showjumping phase adds five penalties to the score, which meant that while Mark had a fence to spare over Richard Meade, there was no margin for error at all between him and Sandy Pflueger – just one fence down and he could kiss goodbye to the Badminton title if Sandy went clear.

As the list of the top twenty riders was ticked off one after another, fortunes rose and fell like a barometer. Lucinda dropped from sixth to twelfth on Mairangi Bay after knocking down two fences, though the Swedish horse Ultimus pulled up from eighth to fourth with a clear round. Mark watched from the edge of the collecting-ring and admitted to feeling 'as sick as a dog' with the memory of the previous year's competition at Burghley still crystal-clear in his mind – when he went into the showjumping-ring in the lead, and came out in second position after having two fences down. A quarter to four, and just three riders to go. Richard Meade on Kilcashel had two fences down – and hung on to third position. Sandy Pflueger rode with care and precision, obviously going for a clear, but two fences down on the course gave her a total of 73·2. Mark Phillips rode into the ring knowing that he could make two mistakes and still emerge a winner; three, and he'd be the fallen hero again.

He rode at a gentle canter into the centre of the ring, stopped in front of the Royal Box and tipped his hat in formal salute to his mother-in-law – Her Majesty the Queen. The crowd roared its approval and Mark turned right-handed away to the top of the ring; 'I

Simon (Going Places) after jumping a clear round at Tidworth 1981. Five minutes earlier he had failed to jump the practice fence properly, kicking the pole out. There was money won and lost in the collecting-ring on his eventual clear round! He finished third and qualified for the Windsor Three-Day Event, but that event was later cancelled

deliberately turned away from the start,' he admits, 'just to give myself and the horse time to get used to the atmosphere. There's a lot of tension in that ring, a lot of pressure, you can almost hear a pin drop – so I went round first on one leg, then the other, said "click, click, come on, we're off" and then just tried to attack the course as if we were at home.' Like the riders that had gone before, Mark knew this would not be an easy track to ride. No doddle this after the rigours of the day before, but a twisting course with related fences needing precise and accurate riding on every stride – and soft going to contend with.

Lincoln took the first three fences well and Mark remembers thinking '"you'll do". He had a good look at the water but I had a good stride, so no problem – but then half-way round he got a bit strong with me. Coming into the gate he suddenly said "come on – I'm off" and it was difficult trying to keep him balanced and riding forward. He touched the gate behind, and I didn't know whether it had come down or not. And then stupidly, out of the soft going on the landing, I let him freewheel a bit into the next fence and he kicked it out. It was the first fence where I had let him off the hook – and it was bad riding. As we came into the wall I didn't have time to organise myself, so he just clipped it somehow and I decided that this was all getting just a bit hairy. I stopped him and thought I've got to calm this effort down a bit and start again before we come into this last combination, because I didn't know if I'd had the gate down or not, so I had to jump the combination clear to win. Anyway, I settled him down, and he came to the last triple and just popped in and jumped it like a real one.' The roar that erupted as he made a clean touch-down after the last fence was all Mark needed to tell him that he'd won. He had only had the one fence down, and that wasn't enough to rob him of victory. Lincoln had won the Badminton Three-Day Event against all the odds and understandably no-one was more surprised – or delighted – than the man who'd ridden him. Captain Mark Phillips grinned from ear to ear like the cat who'd got the cream.

Shelley burst into tears, Mark's father, Mr Peter Phillips, was speechless with pride and emotion, and Mrs Anne Phillips declared 'why on earth didn't I put a table-tennis bat in his hand when he was a youngster – it would have been far less nerve-wracking'. But they were the sentiments of a mother who knew that she wouldn't have missed the triumph of that moment for anything in the world, and she slipped almost unnoticed into the crush of people in front of the presentation table to watch her son receive the Whitbread Trophy of a silver horse and rider from the Queen and earn his place in the record books as only the second rider ever to win Badminton on four occasions.

Monday morning after Badminton 1981 – well-earned rest and relaxation for Lincoln in the paddock at Gatcombe. Three weeks later he came in for the night with a bump on his leg which put him out for the rest of the year

Epilogue

The next three hours floated by on champagne and euphoria, first at the Whitbread stand in the company of the competition sponsors and then with the men from Range Rover. As the registered owners of Lincoln and sponsors of the Range Rover Team they would keep the Whitbread Trophy, and on the following morning the elegant silver horseman graced the table in front of Sir Michael Edwardes at a board meeting of the Range Rover Division of British Leyland Cars. But the huge silver Butler Challenge Trophy presented to the leading British rider was Mark's to keep for a year; although it was destined to take pride of place in the centre of the dining-table at Gatcombe, in those first few hours after the presentation pints of golden, frothy champagne sloshed around inside it as it was handed from one guest to another, each toasting Mark's success in delicate, cat-like sips, trying not to spill the whole lot over their chins.

The journey back to the stable was delayed by just five minutes to collect a signed Snaffles print of 'The Huntsman' from one of the print dealers. Mark had picked it out before the competition had even begun and decided that it would be his own prize to himself if he won – but admitted that it probably would have ended up at Gatcombe anyway 'as a jolly nice consolation prize if we'd lost!'.

He'd talked very little about the win, enjoying the fact of it rather than analysing the emotions. But now that the back-slapping and toasting were finished came the realisation of what he'd achieved. 'And I still don't really believe it,' was his reaction. 'You don't win a three-day event every day of the week, and you can really only hope to win Badminton once in a lifetime. I know when I won it for the first time, it was the realisation of a lifetime's ambition. The second time around was unreal, and only happened because Richard Meade made a mistake in the showjumping. When I did it the third time on Columbus in '74, I really believed he deserved to win – but to win for a fourth time is just unreal.' His attitude was that of any sportsman savouring the pleasure of a win, but for Mark there was the added pleasure of a personal triumph over his critics. 'Winning this Badminton is a very sweet experience,' he admitted. 'It's seven years since I did it last – and there's no fame shorter than sporting fame. The

Success! Mark and Lincoln with David Andrews, the Chairman of Range Rover who holds the Whitbread Trophy (*Jim Bennett*)

day you ride the winner you're everybody's friend, and the day you get beaten nobody wants to know you. In the past few years I've had a lot of criticism over my sponsorship and a lot of criticism about my horse, so winning this Badminton is particularly satisfying and should give my critics something to think about.' It was a statement made without rancour, but a frank acceptance of the fact that, even in an amateur sport where most people ride for pleasure, not glory, the back-biting and jealousy have to be met, and ridden, with the same forthright attitude as the fences themselves. There was no bitterness, just a competitor's honesty when he added: 'They'll all be very quiet now for a few months – until I get beaten again. Then they'll start afresh – but that's the sport, that's what you live with.'

Perhaps in the months ahead there would be jealousy and back-biting to contend with, but on the evening of Sunday, 12 April, there was nothing but joy and celebration in the air.

At Gatcombe the rose-bowl was filled yet again with more champagne; there were four bottles to consume – a gift from Tim Adkin. Captain Phillips explained: 'When I won the competition the first time my godmother's husband heard the news on the car radio and drove to my home with a celebration bottle. When I won it the second time he sent two bottles, three on the third occasion, and tonight there were four waiting for me.' This time the bubbly was shared with the stable staff who rise early and work late, and give their all for a horse and rider they admire and believe in.

Lincoln was back in his home stable knee-deep in straw, eating his head off, with the Badminton winner's rosette pinned predominantly on the stable-door. After his own supper, Mark and Princess Anne settled down for a quiet evening's television, and when the late night news showed the triumph of his winning round, Captain Mark Phillips was slumped in his favourite armchair in front of the screen – fast asleep.

PART THREE   RIDING

General Hints

On 4 May 1981 five young riders, nominated by the British Horse Society, arrived at Gatcombe Park in Gloucestershire to receive four days of instruction from Captain Mark Phillips. The five were all girls – Nicola May, Ginny Strawsen, Sue Berbeck, Frances Hunter and Joanna Wrigglesworth – and each one had already achieved an outstanding record in Junior events during the previous year.

Captain Phillips does not hold regular classes at Gatcombe. He becomes a 'trainer' just three times a year as part of the sponsorship deal he has with Range Rover cars to make a positive and personal contribution towards the future of eventing in this country. He doesn't set out to teach 'The Mark Phillips Method of Riding', only to pass on some of the wealth of knowledge and experience he's gained after a lifetime of top national and international competition and to demonstrate, by his own example of fine horsemanship, a standard at which to aim. Because the numbers, and his time, are limited it means that barely eighteen riders a year have the opportunity of learning from one of the finest three-day event riders in the country. But in May, I joined the five girls on their course and later got Captain Phillips to summarise the main areas he'd been working on, both in general technique and 'arenacraft'. He makes no claim that he holds the key to perfect riding; what he does believe is that riders should draw on as wide a pool of knowledge as possible, and that perhaps some of the ideas and methods that worked for him will work for others. As he says, 'if it works – it's right'.

HANDS

I think 'bad' hands are the most common fault of all; very rarely do you see people with good hands. Too often people ride along with their knuckles uppermost which means they're bound to have a stiff wrist and a stiff arm so they're not getting the proper contact with the horse's mouth. It's much better to ride with your palms uppermost or at least vertical and flex your fingers and wrists towards you. Hands must feel the horse's mouth all the time so that one second they can be really quite strong, the next just as soft as silk. When people start to ride, basically they pull the horse to stop and kick the thing to go. What we're doing is to push the horse up on to the bit by using your seat to bring the horse's hind legs underneath him. Just by holding with your fingers and pushing the horse up to your hands with your

Mark demonstrating his recommended positioning of hands and reins to Frances Hunter, a Range Rover Bursary scheme pupil riding Strike a Light (*Jim Bennett*)

seat, thereby increasing the pressure on the horse's mouth, it will stop – not because you've pulled, but because it's having its back end pushed up to its mouth. What that means is that it stops four square on its hocks and in balance, whereas if you just pull, everything falls apart and it stops on its head, like a car with its bonnet dipping.

ARMS, WRISTS, ELBOWS

There's one girl I've taught who rides very nicely, but she has a bad habit of riding along with her elbows sticking out. It looks awful and means as a result that she's stiff in her shoulders and has no feeling in her hands or fingers at all – all the movement is coming from the elbow. I like to see a rider sitting totally loose with the elbows naturally at your side and with your hands just above the horse's withers, so that you can see the palms of your hands. If you hold your elbows out, then you're creating a resistance and must be stiffening up somewhere.

SEAT

Basically riding is about your seat. The strength of your seat and what you do with it to a large extent determines the degree of movement you can achieve with a horse. Your fingers, hands and legs play a comparatively small part. You use your legs to give certain aids and to keep the horse straight, and your hands likewise. But the whole way of movement and the forward momentum and the balance of the horse is generated from your seat. If someone is doing a sitting trot, bouncing up and down on top of the horse as opposed to being part of it, then no way are you going to be able to keep your hands still because you must be tensing up against the horse's movement somewhere in your body. And if you're doing that you're not going to keep a true, hundred per cent contact with the horse's mouth and achieve any kind of balance or movement at all. This sets off a vicious circle; if the horse has got your weight bumping up and down on its back, it will stiffen its back against the weight, and of course as soon as the horse stiffens its back, it makes the rider bounce about even more.

On the other hand someone with a deep seat looks as though their seat bones will never leave the saddle, and all movement can be absorbed or transmitted through the rider's seat. You have to be able to sit quite still in the saddle and let your hips, tummy and back absorb all the movement. I know it's a very difficult thing to explain to people and ultimately the best way of achieving the right feeling is to spend hours riding without stirrups. In the end you get bored bouncing up and down because everything starts to hurt. That's when you make yourself totally relaxed because the pain starts to dictate that you should. Once you've achieved it you can either sit in the saddle and just absorb the movement or you can use your seat to be heavier, or firmer, and really push to get good movement and extensions.

The canter is effectively exactly the same movement as the walk, and most people manage to move their hips backwards and forwards without bouncing up and down in the saddle when they're walking. But at the canter you see them waving about on top like windmills. Their whole body is swaying backwards and forwards with every stride, and if they're doing that they can't possibly be sitting still on top of the horse which doesn't give the animal a chance to get its balance. Just imagine if you were carrying a weight on your shoulders and it kept jumping about from one side to another, forwards and backwards – what would you do? You'd have to keep counteracting the shifting weight to keep your balance. That's exactly what the horse is having to do, and there we are expecting it to stay on a nice balanced stride, go in a straight line up the centre of the dressage arena and keep its balance as it goes round the corner, then do movements and extensions. Well, unless you keep still on top the poor horse hasn't got a hope of keeping its own balance if you can't keep yours. The more you move your weight about, the more difficult you are making it

for the horse. I know it's not an easy thing to master because every time the horse goes up and down he tends to throw you out of the saddle – which is why you have to work at absorbing the action through the pelvic area.

SITTING CORRECTLY

A common fault of people who work on their own is that after a while they start tipping forward in the saddle instead of sitting up. I know because I do it myself, it's one of my bad habits. What happens is you tend to be thinking so much about the horse's mouth and head and what it's doing that your line of vision tends to get transfixed down towards the horse's mouth and inevitably your head goes forward a bit, then your shoulders come forward a bit, and then of course you can't ride properly because you're losing a lot of the strength out of your seat because everything is tipping forward. So it's good to make the conscious effort of saying 'sit up, put your shoulders, your hips and heels in a vertical line'. Certainly just before I go into a dressage arena I always say to myself 'Come on – sit up, make yourself smarter, use your seat a bit more.'

LEGS

I'm a great believer in sitting still on a horse. Some of the time I just have my legs resting on my horse's side. Some of the time I can be quite strong with my legs, even though I'm not necessarily showing it. I don't believe in going boot, boot, boot all the time, because if you're niggling with the leg eventually the horse isn't going to take a blind bit of notice – it'll become dead to the leg. But if the horse is used to having the legs just resting on its side, I find I can be quite strong enough just to squeeze and squeeze. Certainly if the squeeze doesn't get you what you want, then you need to give just one sharp reminder, and the next time you ask you should get the right reaction. But I must admit I don't use my legs as much as some people; I prefer to use my seat. I was most impressed with two dressage riders from the Spanish Riding School. They were both such tiny people, with no strength in terms of lifting dumb-bells and things, but to get a horse moving they were fantastic. They had incredible strength in their seat and perfect timing and balance. The horses were suddenly doing things we lesser mortals would never have thought they could manage, fantastic extended trots and marvellous elevation, working themselves up into a sweat with the exertion of it all. But the riders didn't turn a hair because they were hardly using their legs, just going tap, tap, with most of the power coming straight from their seat.

Further instruction to Ginny Strawsen, a Bursary scheme pupil, on the seat; Ginny won the 1981 Range Rover Young Rider of the Year award (*Jim Bennett*)

Mark demonstrating his method of training for the forward seat for riding across country, with stirrups crossed over the saddle (*Jim Bennett*)

POSITION IN THE SADDLE ACROSS COUNTRY

Too many riders still go across country bumping up and down in the saddle instead of getting up and standing in their stirrups with their weight over their knees and the balls of their feet, so the poor horse is going for miles with Ten Ton Tessie bouncing up and down on its back. It would find life much easier if the jockey got out of the saddle and sat still. That way the horse can go fast, and still have enough energy to jump a big fence at the end of the course. One of the things I get the young riders to do is put their stirrups to jumping length and then cross them over the saddle. I then tell them to put their feet in the stirrups at that length and canter the horse round. When they're perched up in the air, virtually standing on the saddle, that's when they start to understand about balance, absorbing the horse's movement in their knees and getting their bottoms off the horse's back.

Note: I tried it, and it's not easy! I would also suggest that other riders only attempt this rather diabolical and precarious exercise on a totally bomb-proof horse and in an enclosed area – with at least one other person present to pick up the pieces!!

HORSES THAT 'RUN ON'

Ninety-nine times out of a hundred if a horse is running on it will also be running with its head down, out of balance. Therefore, if you just pull it back, all you'll be doing is slowing it up, so it will still be 'running on' – only slower. What you have to do is change its attitude. Instead of pulling, you have to push with your seat and bring its hocks underneath and its head up. Once you've got the hindlegs coming right underneath the horse, you can feel the horse's mouth and get the animal nicely balanced and then start to ride it forward in the correct manner.

Once the horse is properly balanced it will find it easier to move properly. It's like you – when you run you balance yourself so that you don't fall over, but if you're suddenly made to run with your head tipped forward you wouldn't be able to stop, you'd be tipping forward trying to catch yourself. Which is just what happens to the horse. But as soon as you get the balance right you can move freer and take longer strides, which is just what you're trying to get the horse to do.

THE HORSE THAT 'SETS' ITS JAW

This is a difficult one. The commonest thing is for a horse to set its jaw and then stick its head in the air. Because it's tensing against your hand, it's tense all down through its back and not really engaging its hindquarters, so it has a hollow back and the hindlegs are a long way out. I think that's the time when it's very important to have a strong and supple seat. What you have to do is get the horse to relax its back. Now it's not going to do that if you're bouncing up and down, so sit deep in the saddle, work with your hips, and push the horse up into your hands. Move the bit in the mouth and try to break the horse's resistance. Play with the bit, don't give a solid hand for him to resist against; the horse will only lean against you if you give it something to lean on. Therefore you must keep giving and taking with emphasis on the giving – only taking to assist the steerage.

USING THE FIGURE-OF-EIGHT

I use the figure-of-eight quite often if I have a horse that's a bit fresh, being a bit stupid if you like, or resisting, not wanting to concentrate on its work. If you just go round and round in circles they get fairly bored with that, and the thing tends to become a bit one-sided, and if they're really being bloody-minded then they set up a resistance on one side or the other. But with the figure-of-eight they have to keep listening and concentrating so they come into your hand quite quickly and hopefully in an equal-sided way, because you are always changing direction.

RIDING FORWARD

A common fault with many people is that they don't ride their horses forward enough. If people aren't sitting in the saddle deeply enough it's quite difficult to get the horse to really become balanced and move well, so they tend not to ask for much. They trot about the arena doing a nice steady one, two, three, four, which looks reasonably nice and they're not doing anything wrong, and up to a point they'll get away with it. But once you start to get into really serious competition you'll be slated for not getting a proper movement out of the horse, not going forward enough.

You watch Rachel Bayliss when she's warming up outside a dressage arena. She has her horse so balanced and going forward so beautifully that her working trot is like most other people's extended trot, and her extended trot just floats over the ground. That's what people ought to be aiming for.

Mark on Ginny Strawsen's horse, Greek Herb, discussing problems with her having ridden her horse (*Jim Bennett*)

BRIDLES

I don't use a dropped noseband at all. I hate them. I think they tend to create more resistance than they save. If you do it up loose there's no point in having it on, and if you do it up tight it's like having a muzzle on the horse and he's going to resist it. Also I find people tend to put them on much too low so that they slightly restrict the passage of air up the nose. I use mostly an ordinary cavesson noseband, done up quite tight on some horses. But I always set it quite high, just underneath the cheekbone where it isn't creating any resistance. When I use a crossed noseband, again I do the top element fairly tight, but the bottom part comparatively loose. As for a double bridle – I always regard it personally as a slight admission of defeat if I have to use one on a horse. It means I haven't been able to get the tune right and I've had to use the double to anchor him. I did use a double quite a lot on Lincoln when I first had him – but now I don't find it necessary, and he goes much better in a snaffle.

Arenacraft, or The Art of Riding a Dressage Test

PREPARATION

The main thing is to try to keep very quiet and very still yourself and not let any competition nerves transfer to the horse. Use the time immediately after you are called by the steward, and before the bell that signals the start of the test, to get your horse used to its new surroundings. Canter or trot quietly around the outside of the arena; if the horse has still got its head stuck in the air, that is the time to do a few figures-of-eight or turns so that it gets the message that it is about to ride a test and not going off for a jolly. As soon as you have really got the horse settled that is the time to do your best movement. Something that will catch the judges' eyes just before they ring the bell. Then in their sub-conscious they are bound to be thinking 'oh – this is going to be good', so even before you go into the ring they are already thinking in sixes and sevens. If all you can do is just canter around in a nice balance and with a nice outline, then do that. But if they see you struggling with the horse, then they are bound to start thinking 'oh Lord this is going to be a mess', so they will be thinking in threes and fours as you enter the ring, regardless of how good the test is.

THE APPROACH TO A

It is very important to come into the arena off a circle, as that way you have got a better chance of hitting a straight line and staying there. But if you come in off a right-handed circle and go to the left side of the letter A, then you virtually have to turn back on the centre line again, almost like a counter canter, and you never end up on the centre line at all because you are always correcting the last turn, so you wiggle down the line instead of making a nice straight approach. If you come in on the right-hand side of the marker, at a tangent, you stand a much better chance of going straight. Come in on as good and strong a movement as you can whether it's a canter or a trot, so that the judges can see you are starting with plenty of confidence, plenty of movement and presence with a good outline. Do that and immediately they start thinking 'well this is good confident stuff'.

GOING DOWN THE CENTRE LINE

The minute you start to go straight down the centre, because you are straight on to the judges, they can't really see how much movement you've got or whether you are still going 'forward'. The important thing is to keep going straight. As you approach X throttle down a little so that you come to a halt smoothly. Again if you're not *exactly* on X don't worry too much because the chances are that the judges can't really see, though obviously you should aim to be as near and as accurate as possible. When you move off, make it smooth and straight.

THE FIRST MOVEMENT

When you turn at the bottom of the arena at C you're turning your back on the judges for the first time, and that's the best chance you've got to reorganise yourself if the horse hasn't settled properly. Rebalance the horse a little and get things going as you want before you ride into the next movement. Remember that as you turn your back, that's when they can't see what you're up to. But as soon as you are in full view again you want to be looking smart and confident without a care in the world. It's very important that you're sitting up and looking a million dollars, and pretending that the horse is looking a million dollars as well – even if it isn't doing everything perfectly. Keep your shoulders back and your head up as if you're saying to them 'well look at me – this is the best thing since sliced bread', because that aura of confidence is very important.

MISTAKES

The first rule is never upset the horse if it makes a mistake. If you do, then it's not just that movement that's going to go; it's the next one and probably even two or three after that. So the first thing to do is just keep very calm and almost pretend that nothing has happened. If you have a wrong strike-off to canter, OK, just very quietly come back to trot and try again. If you get another bad strike off, pretend it hasn't happened again; go a few paces at the trot so the horse forgets all about it for a bit, then try again. By then you're probably at a corner or a bit of a turn when you can use the corner to advantage and get the horse on the correct leg. But the more the horse misbehaves, the more you must pretend that it's nothing unusual and that he always plays up. Just keep calm. Don't ever be over-severe with your hands or legs and say 'now look here'. Do that and immediately the judges will think 'that was a dreadful mistake' – and give you a two. If you just ride through it calmly, by the end of the movement the judges will be better inclined to mark you slightly higher for good riding – say four or five – so just by staying calm you've earned yourself a couple of extra marks.

CIRCLES

Ideally, if everything is going well you ought to be able to ride a perfect circle, with the four 'points' touching the sides of the arena or the markers in exactly the right place. But if you're in trouble, then you can give yourself a chance by creating a little extra room and riding further up the arena away from the judges so that the circle is more of an oval. It just gives you a little more scope because the judges can't see exactly how far up the arena you're going, especially if you're heading towards A, so it's just a way of giving yourself breathing space to settle the horse and prepare for the next movement.

SHOWING A DIFFERENCE IN PACE

If the trot says 'at H, lengthen your stride and show a difference in pace', and all you do is continue at exactly the same pace without showing any difference at all, then the judges are bound to mark you down. The thing to remember is that you are expected to 'show a *difference*' so, if you know that your horse isn't going to be able to do a proper extended trot, just before you get to the marker throttle back a bit and shorten the stride. Then as soon as you go into the new movement you can go back to your ordinary working trot, and show a difference. The fact that you're not really doing an extension will obviously lose you some marks, but at least you'll have shown a difference. When you get to the end of the 'extended' movement, throttle back again so that you make the difference really marked, and do a few strides in the much shorter trot before going back into the working trot for the rest of the test. It's not strictly an extension, and you should still work at home to achieve that ultimately, but while you're still working at it, you will at least be achieving a 'difference' and that's what the judges are looking for.

THE WALK

This can be the most difficult thing to do properly in a test because it tends to be the thing you practise least. Most people will pick up the reins and start trotting; then when they've got the trot settled, they go on to canter work. When they've got that sorted out, they think 'oh good', drop the reins and walk home and forget all about working on the walk. What I try to do with people who come here is get them to just squeeze with the legs. Use the right leg when the off-fore is going forward and the left leg when the near-fore is going forward, so that the horse is being pushed, gently, up into the hands and going forward with a steady, strong, forward movement, not just slopping along without any purpose.

THE REIN BACK

Take your weight off your seat bones, and ask the horse to move back by squeezing with the right leg as the off-fore comes back, and your left leg as the near-fore starts to move – exactly the opposite of what you do for a forward movement. It helps the horse to come back in a steady two-time instead of four-time. It also helps give a much smoother action without any resistance.

ACCURACY

I can't stress how important accuracy is. You can do a diabolical test in that you have little movement or no extensions, but if you ride an accurate test hitting each marker bang on at the start and finish of a movement, you're bound to get five or six out of ten for having ridden accurately. If you can show good movement on top of that, then you're starting to build up a good mark. One of the problems is that if you have a horse with an extravagant movement – as I have with Lincoln – then you have a real problem with accuracy because, if you do a really super extravagant extended trot, you risk overshooting the marker at the end, so you have to find the right balance. Do you bring the horse back and settle for a few short strides before you get to the marker, or keep the action and run the risk of overshooting? In the end I think, unfortunately, that accuracy will probably win. Not all judges but most would settle for a little less movement, and an accurate test.

SHOWMANSHIP

When you go into the ring you must be a showman. If you're quite convinced you're going to do a brilliant test, then OK, but most people will be trying to cover up what they haven't got, and pretending that they really are going to be worth watching, and every little bit of extra care you take with your general appearance and attitude will help.

Mark training a three-year-old, Spanish Pearl, on the lunge rein in the covered school at Gatcombe (*Jim Bennett*)

Make sure that your boots are super shiny, that your horse is gleaming, with any white socks really white, his hooves black and oiled, tail pulled and trimmed, mane perfectly plaited. Give your coat a good brushing, and your hat. If you're a lady, tuck your hair into a net – don't have bits flying loose and untidy. Make sure the number is tidy, and your hat is on straight. In other words, ensure that both you and the horse are turned out to perfection. One of the things I hate in dressage is to see people riding in white gloves, because then everything that you do with your hands is just beamed and flashed across the arena. If you wear a dark pair of gloves and you want a bit of a fidget with the reins, or move your hands out a bit, or whatever, then you're not telegraphing every movement to the judges. I have a pair of dark leather gloves that mingle with the natural colour of the horse. It's only a little point but everything helps when you're looking for good marks.

LEARNING THE TEST

I never practise the test while training by riding it through from beginning to end. If you do that, the horse is usually going to cotton on to the movements very quickly, and he'll start remembering that the canter comes off a circle, or the half-pass follows the trot round the far corner, and so on. It's a nightmare doing a test on an older, more experienced horse, because they always pre-empt the halt at X and as you come into the arena, up the centre line, they start slowing down yards before you get to X; you have to keep working and working to get there before grinding to a halt. So when you're practising, do each movement individually jumbled up in the middle of others so that the horse never learns the set pattern of any dressage test. That way they aren't thinking for you and anticipating every move, so that when you come to do the test in the arena they stay alert, make each movement when you ask for it, and perform a much smoother test as a result.

Showjumping

People talk an awful lot about seeing strides. I don't think there is such a thing as 'seeing a stride' and when you hear people say they knocked a fence down because 'oh – I couldn't see my stride' the trouble is they were looking for one! In all jumping you have to keep coming at the fence with your horse going forward in a round, bouncy canter in a nice steady rhythm. If you are going in deep, or going to be off a fence, you either shorten or lengthen the rhythm, and keep the horse bouncing so that it can pop over well-balanced with plenty of power and impulsion. You see so many people coming up to a fence and going check, check, pulling on the front end with no push from the back. And the more they pull the more the horse falls apart. Suddenly they see a stride but by the time they get to the fence, they've flattened the horse out from 'here to Land's End' and they end up falling over the fence. As soon as a horse is strung out, he's off balance, and then you haven't got a clue whether he's going to go on to the bottom of the fence, or stand off it. And you haven't got any say in the matter either because the horse is strung out; it means you haven't got your legs on it keeping it going forward to the fence – so you don't have any control over it.

What you should be aiming for is what we were talking about with the dressage movements. Everything should be going through your hands, to your seat and your legs. If you've got it right, then everything should be under control and you can keep the horse balanced and bouncing on a steady, strong rhythmic stride. If you look at the good people like Lucinda, Richard Walker or David Broome, they're always on a strong bouncing stride, whether it's the first round, the jump-off, or whatever. People who ride flat out across country and try to do the same in the showjumping ring are not going to go well against the clock. They get about a hundred yards from the fence, start heaving and pulling, pop out over the fence, then go flat out to the next one, and start heaving and pulling again. They're always slower than the man who just keeps coming on a steady, bouncing rhythm. David Broome just keeps the same rhythm all the way to the fence, over and then on to the next. They're always faster against the clock, because they keep the whole thing smooth, and that gives them speed. The rider who's hooking and checking is breaking the cycle of balance and rhythm so they've never got enough coming from behind to make a really good jump.

In a three-day event the thing you have to remember is that the showjumping phase is totally different to any showjumping in any other competition, or anything you may have done with the horse at home. You may jump the horse every day of the week at home and really feel you've got something smart, but then you take it to an event and jump it on the third day and think you've got an entirely different animal. Probably all week it has gone up to a fence and pinged off the ground; now suddenly it has lost its 'ping' because it is bound to be a bit tired and stiff, so you have to make allowances. When a horse is fresh you can put it deep into a fence and expect it to fire off the ground and jump nicely. If it's tired, you don't want to be doing that; you must be prepared to jump it slightly further off the fence. Similarly, if you are jumping off very boggy going you can't expect a horse to go in as deep and come out of the bog in the same way as if you were on good going. You have to make it easier for him by standing away from the fence, and putting a bit more pace in the stride.

USEFUL JUMPING EXERCISES

I think that getting a horse to jump down a 'grid' of fences is one of the best exercises. I like the grid to have four fences starting with a pole on the ground, then a cavaletti, then a fence at 2ft to 2ft 6in, and finally a parallel bar or an upright at 3ft to 3ft 6in. The first three fences have just a bounce between them with a single stride to the last fence. You can play with the distances on the last one making the stride either short or long, so that it really has to explode off the ground, and use itself to get out over the fence. The grid is particularly useful if you have a horse who's a bit headstrong. Then I set the fences so that you have one stride, then three strides, then one, then three, and so on up the grid. The horse sees a line of fences, and once he starts jumping he has to concentrate – he can't go rushing off. It makes him steady up, look and think, and start to use himself.

It would be true to say that you can make an infinite number of different grids, all of which could be good. You must therefore think about the problem you have with your horse, and build a grid to try to help the horse overcome that problem.

THE HORSE THAT RUNS OUT

Usually this happens when the horse is being naughty and finds he can get away with it. I recently started a youngster on quite a small fence and found that when I sat quite still he would try and run out first to the left, then to the right. So I kept him on a good, strong, bouncing stride and really made him approach the fence dead straight. When he tried to duck out I was ready for him with a strong leg, so over he went. A few more times and he ran out again, but that was my fault because I stopped trying so hard, and didn't keep a bouncy rhythm going, so he was a bit long and flat when he came to the fence, which meant that he had the whip-hand and I wasn't able to control him, so he took full advantage of it. Once a horse is in charge there's not a lot you can do about it. So you have to keep a good contact, keep command at the fence on a good, strong forward stride, in balance – and then *you're* back in charge.

KEEPING BALANCED

In showjumping riders always aim to turn corners and ride into fences 'on the right leg' but really I find it's more important to keep your horse balanced rather than have an argument with him over which leg he should be cantering on. Take Town and County for instance; he always leads with the leg closest to the collecting-ring, regardless of which way he's actually going. I could bring him back to a trot and try to get him on the right leg, but if it wasn't the one *he* wanted to lead with I'd still be there in a week's time, and he wouldn't do it. Therefore, I know with him I just have to ignore that, and come round the corner in a nice balance – even if it's in counter canter. I know that's going to upset him much less than if I spent the entire round trying to get him to jump fences *and* change legs. Even though the showjumping phase of the three- (and one-) day event is timed so strictly, and the time penalties for going over the top are massive, there

Spanish Pearl with a rider – Hamish Cameron – on board for the first time, while Mark and Jane keep him calm (*Jim Bennett*)

are times when it pays to lose a few seconds and slow your horse back to a trot to get him settled. In Lincoln's case, for instance, after he jumped three or four fences in the final at Badminton in 1981 he stuck his head in the air and went absolutely rigid on me – all the way down through his mouth and back so that his hind legs weren't engaged – and he was a disaster. What I've found is that if you just bring him back to a trot, that can just relax everything, so that when you strike off to a canter he comes back to your hand quite quickly. I find I sometimes have the same problem with Classic Lines who just gets stronger and stronger. It's certainly worth just coming back to a trot for a few seconds, especially if you have a difficult line of fences coming up or a combination, so that you can get them perfectly balanced before they start and then you can make up the lost time elsewhere on the course.

LOOKING BACK

Never ever look back at the fence you've just jumped to see what you've done to it. Whatever has happened, it's too late to do anything about it, and by looking back you're likely to be totally off-balance to jump the next fence and you're absolutely guaranteed to have it down. What happens is that as you look back you're also looking down, so that your weight tends to go forward and you get in front of the horse's movement, and effectively put your weight over the horse's forehead; that's totally counter-productive to what you're trying to do, which is to keep the horse's weight and balance back on his hocks. But if you keep looking up, always with your eye on the next fence, then your weight is still in a vertical position and therefore where the horse finds it more easy to canter – and to jump without getting into trouble.

Crosscountry

We all spend so much time and effort working on dressage these days, but I think that crosscountry riding is as much, if not more, of a skill than some basic dressage, and some people don't spend nearly enough time perfecting the art of really good crosscountry technique. To begin with the rider's position is very important – not only from the weight-carrying point of view in that you should be up on your knees, in a good forward position to make it easy for the horse to carry you, but also with regard to your position when you're actually jumping the fence.

I would think that nine people out of ten fall off their horses rather than part company with them because the horse has actually come down. The main problem is that when they go over the fence they bring their heels up which is their weakest position; if the horse is about to peck, or anything untoward happens, all their weight is going forward and the rider is going to complete that momentum by toppling out of the front door, because there's nothing there to keep him in the saddle. It's all balance really. You see a racing jockey landing over a fence and he'll have his lower leg forward, and at the same time be sitting forward to go with the movement of the horse.

It's the same in Horse Trials, only not quite so exaggerated. You must put your leg forward so that when the horse lands you can feel all the movement through your legs and 'catch' yourself with your heel if the horse feels as though it's going to peck or land badly. Look at any picture of Lucinda Prior-Palmer and you'll see she always has a beautiful position over a fence. She is always behind her lower leg and that is why she very rarely falls off, and wins so many competitions. If you combine that with also slipping your reins, when things really go wrong you're able to open your hands and let the reins slip through so that the horse has all the room it needs to sort itself out. Then when you land you can close your hands and pick the horse up off the deck with some strength. What you see people do time and time again is put their heels back as they jump and then fall onto the horse's neck, just when the horse needs all the help and support it can get on its front end to bring it back up. Instead it gets buried with ten stone of jockey landing between its ears and hasn't got any chance at all of getting up. It's something I feel desperately strongly about. If only more riders stopped to think about it, and spent the odd half hour working on it, they'd improve a lot. But people just don't bother. They get to a competition, find things go wrong, and then wish they had worked on the problem at home. That's one of the main differences between the top people and the ones who keep knocking on the door – but never quite make it. They get so far, then keep toppling off!

CHOOSING A ROUTE

I've always believed the shortest way is the quickest way, which doesn't always mean the biggest element of the fence. Sometimes discretion is the better part of valour. If the biggest part of the fence creates too much of a risk or gamble with the particular horse you're riding, you take time out and go a longer way round, then try to make up a bit of time elsewhere. But just the way you turn into a fence can make a lot of difference. Very often people wing out and take a great sweeping approach to a fence when there's absolutely no need. If you've got a good steady rhythm you can often approach a fence and jump it off a turn – it might even be easier.

You also very rarely these days see people turn in mid-air but, just as with showjumping, if while you are in the air you pull to either the right or left depending on which way you have to go, you can often land with the correct leg leading and be off towards the next fence without losing any time. But I often see people land, and then go on for two or three strides congratulating themselves on having jumped the fence before they even think about turning. What you have to remember is that, in crosscountry riding, for every ten feet you cut off your route you save a second, and in four-and-a-half miles there's an awful lot of seconds to be saved.

JUMPING A FENCE DOWNHILL

You must keep your horse's hocks underneath him, and hold him in balance on a steady rhythm. Unless you do that and set the horse up with enough energy and bounce on the approach so that it can actually jump, then you're wasting your time. If what you are approaching is a fairly complicated fence like a coffin or a sunken road, then you don't need a lot of speed or pace – just plenty of bounce. As you get to the fence, right or wrong, you've got to go – chicken out, and everything will just stop.

JUMPING UPHILL

Whenever a horse is going uphill it's bringing its hind legs much further underneath it than it does when it's on the flat, and so it's able to jump a much greater height – it's quite extraordinary. All you really have to do is put a hand to the mane or neck-strap and make sure you go with it and don't get left behind.

JUMPING INTO WATER

The important thing is not to come into it too fast. Once you've taken off it's one of the few times when it's almost excusable to have a feel of the horse's back teeth with the bit so that it lands with its head up. If you can just bring the head up a little as it goes into the water, that will bring its feet out in front and, especially if it's fairly deepish water, that will act as a brake. The Lake at Badminton and the Trout Hatchery at Burghley are probably the most famous water 'fences' in Britain, and the Hatchery in particular is certainly not an easy fence. You approach it downhill so you have to keep the horse balanced, almost holding him back, but then as you get to the log at the bottom of the slope you go from the 'backward' movement to asking the horse to go forward and jump straight out and down over the log into the water. It's not easy. You have to be strong and determined, and keep the forward momentum going as best you can. Once you're in the water hopefully you'll land with the horse's feet out in front; that way you're less likely to topple over and get a ducking!

JUMPING A FENCE IN WATER

I was always taught that you should trot through water because then the horse always has one foot on the ground, and therefore he can always take off to jump a pole in the middle, but some of the fences you have to jump in water nowadays are really quite big. They're decent fences to jump from a trot on dry ground, let alone out of water. That means you now see a tendency for people to canter through water with a bit more pace. I think at the end of the day it all depends on the depth of the water, the fence you've got to jump, and the horse itself. The only important thing to remember, whether you opt to trot or canter, is to keep going forward and attack the fence with as much momentum as possible, while keeping the horse balanced.

DITCHES

If I see an open ditch on a course I'm always rather pleased and regard it rather like a triple bar. You come in to it and get your horse as close to the edge of the ditch as you can, then just jump it as you would a triple bar, regardless of whether it has a rail or a hedge or just open ground behind it. It's the same with a trakener. You only get into trouble if you try and stand off; provided that you keep coming on a strong, bouncy stride and come to the bottom of it, you've got to jump it well.

DROP FENCES

One of the bad fences on a course will always be the obstacle that asks you to jump a spread with a drop because usually if you've got a drop fence the horse will tend to lower itself over the fence, like the Leaf Pit at Burghley. But if you get a spread before the drop, then you're asking the horse to jump up and out, before it starts going down. It's rather like a person who's sitting in a house and looking out of a window. He doesn't know if he jumps out whether he'll be just a few feet off the ground, or several floors. It's the same for the horse. So you must bring it up to the fence on a steady stride and put it in a position so that it can jump the fence in the easiest possible way. Approach too fast and he's going to start putting on the brakes, but if you make a steady approach, they can sum up the situation and jump with confidence.

PACING

Something I feel very strongly about is pacing yourself on your ride across country so that you've always got enough petrol left in the tank at the end. You must ride the course according to the conditions on the day, taking into consideration the weather, the going and the demands of the fences. If there's a really big fence at the end of the course, then it's no good going flat out over the first half of the course and hoping that the horse will have enough energy to tackle the important obstacle at the end. I believe you should always ride at a steady, sensible pace until you've jumped all the fences you think are likely to give problems or demand that extra bit of effort. After that you can start to unwind, and if you finish with a horse that's pulling your arms out, you'll know that the next time you can perhaps ask for a little more speed or a little more effort. I think perhaps you see some of the worst riding on the steeplechase course. People go round so fast that they finish some fifteen or twenty seconds under the time allowed, and then wonder why their horses are worn out when they tackle the crosscountry. It's simple. They haven't paced themselves or their horses properly, and when they get halfway round, there isn't any more petrol in the tank.

Summary

These days people work very hard at their dressage to get good marks right at the start of the competition, but the crosscountry is by far the most important of the three phases, and what the competition is all about. Anyone who wants to be really successful at the sport knows that the first thing they have to do is find themselves a really good consistent, fast crosscountry horse. You hear a lot of criticism from some people about the way that sponsorship is helping to keep just a few riders at the top – but it's just not true. The opportunities are wide open for anyone to come in and be successful, and even though we 'old riders' are still at the top of the sport, it will only take a few determined and talented young riders to knock us off. The difference is that the younger generation seem to be more content to do circuits and bumps rather than learn how to cross the country with speed and accuracy. The more that trend continues, then the more likely it is that people like Lucinda, Richard and myself will be there in the years to come.

Index